KT-423-907

Contents

CN 361.61
AN 10688

SOCIAL POLICY REVIEW 13

LIBRARY AND LEARNING RESOURCES CENTRE
Northern College Barnsley   S75 3ET

NORTHERN
COLLEGE

Please return

9   /1   01

11. 1. 0,

..., Catherine Bochel and

The POLICY
PP
PRESS

THE NORTHERN COLLEGE

Northern College
Library

CANCELLED

NC01445

BARNSLEY

First published in Great Britain in July 2001 by

The Policy Press
34 Tyndall's Park Road
Bristol BS8 1PY
UK

Tel +44 (0)117 954 6800
Fax +44 (0)117 973 7308
e-mail tpp@bristol.ac.uk
www.policypress.org.uk

© The Policy Press/Social Policy Association 2001

British Library Cataloguing in Publication Data

A catalogue record for this book is available from the British Library

ISBN 1 86134 291 8 paperback
A hardcover version of this book is also available

Robert Sykes is Principal Lecturer in Social Policy in the School of Social Sciences and Law, Sheffield Hallam University, **Catherine Bochel** is Senior Lecturer in Social Policy in the Department of Policy Studies, University of Lincolnshire and Humberside, and **Nick Ellison** is Senior Lecturer and Head of Department of the Department of Sociology and Social Policy, University of Durham.

Cover design by Qube Design Associates, Bristol.

Front cover: Photograph supplied by kind permission of Phill Rushen.

The right of Robert Sykes, Catherine Bochel and Nick Ellison to be identified as editors of this work has been asserted by them in accordance with the 1988 Copyright, Designs and Patents Act.

All rights reserved: no part of this publication may be reproduced, stored in a retrieval system, or transmitted in any form or by any means, electronic, mechanical, photocopying, recording, or otherwise without the prior permission of The Policy Press.

The statements and opinions contained within this publication are solely those of the editors and contributors and not of The University of Bristol or The Policy Press. The University of Bristol and The Policy Press disclaim responsibility for any injury to persons or property resulting from any material published in this publication.

The Policy Press works to counter discrimination on grounds of gender, race, disability, age and sexuality.

Printed and bound in Great Britain by Hobbs the Printers Ltd, Southampton.

Notes on contributors

Christian Aspalter is Lecturer in Comparative Social Policy at the University of Linz, Austria.

Andrea Beckmann is Lecturer in Criminology in the Department of Policy Studies, University of Lincolnshire and Humberside.

Lee Berney is a researcher in the Faculty of Health and Social Care Sciences, St George's Hospital Medical School.

Catherine Bochel is Senior Lecturer at the School of Policy Studies, University of Lincolnshire and Humberside.

Jean Carabine is Lecturer in Social Policy at the Open University.

John Dixon is Professor of International Social Policy at the Department of Social Policy and Social Work, University of Plymouth.

Nick Ellison is Senior Lecturer and Head of Department, Department of Sociology and Social Policy, University of Durham.

Mark Exworthy is Research Fellow at LSE Health, London.

Tony Fitzpatrick is Lecturer in Social Policy at the School of Sociology and Social Policy, University of Nottingham.

Emma Heron is Senior Lecturer in Social Policy at the School of Social Science and Law, Sheffield Hallam University.

Martin Hewitt is Secretary to the Social Policy Board, Institute of Actuaries, London.

Zoë Irving is Senior Lecturer in Social Policy at the School of Applied Social Sciences, Leeds Metropolitan University.

Leigh Keeble is Research Fellow at CIRA, University of Teesside.

Nick Manning is Professor of Social Policy and Sociology at the School of Sociology and Social Policy, University of Nottingham.

Paul Nixon is Senior Lecturer in Political Science, HEBO Haagse Hogeschool, Netherlands.

Jan Pahl is Professor of Social Policy at the University of Kent at Canterbury.

Martin Powell is Senior Lecturer in Social Policy in the Department of Social and Policy Sciences, University of Bath.

Robert Sykes is Principal Lecturer in Social Policy, School of Social Sciences and Law, Sheffield Hallam University.

ONE

The year in social policy

Robert Sykes, Catherine Bochel and Nick Ellison

Introduction

Over the last year, and as we enter the 'real' new millennium in 2001, a number of changes have been made to *Social Policy Review* (*SPR*). First, the Social Policy Association (SPA), which has been publishing *SPR* for 12 years, has entered into a partnership with The Policy Press to publish and distribute the *Review*. We are very enthusiastic about this development at the SPA since The Policy Press has a fast-growing reputation among academics and policy practitioners for the quality of its publications, and is at the leading edge of publishing topical and more reflective new work on policy issues. To mark this development, the *Review* has a new look, which we hope will become familiar to our existing readers in universities and elsewhere, and also become a symbol to old and new readers alike of high quality, incisive, polemical and interesting reading on developments in social policy, year by year.

Second, the editors have introduced some new features to the content of the *Review*. The first of these is this introductory chapter, 'The year in social policy', which the editors will use to cast a critical eye over selected developments in social policy in the last year (2000). To put such a time frame on historical and conceptual developments is not really possible, of course, and nor will we be able to cover all the developments that our readers may themselves have selected. So, while the introductory chapter will reflect the three main sections of the rest of the *Review* (UK developments, international developments, and conceptual and historical dimensions), the content and discussion will also reflect the particular slant on the past year's developments and issues taken by the editors. It should not be seen as an attempt to summarise objectively what has happened in the previous year, but rather to provide further analysis and argument at a more general level to complement the more specific foci of the remaining chapters in the review.

Third, this year we have introduced short section introductions for each of the three parts of the *Review*, summarising the chapter contents and arguments, and providing the reader with a quick guide to what our various authors have to say.

UK developments

It is a particularly apt time at present to take stock of the progress of New Labour. As we go to press, a General Election has been called and New Labour is clearly targeting increases in the numbers of doctors, nurses and teachers, and an improvement in the quality of public services as a major vote-catcher. Whether such promises come to fruition remains to be seen, however, and if its past practice is anything to go by, a re-elected New Labour government will need to be kept under pressure to deliver all its promises in the social policy field. Rather like London's Millennium Bridge represented on our cover, a comment on New Labour's social policy since 1997 might be: 'Nice idea. Delivery could be better'. Where social policy is concerned, debates about New Labour's approach have varied widely, ranging, from concerns with the ideological underpinnings (if any) of the government's policies, to consideration of the 'Third Way', through discussion of the principles and processes of policy making and implementation, to analysis of the success or failure of policy and provision. In addition, the framework within which the government has been operating, and within which social policy has been formed, has been complex and multifaceted. From 1997 to 2001 the Labour government was fortunate, or proficient enough, to have benefited from a buoyant economy, making some increases in public expenditure both possible and relatively uncontroversial, while giving Gordon Brown's increasingly clear promises of a move towards full employment greater credence. Labour's credibility was also strengthened by the close relationship with the Clinton presidency in the United States, and the strength of the US economy for much of this period. However, with George W. Bush in office, and a weaker-looking US economy, the economic challenges from 2001 onwards may be sterner.

Within the world of social policy there has been much debate about the extent of Labour's achievements in their first term in office, and the extent to which these achievements reflect different patterns of ideology, provision and resourcing. The range of policy areas affected is, it is true, impressive. For example, social policy issues such as poverty have, to a greater or lesser extent, been addressed through the introduction of the minimum wage, increases in child benefit, the national childcare strategy, new tax credits and the New Deal. There have also been significant changes in fields such as health, education, and disability.

Perhaps of equal importance, the past four years have seen increased Treasury involvement in social policy, whether in controlling public expenditure, in anti-poverty measures, or through the emerging possibility of a new commitment to a policy of full employment.

In the policy practice sphere there has been a new emphasis on evidence-based research, together with an apparent willingness to consult (and to some extent to listen), while concepts such as partnerships and joined-up government have received attention. Some of these ideas can be seen to be reflected in the government's own work and research, for example through the work of the Social Exclusion Unit, the attempts at consultations with women, as well as through policies on local government and the health service which have attempted to develop reforms reflecting this perspective.

To all this should be added New Labour's constitutional and governmental changes. These include developments such as the incorporation of the European Convention on Human Rights into UK law, devolution to Scotland, Wales and Northern Ireland, and reforms to local government, including the introduction of Best Value. The full effect of these changes has yet to be seen, but there is clear potential for a significant and long-lasting impact on the future shape of social policy. Arguably, devolution represents a different dimension of New Labour politics in contrast to its more normal emphasis by the higher echelons of the party on central control, and the need for all government actors to be 'on-message'. In social policy terms, there have already been small but significant departures from the overall UK position: see, for example, the abolition of student tuition fees and the repeal of Section 28 in Scotland, and moves in Northern Ireland to scrap school league tables.

However, despite the array of policies and legislation, there is popular dissatisfaction with New Labour policies, and the view expressed by Coote (in relation to New Labour and women) that "... if this is as good as it gets, it is not good enough" (Coote, 2000, p 1) seems to have a wider resonance. Over the past year, discontent has been expressed in a variety of ways, including the protests over the price of fuel, public concern over pensions (especially the very small increase in pensions in 2000), and the slow-handclapping of Tony Blair by the Women's Institute. Other signs of dissent with potential for significant political impact include the campaign by the Countryside Alliance, particularly over the issue of foxhunting, but apparently drawing on a much wider dissatisfaction with New Labour from broader, rurally-focused groups.

The issue of racism has refused to die away with the continuing repercussions of the MacPherson Report on the Metropolitan Police's investigation into the death of Stephen Lawrence, reinforced by incidents such as the killing of Damilola Taylor. In another area, fuelled by the *News of the World*'s 'Name and Shame' campaign, a number of anti-paedophile protests were seen across the country, with a resurgence after the murder of Sarah Payne. A so-called 'Sarah's Law' has been proposed which would allow local people access to information about sex offenders living in their neighbourhoods.

Internationally, a range of campaigns has been taken up by sections of the British population. As part of a growing awareness of the potential impacts of globalisation and unfettered free trade, a number of anti-capitalist protests against the growing power of companies such as Starbucks, Microsoft and the developers of GM foods have taken place in several countries, including Britain. More 'home-grown' have been growing uncertainties expressed over the future of the pound, and the United Kingdom's possible entry into the European Union's single currency network, commonly known as the Euro-Zone. Economic concerns about such moves have been combined with broader debates over proposals for the broadening and deepening of the EU and its impact on Britain.

Perhaps these home-grown protests, combined with the global protests from Seattle to Prague (see below), may signal the emergence of a different kind of social and political movement, or form of social action, where people give voice to their feelings on the streets rather than through institutionalised political forms. Be this as it may, and only time will tell whether such political and social shifts become more permanent features, Labour has continued to enjoy a comfortable lead in opinion polls, aside from a major 'blip' at the time of the fuel price protest. This may be attributable to a number of factors, from the relative strength of the economy, to the persistent problems and weaknesses of the opposition parties. Arguably, both the Liberal Democrats and the Scottish National Party have suffered from the resignations of their established leaders, and the lack of immediate impact of the new leaders. The Conservatives have continued to experience similar problems to those faced by Labour during the 1980s, of factional infighting, unclear leadership, a frequently sceptical and sometimes hostile press, and a general lack of credibility in the eyes of the public. Nevertheless, by late 2000 it was clear that the Labour government was concerned over its lack of strong support, and its concern was demonstrated in the manner of its responses to the petrol protests, by a robust attack by Tony Blair on Thatcherism, and the attempts to rally the party's core voters.

What can the government do to address this discontent, particularly with regard to social policy issues? It can continue with the start it has made in terms of using evidence-based research to underpin its policies and legislation, perhaps broadening this to take notice of the work of some of its critics. It may also need to reconsider the unifying role of ideology in presenting a clear view of what a government is seeking to achieve. The Third Way has so far failed to establish itself as a comprehensive approach that can be used to underpin the role of government, and indeed seems as far from doing so as it has ever done. From another perspective, it may be that the government needs to re-examine the approaches and means by which it seeks to translate policy into practice, and to consider what is necessary for the successful implementation of policies.

What can the social policy community contribute to this? It can criticise constructively, as it has always done, but it is capable of doing more than this. In keeping with the government's own focus, it can continue to undertake policy relevant research and seek to use this to influence government policy and practice. For example, Pahl's chapter (Chapter Two) demonstrates the potentially major contributions that could be made by helping people understand the better management of family finances. Similarly, the conceptual framework by which interagency partnerships can be appraised, developed by Powell et al (Chapter Three), although described by the authors as 'rudimentary', highlights very real problems with the notion of partnership as used by the government, and adds significantly to the existing literature through its suggestions for improved working.

Given the impetus and enthusiasm to bridge the gap between rhetoric and reality in policy making, there is clearly the potential for greater involvement of the social policy community, broadly defined, to have a significant impact on policy, assuming the government is willing to listen and to take note. At the same time, those involved in the study and provision of social policy need to recognise the social, environmental and political constraints under which governments necessarily operate and, where appropriate, tailor their demands and suggestions accordingly.

International developments

During 2000 a lot has been said and written, much of it polemical, impassioned and opinionated, about the impact of globalisation, international organisations such as the World Bank and International Monetary Fund (IMF), and of transnational corporations (TNCs) on national and regional economies and on the welfare of citizens around the world. In Seattle, in Prague and, although largely suffocated by local police action, in Davos, where these international organisations and leading economic and political actors have met, we have witnessed vociferous, sometimes violent and always well-reported protests against the impact of global capitalism and its alleged agents, the governments and corporations of the rich capitalist world. Protests have focused mainly on the alleged negative economic and social welfare effects of 'globalised capitalism', and the way in which the governments of the rich North have become more or less willing agents of the self-interested and essentially damaging actions of capitalist corporations who pursue profit before welfare. The effects on the economies and peoples of the developing South, and indeed on large sections of the poor and socially-excluded in the North are, it is alleged, essentially negative and reduce the welfare of all but the richest and most powerful around the world.

For their part, the World Bank, the IMF, the EU, governments of the richer countries, and individuals such as George Soros, have defended trade liberalisation, and fuller integration of the world's poorer countries into the global economy and argued for the essentially beneficial effects of globalisation qua international economic liberalisation, and further capitalist integration across the world. Some would argue that it is the very force and visibility of the protests over recent years which has stung such 'pro-globalisation' bodies into defending their actions and policies in ways which stress their welfare-friendly character. Whether what they allege about these benefits can be accepted, or even assessed, is usually, however, lost in the ongoing diatribe that has characterised both popular and even some supposedly academic debates on this topic.

While not necessarily disagreeing with the critical elements of this discourse, objective policy analysis of globalisation and other factors on social policy internationally requires a somewhat less impassioned and polemical tone, and a rather more analytic approach to what is actually occurring. Globalisation and international economic change have indeed become the focal point of a growing number of academic studies of social and economic policy in recent years (see, for example, Mishra, 1999;

Scharpf and Schmidt, 2000; Sykes et al, 2001). What these and other studies suggest is that a rather more sanguine approach to the issues generates a much more complex and ambivalent picture of international social policy developments and the impact of globalisation, international organisations and economic change than both the most 'pro' and 'anti' polemicists suggest.

What, then, have international organisations such as the World Bank, the IMF, and the EU been doing in the last year that may be likely to affect international social policy developments? We shall focus here on just two bodies, the World Bank and the EU.

During 2000 the World Bank released two major studies on world poverty and economic growth: *World development report 2000/2001: Attacking poverty* (2000), and *The quality of growth* (Vinod et al, 2000). Both focus on the continuing existence and widening disparities in poverty across the globe. The *World development report* focuses on the continuing existence of poverty:

> Of the world's 6 billion people, 2.8 billion ... live on less than $2 a day, and 1.2 billion ... live on less than $1 a day, with 44 percent living in South Asia. In rich countries fewer than 1 child in 100 does not reach its fifth birthday, while in the poorest countries as many as a fifth of children do not. (World Bank 2000, p 3)

Yet, the report argues, major reductions in all the main dimensions of poverty are possible. Rather than arguing for increased investment in physical capital and infrastructure, or the development of health and education provision, or indeed in promoting labour-intensive economic growth as earlier World Bank studies have done, this most recent report moves the emphasis towards issues of governance and institutional development in poorer countries. Actions to reduce world poverty are needed in three areas: the promotion of economic opportunities for poor people through more 'equitable growth' and better access to world markets; making state institutions in poorer countries more responsive to poor people and removing barriers for women, ethnic and racial groups and the socially disadvantaged; and more 'security', meaning the better management of economies to avoid the crises which, because of their vulnerability, affect poorest people most (see World Bank, 2000, pp 31-41). Thus economic growth is still at the centre of the World Bank's strategy to tackle poverty, but there is now a greater emphasis on the 'quality' of such growth to make it more likely to benefit the poor, as well as the better-off.

It is this issue of the *quality* of economic growth that sits at the heart of the World Bank's other major study and provides its title. *The quality of growth* argues that four dimensions are especially relevant for outcomes affecting poverty reduction and, indeed, more widespread improvements in the quality of life of the population at large. Briefly, these are the manner in which economic opportunities are distributed in the process of growth; the sustainability of the environment; the impact of global risks and how these are managed; and the way in which the economy and society are governed. The emphasis in growth should now shift away from physical capital towards human and natural capital.

Not surprisingly, anti-capitalist and anti-globalisation protesters of various sorts have not found the Bank's recipes to its liking. What is more surprising is that a growing range of critics of the World Bank's recent approach can also be found among economic commentators that have previously supported its market-led approach. Some have been extremely sceptical of the bank's more apologetic style, and accuse it of conceding to pressures from a mixture of street protests, rich-country non-governmental organisations (NGOs), and rich country governments "... that care more about seeming enlightened and caring than about doing what is right" (*Economist*, 21-28 September 2000).

Turning to the EU, there have been two major developments during 2000 which are likely to have some sort of impact on social policy development across the EU member states, and, arguably, across European welfare states more generally. The first was the publication and adoption by the Commission of the new *Social policy agenda* (Commission of the European Communities, 2000). The second was the adoption by the European Council in December 2000 of the *Charter of Fundamental Rights of the European Union* (EU, 2000).

The EU's new social policy agenda, intended to cover the period 2000 to 2005, is not really new at all: most of its targets and its methods are extensions of those developed out of the economic and social policy white papers of 1994, and subsequent action programmes. EU social policy is fundamentally focused on economic policy, and in particular employment policy: the key phrase now is 'social policy as a productive factor'. The emphasis continues to be on sustained economic growth combined with low inflation and sound public finances. While social inclusion and the fight against poverty have now become an even more central concern of the EU's social policy agenda, the message is clear as to how exclusion may be transformed into inclusion, and poverty tackled: 'more and better jobs', to use the EU's own phraseology.

Does this then mean that the EU's new social policy agenda is simply old wine in new bottles? Not entirely. As is so often the case with the policy statements and declarations of the EU, and as committed EU-watchers will know, the formal statements represent carefully worded compromises between the positions of different member states and other constituencies involved. Once agreed on, however, these policy statements provide various 'windows of opportunity' to be exploited by different interest groups within the member states, in the various directorates of the Commission, and among various NGOs, trades unions, and citizens' groups seeking to pressure the EU for policy development. While the new social policy agenda itself may not seem to represent an especially novel or different departure for EU policy development, only time will tell whether the combination of this agenda along with, for example, the EU enlargement process, the success (or failure) of European Monetary Union (EMU) and the single currency, and the impact of international economic downturn will generate different social policy initiatives in the EU. At present, it is clear that both member states and the Commission, if not the European Parliament, are content to leave social policy very much to national governments to control – 'subsidiarity rules' – while otherwise committing themselves to the same sort of rhetoric on economic policy and its welfare effects which the Bretton Woods organisations are promoting elsewhere.

Potentially more significant for social policy in the EU is the *Declaration of Fundamental Human Rights*. While it is still too early to say what the effects of the new Charter will be (and it has not yet even been agreed by the European Council, that is, the member states, how it should be implemented), experience with respect to incorporation of the Council of Europe's European Declaration of Human Rights into national law suggests that the combined effect of these two declarations could, indeed, be very significant. For example, the interpretation of what Article 23 on equality between men and women, Article 24 on the rights of the child, and Article 26 on the integration of a person with disabilities mean in terms of access to social policy provision in different EU member states might lead to fundamental legal challenges to existing policy and practice. If we turn to Articles 34 (on social security and social assistance) and 35 (on health care) one can envisage how various pressure groups could use such provisions to mount significant legal challenges to existing imbalances in provision across the EU.

Conceptual and historical developments

Constraints affecting governments can also have an influence in civil society more generally, and in ways that challenge abiding perceptions of the relationship between the individual and the state. Many of the chapters in this volume suggest that what counts as 'social policy' is continually changing, with certain chapters in Part 3, for example, exploring the implications of scientific advances in genetics and the increasing impact of the new information and communication technologies. Developments in these areas clearly have consequences not only for governments as they struggle to come to terms with the social and political effects of these changes, but for citizens too. The emergence of new areas of this kind raises the basic 'social policy' issues about forms of poverty, exclusion and social justice, but in a manner that challenges accepted understandings of these key terms. Whereas traditional interpretations of citizenship and social policy looked first and foremost to forms of material provision as indicators of social equality – or at least equity – the degree of material provision alone may not be sufficient to anchor a sense of citizenship in the future. To what extent, for example, will citizens be able to have access to electronic forms of information? Might limited and unequal access create new divisions of 'information-rich' and 'information-poor'? Again, while access to new and expensive forms of medical care has always been limited, and this could reasonably be counted as a 'material' issue, the advent of the new genetic technologies may lead to a rather different set of problems. If 'genetic engineering' works to undermine genetic diversity, one consequence is likely to be the (further) marginalisation of people with disabilities, a form of exclusion and inequality that no amount of extra material resources could rectify.

The point here is simply to raise the issue of how academics and policy makers might reconceptualise notions of social justice better to accord with the increasingly complex range of concerns with which we are faced. Questions of the kind posed above prompt us to think more broadly about the nature of citizenship and social belonging in the developed economies in ways that are likely to challenge traditional perceptions of the role and nature of the welfare state. To be sure, the welfare state in the UK, as well as elsewhere, is no stranger to change as the briefest glance at the history of the past 20 years or so would demonstrate. The significant thing now, however, is that the *direction* of change is less clear and there appear to be no sure principles by which to gauge the relative merits of competing claims and demands. If there is good reason to suppose that the core ideological convictions around which social policy debates were once organised – notably socialism and market liberalism – have become less influential, the difficulty is that no alternative normative theories have emerged to replace them.

Of course, it is no longer clear that such theories (that is, internally coherent systems of thought capable of providing reasoned, if contestable, sets of principles and able to inform distinct attitudes to social policy making) actually *could* be developed. The variety of theoretical and empirical issues which need to be taken into account in the development of such perspectives, and the increasing number of sectional interests in civil society that could produce 'privileged readings' or interpretations of such issues, would defy even the most sophisticated efforts to produce a meaningful, though flexible, conception of the common good. To illustrate this point, Gail Lewis (2000, p 2) indicates one specific difficulty that immediately reduces prospects for a new normative synthesis. Complexity, she suggests, is compounded by the points of theoretical and political tension that result from the

> ... intersection of two issues that potentially pull in opposite directions ... on the one hand, rethinking social policy involves trying to think through an agenda that will ensure greater equality across numerous social divisions. On the other hand, this requires recognition of the specificity of particular relations of inequality without privileging any one of these relations as primary. (Lewis, 2000, p 2)

If this formulation is correct, and the sheer number of sectional interests demanding recognition in the public sphere suggests that it is, then how plausible is it to think in terms of a principled 'way forward' in social policy which is sufficiently robust to be able to resolve – or at least ameliorate – the fundamental tension that Lewis describes?

It is not the purpose of this introduction to provide definitive 'answers'. However, it is worth briefly indicating the 'contours' of two potential answers that deserve much greater consideration than can be given to them here. The first makes a virtue of pragmatism in social policy making, the argument being that such an orientation in formulating and implementing social policies is no bad thing. In fact it may be that no necessary connection exists between the development of coherent ideological principles and their application and, indeed, the absence of such principles could allow a greater diversity of policy practices to flourish. As Will Kymlicka (2001, p 5) observes in relation to the rights of minority groups, it is possible that excessive concern with principle contributes to a hardening of attitudes and an unwillingness to contemplate alternative policy approaches. In this regard, it could be argued that the 'Third Way' provides a range of practices sufficient to this task. After all, the notion of finding a 'middle way' between state and market, utilising the advantages of both in the interests of the more efficient provision of social goods and services to a wide range of citizen groups, suggests an acceptance of pragmatism in social policy that could provide a welcome change from the ideological struggles – and stalemates – of the past. The fact that Third Way solutions vary substantially among different countries, the Clinton era in the USA or Schroeder's contemporary Germany exhibiting quite different policy priorities from Blair's UK, suggests that policies developed under this rubric owe more to pragmatism than principle; there is certainly no 'new politics' here, as the Institute of Public Policy Research's Matthew Taylor has recently intimated (quoted by Beckett, 2001).

But are such solutions really enough in the sense that they provide a means of underpinning policy formulation and implementation in ways acceptable to an ever-increasing plurality of social, economic and political interests? Having questioned the role of normative theory, asking whether it is useful at all, Kymlicka (2001, p 6) hints at a second, and different, response to the question posed above. In his view such theory does have a role. So far as minority rights are concerned, he argues that the elaboration of normative theory is important because it provides a basis for distinguishing between fundamental principles and 'contingent practices'. Translating Kymlicka's concerns into issues directly relevant to social policy, there is a need to distinguish, for example, between two types of demand: first, 'citizen' demands for particular resources or the meeting of specific claims which, however different they may be in terms of nature and pattern of delivery across different groups, nevertheless contribute to the realisation of fundamental principles such as increasing the total sum of social and economic equality, or at least reducing poverty. Second, purely 'sectional' demands, though they may draw attention to considerations of 'difference', might do so in a highly contingent manner, which undermines normative understandings by justifying inegalitarian practices.

This formulation is in no way intended to undermine developing notions of 'difference' – far from it. But it is employed to suggest that the validity of competing claims needs to be understood by reference to principles which are based on more than the possession of raw power, whether this takes the form of physical violence or 'voice'. It is notable in this regard that where such principles are *not* brought into play, the clash of interests can get ugly indeed. The summary actions of farmers and road hauliers in the early autumn of 2000, although arguably a form of citizen action (Ellison, 2000), nevertheless pointed up the potential ways in which groups can mobilise certain key resources in a manner which is detrimental to the 'common good'. To be sure, the presence of normative theory in social policy is unlikely to reduce the immediate heat of argument, but it might serve as a guide to others who are responsible for allocating the scarce resources under threat. In this sense, of course, 'principled' claims for 'difference' have some degree of protection against the vagaries of sectional demands.

A final point for consideration is the inevitable issue of how normative principles can be 'grounded' in this post-ideological' age. If the 'old-fashioned' answer is to look to forms of democratic control, the gloss on this response must be to make it clear that what stands as 'democracy' must somehow include adequate recognition of an evermore bewildering array of competing demands. There is no space here to explore the possibilities for new forms of democratic organisation (and participation), but the emphasis should be firmly on increasingly sophisticated forms of consultation, and even 'deliberation', which need to be introduced into democratic procedures. To this degree, it is important that normative principles of social policy include an awareness of the 'political'.

References

Beckett, A. (2001) 'Dulling down' , *The Guardian*, 5 March.

Commission of the European Communities (2000) *Social policy agenda*, COM 379 Final, Brussels: Commission of the European Communities.

Coote, A. (2000) 'Introduction', in A. Coote (ed) *A new gender agenda*, London: Institute of Public Policy Research.

Ellison, N. (2000) 'Proactive and defensive engagement: social citizenship in a changing public sphere', *Sociological Research Online*, vol 5, no 4.

European Union (2000) *Charter of Fundamental Rights of the European Union*, 2000C 364/01, Luxembourg: OOPEC.

Economist (2000) 'Economic focus: quantity and quality', 21-28 September.

Kymlicka, W. (2001) *Politics in the vernacular: Nationalism, multiculturalism, and citizenship*, Oxford: Oxford University Press.

Lewis, G. (2000) 'Introduction: expanding the social policy imaginary', in G. Lewis, S. Gewirtz and J. Clarke (eds) *Rethinking social policy*, London: Sage Publications.

Mishra, R. (1999) *Globalization and the welfare state*, Cheltenham: Edward Elgar.

Scharpf, F. and Schmidt, V. (eds) (2000) *Welfare and work in open economies* (2 vols), Oxford: Oxford University Press.

Sykes, R., Palier, B. and Prior, P.M. (2001) *Globalization and European welfare states*, Basingstoke: Palgrave.

World Bank (2000) *World development report 2000/2001*, Washington, DC: World Bank/Oxford University Press.

Vinod, T., Dhareshwar, A., Lopez, R., Wang, Y., Kishnor, N., Dailimi, M. and Kaufmann, D. (2000) *The quality of growth*, Washington, DC: World Bank/Oxford University Press.

Part One:
UK developments

The work of the authors in this section draws on a wide variety of approaches and the analysis of very different policy areas, but when taken together they serve to highlight some key issues for the study of social policy. These include not only the currently much-debated strengths of evidence-based research and its implications for policy and practice, but also the variety of processes which reflect the important role of ideas in social policy and which can contribute to our understanding of contemporary society and politics. They also serve to reinforce the recognition that the making and implementation of social policy is inevitably a continuous and sometimes cyclical process. In addition, several of the pieces make clear that while academic research can be both interesting and insightful on its own account, it can also have very significant implications for policy and practice.

For example, Pahl's chapter (Chapter Two) considers family finances and looks at why some people make what are apparently irrational financial decisions. This draws on a variety of theoretical perspectives and applies these to practical case study examples to highlight issues such as the limited rationality of many consumers in their financial decision making; access to financial services; and increasing concern about the 'digital divide'. Given recent and likely future developments in financial services Pahl's chapter raises a number of what should be significant concerns for policy makers in this field. Similarly the work of Powell, Exworthy and Berney (Chapter Three) builds on an examination of the rhetoric of New Labour around 'partnership' and goes on to develop a conceptual framework to illustrate its application with empirical material based on the implementation of policy at local levels. This is expressed in terms of 'playing the game of partnership'. The ladder of partnership is examined through an analysis of stakeholders' views on health inequalities policy and includes a number of potential lessons about the relationship between the centre and locality and the development of partnerships, including crucially, the finding that the rules within which they operate are often not clear to local stakeholders.

In Chapter Four, Heron charts the relationship between Etzioni's communitarianism and current British social policy developments in a range of policy areas including social security, education and housing and regeneration. It illustrates the prevalence of communitarian values in New Labour's social policies and the extent to which they echo the spirit of American communitarism.

Finally, the chapter by Beckmann (Chapter Five) brings an added dimension to the social policy sphere with a discussion of consensual sadomasochism and develops some possible implications in the context of disability. This draws on the author's primary research to challenge the selective criminalisation of sadomasochism and to illustrate that a fuller understanding of the ethics and practice of consensual sadomasochism might bring some lessons for the wider society, for example, in challenging stereotypes around sexuality and 'disability', including enabling disabled people to give full expression of their 'sexualities'.

TWO

Couples and their money: theory and practice in personal finances

Jan Pahl

Why do some people make apparently irrational financial decisions, despite the plethora of financial advice and information which is now available? This question arose in the course of my recent study on family finances in the electronic economy. Listening to people talking about money made me realise that their discourse is very different from that of the money advice columns of newspapers or the information offered by consumer organisations, financial advisers and other bodies. In an attempt to make sense of the tangle of meanings that that seemed to be attached to money, I have been examining the data from a variety of theoretical perspectives. In this paper I shall present four of these perspectives, illustrating each with examples from my own and other people's research. The four perspectives draw on:

- economic approaches and rational choice theory;
- social structural approaches and financial exclusion;
- psychological approaches;
- cultural theory and the meanings of money.

The context is a world in which cash is being superseded by cheques, credit cards and Internet banking, in which social security benefits are paid into bank accounts instead of in 'real money', in which 'financial education' is being introduced into the national curriculum and financial services are increasingly part of the 'welfare state' (Pahl, 2001).

The study grew out of a long-running stream of work on the control and allocation of money within the family (Pahl, 1989, 1995). This research showed that couples control and manage their money in a great variety of different ways and that particular systems of money management have significant implications for individuals within couples. Crucially, it underlined the fact that the household cannot be treated as an unproblematic financial unit. Opening up the 'black box' of the domestic economy revealed that complex economic and social processes underlie the financial transfers which take place within the intra-household economy.

However, all this research essentially conceptualised money as cash, or as cash held in a bank account. Over the past 30 years there have been dramatic changes in the ways in which ordinary people receive, hold and spend their money. The first credit card was launched in 1966, to be followed by store cards, debit cards, loyalty cards and smart or chargeable cards (Credit Card Research Group, 1998). Banking by telephone or computer began in the 1980s, with an accelerating expansion in the use of Internet banking services throughout the 1990s. All these developments are described here collectively as 'new forms of money', or 'the electronic economy'.

From the point of view of the banks there are significant differences between different forms of money, not least in terms of the costs of transactions. The cost of withdrawing cash across the counter is just over a pound per transaction, compared with about 42 pence for a withdrawal by cheque or credit card, just over 30 pence for a withdrawal from an Automatic Teller Machine (ATM), around 25 pence for paying with a debit card and around 20 pence for paying by direct debit (Cruickshank, 2000, p 60). Customers also identify differences between different forms of money, although their perspectives are not the same as those of the banks, as we shall see. The research on which this paper is based was concerned with the ways in which new forms of money are being incorporated into the financial arrangements of married and as-married couples. Its aim was to examine the extent to which new forms of money constrain or enhance the access which individuals have to financial resources (Pahl, 1999).

Methods of the study

Three different sources of data were used in the study, in order to gain both quantitative and qualitative information about the issues which were being explored. First, analyses of the Family Expenditure Survey (FES) provided quantitative data about 3,676 married couples, which could be generalised to a larger population because of the nature of the survey (ONS, 1996). Second, seven focus groups took place, involving 59 individuals living in five different parts of England. Finally, face-to-face interviews were carried out with 40 couples, in order to develop a more qualitative understanding of the ways in which individuals and couples managed their finances and made use of new forms of money. Men and women were interviewed separately and privately. (For further details about the methods of the study, see Pahl, 1999.)

Economic approaches and rational choice theory

According to classical economic theory, money has four main functions: it is a medium of exchange, a store of value, a unit of account, and a standard of deferred payment. The words are neutral and unemotional and it is inherent in this approach that money is essentially defined as subject to reason rather than emotion.

There is, of course, an extensive economics literature on money, but most of it is concerned with the place of money in a modern economy, with rates of interest, financial markets, monetary policy, techniques of monetary control, the international financial system and so on (see, for example, Crockett, 1979). Most have no entry in the index for words such as 'individuals', 'households', 'consumers' and other ways of designating the world of personal finances with which we are concerned here. However, there are some theoretical perspectives within economic theory which are very relevant to personal finances and I would like to highlight two of these.

First, there is the issue of fungibility. This notion is standard in classical economic theory and means that money is considered to be neutral and interchangeable, so that any unit of wealth is substitutable for any other (McCloskey, 1987).

Second, classical economic theory has developed the idea of rational choice theory. This assumes that people make reasoned choices in order to maximise their overall welfare or utility; the theory was applied to the economics of the family by Becker (1993). Rational choice theory lays stress on the importance of information in facilitating the efficient working of markets and of consumer choice. This theoretical perspective informed the recent report to the Chancellor of the Exchequer, entitled *Competition in UK banking* (Cruickshank, 2000). The review on which the report was based carried out a detailed investigation of competition in the supply of banking services to personal customers.

The executive summary concluded that:

> Knowledgeable customers provide the best incentive to effective competition. With the right information, customers can take responsibility for their own financial well being, shop around and exert the pressure on suppliers which drive a competitive and innovative market. There are a number of actions which government can take to improve information conditions in retail markets. The costs are small, and the potential gains from catalysing competition are large. (Cruickshank, 2000, p xix)

The review recommended that the government should encourage the Financial Services Authority (FSA) in its promotion of financial awareness among the population. Such promotion should provide consumers with a means of making informed choices about allocating their resources between different types of financial services and different suppliers. In other words, they should behave as rational economic individuals (FSA, 1998).

Recent research from the FSA concluded that many financial consumers fail to shop around, have difficulty in understanding the information they get, and often find it hard to identify products to meet their needs. Interestingly the highest and the lowest social classes were least likely to shop around, and those who were retired were less likely to shop around than those in full-time employment (Levene, 2000, p 11).

Those who took part in my research often presented themselves in the focus groups and interviews as rational economic individuals. Equally often, they revealed the sort of situation which the FSA research documented. Here are two examples.

Daniel and Rosie were both in their 30s, but their approaches to money were strikingly different. Daniel was an executive with a major company, earning over £60,000 per year, while Rosie's work as a part-time art teacher brought in about £8,000; they had two children. Rosie described the way in which they managed their money as "we pool some of our money and keep some of it separately", while Daniel described their system as "we keep the money separate but manage it jointly".

Daniel was very much the rational consumer and banked by 'phone. When asked why he chose telephone banking, he said, "24 hours, there's no queuing and they're very efficient; I hate queuing, haven't got time to queue, I can do it from my desk and I can do it at home, terrific". He had a current account, from which all the bills and Rosie's credit card were paid by direct debit, and went on to describe his other accounts:

"I have a high interest account with First Direct as well. And then I have another savings account which is slightly lower interest. The high interest savings account has a penalty on withdrawals, so I keep a sum of money in there stable which I don't draw on. If I have extra spending, or I need to top up my current account in case I'm going overdrawn, that comes from the third, lower interest account which I keep for small amounts. When I have a surplus at the end of the month in my current account I transfer across to the high interest account as much as I can."

Daniel's economic rationality extended to credit cards and Air Miles. He explained about his American Express Gold Card:

"I use that for my purchases because I get Air Miles on that, so all my purchases I get Air Miles and I transfer that to my various Air Miles accounts. I originally got a Gold Card because they did a special offer, had one free for a year, and so I gave up after a year. Said 'No thank you. I don't want to pay for a card'. Oh well, another card arrives free for a year, so I said, 'Fine'."

Rosie had a very different approach to finances. The way in which her bank accounts reflected her biography has been described elsewhere (Pahl, 1999, p 62). Her interview was full of comments about forgotten pin numbers, penalties imposed for going overdrawn and doubt about the balances in various little-used accounts. When asked about telephone banking, she was emphatic in her rejection of the idea:

"If I've got to have dealings with them for money, I like to know that it's only a certain number of hours.... I like restrictions of banking hours; I do quite like that. I'm old-fashioned, completely opposite to Daniel. If he sees that something is wrong with one of the accounts, he says ring up immediately, but I kind of like stalling everything. I feel sort of secure that at least I can't do anything about it. I have to wait until tomorrow. I think it's quite good not to feel you have to deal with financial matters. You just don't want to have to worry about it. The weekend is the end of work; you don't want to work; you don't go to work."

Daniel and Rosie could afford her lack of economic rationality, but for many people in Britain the effects would have been disastrous. For Andy and Sylvia their approach to financial matters had contributed to a situation in which their house had been repossessed and they were still paying back on various court orders. They were in their mid-40s with three children, and had recently been rehoused in a council flat. Andy was a service engineer and Sylvia a classroom assistant. She described what happened with the mortgage:

> "We had a few arrears ... a little bit of arrears. But they had this policy where they sort of put the interest on top of the mortgage and then you get the interest. And the interest on our little bit of arrears of about £4,000 actually snuggled into £25,000."

Then there was the credit card:

> "When you've got a credit card you can get up to your limit ... which is what happened to us with our credit card. You get to your limit of maybe it's £1,500 and as you get there and you just begin to pay it back, and then they write and say to you, 'We've upped your limit to £2,500'. And you think, 'Ooh, I've got a bit more to spend'. Or 'We'll pay this, we'll do that'. And then you spend that bit more."

Keeping a check on their money became less and less rewarding:

> "I can't say he checks statements. That is one thing he never does. He used to when we were first married – he used to have a book. He used to be able to check and say how much money we had. But then I think we had the kids and it just disappeared. There's not any money there to count [she laughed]."

However, the situation in which Andy and Sylvia found themselves was not solely the result of their mismanagement. With low incomes and no savings, at a time of rising house prices and high interest rates, buying their own house must always have been a risky enterprise. This leads us to a more social structural approach.

Social structural approaches and financial exclusion

While economists have focused on the macro-economy and on the part that money plays in the workings of modern industrial societies, sociologists and social policy analysts have been more concerned with

Figure 1: Financial holdings by socio-economic group

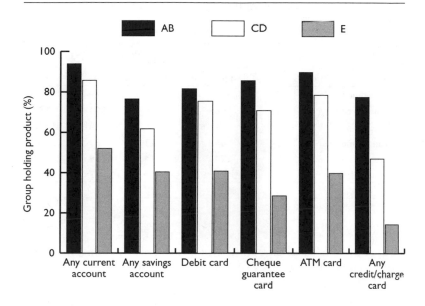

Source: cited in Cruickshank (2000, p 277)

the extent to which different social groups have differential access to money in the forms of wages and salaries, pensions, savings and capital. Feminist theory has been particularly concerned with gender and with the social and economic processes by which women have been excluded from power and have been economically disadvantaged. Marxist theory has pointed to the importance of class and to the very different structural position of the working class, as opposed to the class of owners of the means of production. In a memorable phrase, Marx defined money in terms of the power it conveys. He said,

> Money is impersonal property. It permits me to transport on my person, in my pocket, social power and social relations in general: the substance of society. Money puts social power in material form into the hands of private persons, who exercise it as individuals. (Marx, 1971, p 150)

Certainly there are class differences in the use of new forms of money. Figure 1 shows that the proportion of the population with a current account varies from nearly all of those in social classes A and B to around

Table 1: Percentages of individuals using a credit card to make a purchase by household employment categories

| Household employment categories | Credit card used to make a purchase | | | | Sig/ P ≤ |
| | Men | | Women | | |
	%	No	%	No	
Both full-time	42	350	41	349	ns
Full-time/part-time	42	356	35	304	0.085
Full-time/no paid job	37	256	25	170	0.001
Woman main earner	24	66	23	63	ns
Both retired	21	174	14	119	0.003
Both unemployed	6	9	7	12	ns
All	33	1,221	28	1,017	

Total number = 3,676 couples

Source: Pahl (1999)

a half of those in social class E. Use of credit cards varies too, with only about a tenth of those in social class E holding a credit or charge card (Cruickshank, 2000, p 277).

My own research, using data from the FES expenditure diaries, showed significant variations in the use of credit cards, according to income, employment status, gender, age and education. As Table 1 shows, between a quarter and a third of all those who took part in the survey used a credit card over the two-week period when they were keeping the expenditure diary for the FES, with men being slightly more likely than women to use cards. Gender differences in the use of credit cards were associated with intra-household differences in employment status. When the man and the woman were both in full-time employment they were equally likely to have used a credit card. However, women in part-time employment were less likely, and women without employment very significantly less likely to have used a credit card, by comparison with their employed husbands.

Unemployed and retired people were very much less likely to have used a credit card than those who were in employment. This is consonant with research on access to credit more generally, which shows that when low-income households have to borrow money, they tend to contact more expensive money lenders than the typical credit card company (Ford, 1991; Rowlingson, 1994). There was a significant gender difference among retired people, with men being more likely to use credit cards than women. This may reflect differences in income, a lack of confidence by women in using new technologies, or a tradition of male dominance in marital finances among this age group.

Regression analyses showed that education was a very significant variable: those with more years of education were more likely to make use of credit cards. The conclusion was that those who are 'credit-rich' tend also to be 'work-rich', 'information-rich' and 'education-rich', while those who are 'credit-poor' are likely also to be 'work-poor', 'information-poor' and 'education-poor' (Pahl, 1999, 2000).

The social structural approach has also shaped recent debates about 'financial exclusion', defined as having few or no financial products. Being a full citizen of a Western European country increasingly depends on access to financial products and services, that is, access to credit, banking facilities, mortgages, insurance and so on. Those who have full access to all these products will make savings by comparison with those who are partly or completely financially excluded. However, one-and-a-half million households in Britain lack even the most basic of financial products, such as a current bank account and home contents insurance, while a further 4.4 million are on the margins of financial exclusion, using just one or two financial products (Kempson and Whyley, 1999; FSA, 2000).

Financial exclusion has been shown to be a complex and dynamic process (Kempson and Whyley, 1999). Some people have spent all their lives in a cash-based economy, with pensioners and the long-term unemployed being over-represented among this group. Others have given up using financial services, often because of a drop in income following unemployment, long-term sickness or retirement. Women may cease to use financial services on the death of a partner in whose name the products were held. The majority of people without financial products are excluded by a combination of marketing, pricing and inappropriate product design. Some of those who do have access to financial services use them rarely or inappropriately; others have made a conscious decision not to use particular services, for a variety of different reasons (Kempson and Whyley, 1999; see also FSA, 2000; Treasury, 1999; Lewis, et al, 1997; Molloy and Snape, 1999). Results such as these suggest that social structural approaches cannot explain everything about the use of financial services and new forms of money.

Psychological approaches

There are links between the social structural and psychological approaches. For example, the development of the money economy has been seen as an agent of individualism and modernism. Simmel identified money as a catalyst in the growth of individualism and in the destruction of community, describing it as "the major mechanism that paves the way from *Gemeinschaft to Gesellschaft*". Money for Simmel was the "breeding ground for economic individualism and egoism" (Simmel, 1990, p 437).

Within psychology itself there is a growing interest in money as a topic, evidenced by the success of the *Journal of Economic Psychology*, and by an expanding literature. In the discussion that follows I shall draw especially on the work of Furnham and Lewis (1986). They suggested that, considering its importance in everyday life, there has been relatively little research into the psychology of money, although there have been studies in particular areas. Each of the different branches of psychology has contributed something to the study of money. So, for example, experimental psychology has been concerned with distortions in the perception of familiar and unfamiliar money. Occupational psychology has examined attitudes to money as a reward and incentive for labour. Social psychology has explored individual, group and societal attitudes to money.

Developmental psychology has been concerned with how and when money concepts are learnt. For example, one study examined the ways in which children understood the principles on which banking is based (Jahoda, 1981). They were asked: "Supposing I put £100 into a bank, and after a year I take my money out again, would I get back more, less or the same?" and "Supposing I borrow £100 from a bank to pay back after one year. Would I have to pay back more, or less or the same?" The responses of the children were categorised thus:

- no knowledge of interest (get or pay back same amount);
- interest on deposits only (get back more but pay the same);
- interest on both, but more on deposit;
- interest same on both deposits and loans;
- interest higher on loans (but reason not fully understood);
- interest higher on loans fully understood.

The results showed that only a quarter of British 14 and 16 year olds fully understood the function of the bank, in the sense of understanding why the interest on loans would be higher than the interest on deposits. There was some evidence of class differences, with middle-class children having a slightly higher level of understanding, but the differences were not statistically significant. Replications of the study in other parts of the world showed that Dutch children were twice as likely to understand the concept of interest on deposits and loans as were British children, while in Hong Kong a full understanding of these issues emerged at the age of 10. The researcher concluded:

> The exceptional maturity of the Hong Kong children probably reflected their high level of economic socialisation and consumer activity, and the business ethos of the society at large.... Their maturity represents, in short, a case of socio-economic reality shaping, partly at least, socio-economic understanding. (Ng, 1983, pp 220-1)

One of the problems faced by Andy and Sylvia was that they did not really understand the principles underlying the concept of interest.

In her book, *The secret life of money*, Wilson contrasted economic, or *objective money*, and personal, or *subjective money* (Wilson, 1999, p xv). She argued that subjective money carries emotional baggage, often acquired in childhood, which can severely hamper its use as a neutral medium of exchange. One reason for the antagonism which many people feel towards banks and other financial institutions may be the discrepancy between objective and subjective money:

> Some people need the bank to be like a stern father, to stand between the individual and their childish impulses. Others deeply resent the dependence, the patronising tone, the continuing control. Still others may, unconsciously, both want the control and yet resent it. People often seem stuck in a sort of perpetual adolescence in their relationships with banks. (Wilson, 1999, p 162)

The language associated with money was set out very neatly in *The secret life of money* (Wilson, 1999, p 182).

Wilson pointed to the contrast between the official language of money, which draws on the physical and material sciences, economics, banking and accounting. These disciplines have opted for terms which are low in affect, with terminology which is impersonal, technical and detached. David Hume's metaphor was taken from engineering. He said, "Money is not, properly speaking, one of the subjects of commerce, but only the instrument which men have agreed upon to facilitate the exchange of one commodity for another. It is none of the wheels of trade; it is the oil which renders the motion of the wheels more smooth and easy" (Hume, 1963, p 289).

Figure 2: The language of money

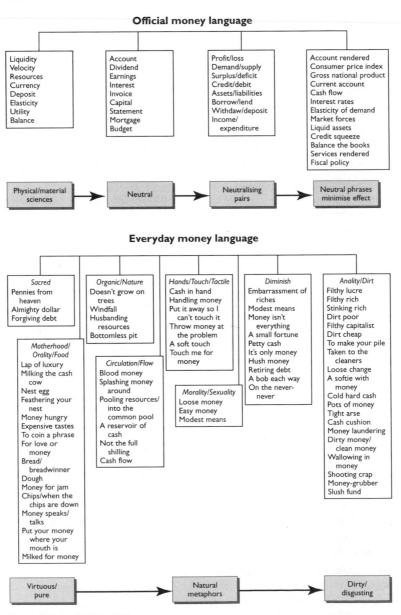

By contrast, everyday money language is rich in sensuality and in emotion. A study in which individuals were asked about the words which they associated with money showed that there was a predominance of negative emotions. From a list of 20 words associated with money, the four most commonly selected were 'anxiety', 'depression', 'anger' and 'helplessness' (Wilson, 1999, p 54).

All of those who took part in the interviews expressed feelings about money and banks during the course of their interviews. Charles and Fiona were both in their 40s. He was a head teacher, while she had been a designer before she gave up her job to look after their three children. He talked about why he preferred paying by cheque as opposed to cash or credit cards:

> "Because I can lie on the cheque stubs. And also the psychology of it – rather than giving sort of £30 cash over to someone, I'll write a cheque for £30, because it's less painful and doesn't seem as much."

Fiona described how she came to take charge of finances:

> "We used to have separate accounts and he was paying some [bills] twice and some not at all. A bank statement would come and he wouldn't bother opening it for, I don't know, about five months. Once he paid the mortgage twice – he never bothered to open his statement."

So they changed to a joint account for which she checked the statement. She described what happened when she came to Charles and his cheque stubs:

> "He'll put down £20 and I know it will be £30. I mean his cheque book's full of blanks and that irritates me because I do a running total and I know that the blanks will be £10 or £15 or £20. When I look at the bank statement and nothing tallies [she laughed]. If I'm in a bad mood sometimes I'll say, 'What's the point in bloody doing this? What's the point in me adding it up?'"

She gave him £30 per week in cash, but he often ran out during the week. Since he was in school all day he could not get to the bank. He then had to do what he called 'creative accounting':

Charles: "I can write a cheque against the school dinner money. They like that in a sense, because it's less cash on the premises."

Interviewer: "Would you tell Fiona about it?"

Charles: "Well, it depends. If I was buying her something.... Maybe I will, maybe I won't. The joke is, I'm in charge of a million-and-a-half pound budget at school, but she wouldn't let me near any of our finances because we'd be bankrupt within a year."

Later in the interview it turned out that Charles was keen to have some cash for which he did not have to account to support his hobbies of buying old silver and betting; he said, "But where I go wrong, 'cos I'm very absent-minded. I leave my betting slips everywhere. So I get found out". However, Fiona had her own source of financial embarrassment. She had opened six building society accounts in the hope of getting bonuses when they demutualised; she commented, "My friend thinks I'm despicable".

Even in this short extract from their interview, Charles and Fiona exhibited a complex mix of feelings, including anxiety, irritation, discomfort, embarrassment, guilt, shame, desire to control and desire to deceive. Charles's discourse, in particular, is very far from that of the rational economic man with which we began. Fiona's final story about the building society accounts is a reminder that the meanings attributed to money are also shaped by the broader cultural context in which they are located.

Cultural theory and the meanings of money

Research in Australia and the United States has cast new light on the meanings which couples and individuals attach to money and has challenged economists' notions of fungibility. In her study of Australian couples, Singh made an illuminating distinction between marriage money and market money (Singh, 1997, p 152). *Marriage money* is personal and private, domestic and cooperative, typically held in a joint account: it is taken on trust and not subject to contract, a fact which may explain some of the resistance to prenuptial contracts. By contrast, *market money* is calculable, impersonal and subject to contract. The contrast between marriage money and banking money becomes striking when couples divorce, or when a wife guarantees a business loan for her husband. When the divorce settlement is made, or when the bank demands repayment of the loan, then marriage money suddenly becomes market money. Financial arrangements that had represented love and trust become revealed as impersonal and contractual. The frequency with which this occurs has given rise to the term, 'sexually transmitted debt' (Lawton, 1991, p 7).

Using historical sources from the USA, Zelizer documented the complex social meanings of money. Her research showed that money is not fungible, in the sense that all currencies are equally exchangeable, but highly differentiated, according to its source, the uses to which it can be put and the person who has the right to use it (Zelizer, 1994). She gave a number of examples:

> People segregate monies *spatially*, using all sorts of domestic containers – labelled envelopes, coloured jars, stockings, piggy banks – or designated institutional accounts, such as Christmas Clubs or vacation funds.... Monies are also distinguished by designating particular *users* for specified currencies: a weekly allowance is for children, not adults; pin money is a female not a male currency; tips are acceptable for waiters, not for lawyers. Or monies are set aside by linking certain *sources* of money to selected uses: income earned by the wife may be reserved for her children's education, while her husband's income pays the mortgage. (Zelizer, 1994, p 209)

Zelizer showed how the social meanings of money are shaped by gender, age and class, so that monetary transactions between two individuals can provide evidence about the degree of equality between them, their level of intimacy and the nature of their relationship.

Cultural theorists have not been concerned with money per se, but rather with the consumption which money makes possible. Nevertheless this can be a fruitful approach to understanding the meanings which individuals can attribute to money. One starting point might be Baudrillard's argument that we have moved from societies that are characterised by production to those of consumption. He suggested that consumption constitutes a system of signs, which enable the individual to relate to the social order through their consumption:

> Consumption does not arise from the objective need of the consumer, a final intention of the subject towards the object; rather there is social production, in a system of exchange, of a material of differences, a code of significations. (Baudrillard, 1981, p 75)

10688   31

Baudrillard argued that an accurate theory of objects will not be established on a theory of needs and their satisfaction, but rather on a theory of prestations and signification. He wrote, "Behind all the superstructures of purchase, market and private property, there is always the mechanism of social prestation ... which is present in our choice, our accumulation and our consumption of objects" (Baudrillard, 1981, p 30).

It might be argued that most of the world's population is not in a position to be concerned about the extent to which their consumption choices constitute a system of signs and significations. However, for the privileged and technologically sophisticated this approach may offer a useful way in which to explore the remarks made by the participants in my research about new forms of money.

The focus groups provided many opportunities for people to use money as a sign for other aspects of their self-identity. Questions about telephone and Internet banking showed some interesting contrasts. Henry, a communications consultant and enthusiast for all things technical, was eager to discuss his experience of Internet banking and to show off his knowledge of telephone banking to his all-male focus group:

> "We needed to go to PC World to buy a computer and buy some stuff, maybe spend three grand. And they said on the 'phone that the money will be transferred within three hours. Well, that's not good enough. The girls wanted to go down to the shop there and then. With online banking like the Royal Bank of Scotland you've got total control. There's no mantras over the 'phone, like the third letter. There's no insecurity like someone else knows a bit of your password. Over the Internet you move that money to there, and off you go and its done there and then."

By contrast, an all-women focus group was scathing about Internet banking, setting up an alternative discourse whose aim seemed to be to validate traditional female identities. The style of the discourse was also in contrast to that of the men's focus group. Compared with Henry's monologue, the discussion in the women-only group took the form of a sequence of brief comments which wove together to make a running train of collective thought:

> "My husband has his private sort of you know – he's got some shares and things. I'm sure he's got his finances on that, but...." (practice nurse)

"Mine plots them and...." (secretary)

"But being as I just don't understand computers at all it's foreign to me." (practice nurse)

"Men have got time...." (secretary)

"I think men like computers more...." (BT complaints officer)

"Yeh – they can play...."

"True – they sit playing or whatever."

"They love their computers." (practice nurse)

"Yeah they do – they do."

"Sometimes he can sit there all day. I say I don't know how you don't go berserk. I would get so frustrated sitting in front of the computer for so long." (practice nurse)

"I do think men are into it." (secretary)

"I think of all the better things I could do." (practice nurse)

"We've got better things to do." (secretary)

"Well, I get annoyed, I get annoyed watching him." (practice nurse)

"We've got a basket of ironing."

"And I've got hundreds of things to do and he's sitting there playing on that all day."

Later it transpired that most of these women must have been accustomed to using computers at work: one was a secretary, one was a complaints officer for BT and another was a practice nurse. Their antagonism to the computers their husbands used at home seemed to reflect some other set of signs and signifiers.

My research showed that typically men were more likely to be banking by 'phone than women, and people in middle-class occupations much more likely than those whose occupations were classified as working class. The same patterns in reverse emerged among those who were not currently using telephone banking, with women being twice as likely as men to express doubts about the idea, and working-class people being more suspicious and less well informed. Internet banking aroused less interest than telephone banking, but the patterns were the same, with men tending to be more interested than women. This finding is in line with international data which shows that male dominance in the use of the Internet occurs in every country for which information is available (Singh and Ryan, 1999).

Credit cards can be understood in terms of the opportunities which they give for status display, in that the colour of the card, and particularly the colours gold and platinum, indicate the holder's income level in a way that cash and cheque books cannot. Michael had a gold card, and admitted that:

> "Depending on who I'm with, if I want to vaguely impress them, I'll get out the gold card. If they get out their gold card, and we're splitting the meal 50/50, then I whack mine on the table and that, er, gives some kind of credibility I suppose."

Perhaps money is becoming not only a means of consumption but also an object of consumption in its own right?

Conclusions

Education and information about personal finances tend to be presented in terms of rational choice theory, but many people are not rational consumers, or their rationality is limited. Policy which is based on rational choice theory, and on the idea of the informed consumer making the best decision, will inevitably miss the target as far as some individuals are concerned.

In their access to financial services, many people are constrained by income, employment status, education, age, gender, ethnicity and the location in which they live. In the future, full citizenship will depend on having access to the full range of financial services. Policy makers will have to consider how to reduce the structural roots of inequality in access to financial services (Oppenheim, 1998; Treasury, 1999).

As more and more financial services are accessed through the Internet, there will be increasing concern about the 'digital divide', whether it is a divide between nations (Brown-Humes, 2000), between the rich and the poor (Grande and Timmins, 2000) or between men and women: interestingly the gender divide is more pronounced in Britain than in many other countries (Kehoe, 2000).

However, beneath all the rationality there is a strong vein of emotion surrounding money, in the form of anxiety, anger, fear, guilt, embarrassment, pride and so on. And increasingly the many new forms which money can take are themselves becoming signs and signifiers of individual identities and patterns of consumption. There is a continuing question about how these aspects of the topic can be built into policy and into financial education and information.

Acknowledgements

This research was funded by the Joseph Rowntree Foundation and the University of Kent at Canterbury: I am pleased to have this opportunity to thank both for their support. I am also grateful to all those who worked on the project, and especially the members of the Advisory Group, who were immensely helpful and generous. Professor Lou Opit worked on the analyses of the FES until four days before his death: this chapter is dedicated to him with my love.

References

Baudrillard, J. (1981) *For a critique of the political economy of the sign*, St Louis: Telos (translation of 1972).

Becker, G. (1993) *A treatise on the family*, London: Harvard University Press.

Brown-Humes, C. (2000) 'E-Vikings blaze the on-line trail', *Financial Times*, 11 May.

Credit Card Research Group (1998) *What's on the cards?*, London: Credit Card Research Group.

Crockett, A. (1979) *Money: Theory, policy and institutions*, London: Nelson.

Cruickshank, D. (2000) *Competition in UK banking: A report to the Chancellor of the Exchequer*, London: The Stationery Office.

FSA (Financial Services Authority) (1998) *Promoting public understanding of financial services: A strategy for consumer education*, London: FSA.

FSA (2000) *In or out? Financial exclusion: A literature and research review*, London: FSA.

Ford, J. (1991) *Consuming credit: Debt and poverty in the UK*, London: Child Poverty Action Group.

Furnham, A. and Lewis, A. (1986) *The economic mind: The social psychology of economic behaviour*, New York, NY: St Martin's Press.

Grande, C. and Timmins, N. (2000) 'Poor left behind as digital divide widens', *Financial Times*, 11 July.

Hume, D. (1963) 'Of money', in D. Hume, *Essays, moral, political and literacy*, Oxford: Oxford University Press.

Jahoda, G. (1981) 'The development of thinking about economic institutions: the bank', *Cahiers de Psychologie Cognitive,* vol 1, pp 55-78.

Kehoe, L. (2000) 'Lost in the web', *Financial Times*, 12 July.

Kempson, E. and Whyley, C. (1999) *Kept out or opted out: Understanding and combating financial exclusion*, Bristol/York: The Policy Press/Joseph Rowntree Foundation.

Lawton, J. (1991) 'What is sexually transmitted debt?', in R. Meikle (ed) *Women and credit: A forum on sexually transmitted debt*, Melbourne, Australia: Ministry of Consumer Affairs.

Levene, T. (2000) 'Naive consumers don't shop around', *The Guardian,* 22 April.

Lewis, A., Betts, H. and Webley, P. (1997) *Financial services: A literature review of consumer attitudes, preferences and perceptions*, Bath: School of Social Sciences, University of Bath.

McCloskey, D. (1987) 'Fungibility', in J. Eatwell, M. Milgate and P. Newman (eds) *The new Palgrave: A dictionary of economics*, London: Macmillan.

Marx, K. (1971, 1859) *A contribution to the critique of political economy*, New York, NY: New World Paperbacks.

Molloy, D. and Snape, D. (1999) *Low income households: Financial organisation and financial exclusion − A review of the literature*, London: DSS.

Ng, S. (1983) 'Children's ideas about bank and shop profit: developmental stages and the influence of cognitive contrasts and conflict', *Journal of Economic Psychology*, vol 4, pp 209-21.

ONS (Office of National Statistics) (1996) *Family Expenditure Survey*, London: HMSO.

Oppenheim, C. (1998) *An inclusive society: Strategies for tackling poverty*, London: Institute for Public Policy Research.

Pahl, J. (1989) *Money and marriage*, London: Macmillan.

Pahl, J. (1995) 'His money, her money: recent research on financial organisation in marriage', *Journal of Economic Psychology*, vol 16, no 3, pp 361-76.

Pahl, J. (1999) *Invisible money: Family finances in the electronic economy*, Bristol/York: The Policy Press/Joseph Rowntree Foundation.

Pahl, J. (2000) 'Money, households and social polarisation', in R. Crompton, M. Savage, F. Devine and J. Scott (eds) *Reviewing class analysis*, Keele: Sociological Review Monograph.

Pahl, J. (2001) 'Widening the scope of social policy: families, financial services and the impact of technology', in R. Edwards and J. Glover (ed) *Risk and citizenship: Key issues in welfare*, London: Macmillan.

Rowlingson, K. (1994) *Moneylenders and their customers*, London: Policy Studies Institute.

Simmel, G. (1990) *The philosophy of money* (2nd edn translated by T. Bottomore and D. Frisby), London: Routledge and Kegan Paul.

Singh, S. (1997) *Marriage money: The social shaping of money in marriage and banking*, St Leonards, Australia: Allen and Unwin.

Singh, S and Ryan, A. (1999) *Gender, design and electronic commerce*, Melbourne, Australia: Centre for International Research on Communication and Information Technologies, RMIT University.

Treasury (1999) *Access to financial services*, London: HM Treasury.

Wilson, V. (1999) *The secret life of money*, St Leonards, Australia: Allen and Unwin.

Zelizer, V. (1994) *The social meaning of money*, New York, NY: Basic Books.

THREE

Playing the game of partnership

Martin Powell, Mark Exworthy and Lee Berney

Introduction

New Labour has emphasised a collaborative discourse (Clarence and Painter, 1998; Huxham, 2000; Ling, 2000). This, they argue, represents a Third Way, "a new model for a new century" which is distinctive from both the hierarchy of Old Labour and the market of the Conservatives (DoH, 1997, p 11; DoH 1999, p 8; Powell, 1999). Partnership is the *zeitgeist* of the Labour government and one of the essential features of the 'third way' (Hudson, 1999). Documents in a number of fields stress notions of partnership, interagency working, coordination and a seamless service (for example, DoH, 1997, 1998a, 1998b, 1998d, 1999, 2000; DETR, 2000). However, Challis et al (1988, p x) point out that partnership is a word in search of ways of giving it effective meaning in practice. In government circulars and ministerial policy pronouncements, it is largely a rhetorical invocation of a vague ideal. Ling (2000, p 82) claims that the partnership literature amounts to "methodological anarchy and definitional chaos". No government appears to have the alchemist's stone to transform base words into golden partnerships. Local partnerships fit well with governance, which has a central characteristic of game playing (Rhodes, 1997). However, although local agencies must work in 'partnership', measures of the extent of and mechanisms to achieve partnership are not fully clear. In other words, local stakeholders are told that they must play the game of partnership without being fully informed of the rules.

In this paper we aim to deduce from both the conceptual literature and from government rhetoric some of the rules of the game, and then illustrate their application with empirical data. The conceptual material involves fusing the ideas of the ladder of participation (Arnstein, 1971) with a continuum of partnership (Hudson et al, 1997; 1999b). This provides the conceptual rungs of the ladder. The dimensions of partnership are based on a review of recent literature, and are examined in terms of policy, process and resource streams (Powell and Exworthy, 2001). Our empirical material is based on data collected as part of a study of how health inequalities policy is implemented at local levels.

Partnerships to reduce health inequalities

The government considers that the end of equity is best achieved through the means of partnership. It claims that the unfairness, 'unacceptable variations' and 'two-tierism' of the internal market would be replaced by cooperation and integrated care (DoH, 1997), and that "connected problems require joined up solutions" (DoH, 1998a, p 12; see Powell and Exworthy, 2001).

Partnership and cooperation is stressed in a number of health documents. The NHS White Paper (DoH, 1997, p 10) claims that the third way is a "system based on partnership". It announced an emphasis on working together within NHS organisations (for example, clinical governance) and between organisations, with a new statutory duty of partnership placed on NHS bodies and local authorities. Moreover, the Green and White papers on public health (DoH, 1998a, 1999) claimed that a three-way partnership between people, communities and government will reorientate the NHS to ensure for the first time that health improvements will be integrated into the local delivery of health care: "the goals of this health strategy will be achieved only by a joint effort" (DoH, 1999, p 119). In seeking to overcome the failings of community care policies, *Partnerships in action* (DoH, 1998b) sets out three levels of joint working (strategic planning, service commissioning and service provision). It also proposes three new types of action: the removal of constraints to joint working, the introduction of new incentives, and closer monitoring of achievements. For the first time, the government has issued national priorities for both the NHS and social services. Some National Service Frameworks require multi-organisational responses. Joint working will also be part of the performance frameworks being established for the two agencies, with progress being jointly monitored by the NHS and social care regional offices. The NHS Plan (DoH, 2000, p 29) stated that partnerships between the NHS and local authorities have historically "not been as close or effective as they could be". Moreover, "the wider inability to forge effective partnerships with local government, business and community organisations has inhibited the NHS' ability to prevent ill health and tackle health inequalities".

The ladder of partnership

For a government that stresses (and even enforces) partnerships, and SMART targets (specific, measurable, achievable, relevant and timed) through the contracts of Public Service Agreements (HM Treasury, 1998), it is surprising that partnership is so vaguely defined. We clearly need some way of conceptualising partnership. In this section, we develop the concept of the ladder of partnership, which can be seen in terms of the vertical rungs of the ladder. In the next section, we turn to the concept of policy streams, which focus on its horizontal dimensions or width of the ladder.

Arnstein (1971) set out a typology, or ladder, of citizen participation. She recognised eight levels or rungs ranging from 'manipulation' to 'citizen control'. The bottom rungs consisted of degrees of 'non-participation'. The middle rungs were composed of 'degrees of tokenism' rising from one-way communication to two-way exchanges. At the top of the ladder are three rungs with degrees of 'citizen power'. Partnership is the sixth rung, below delegated power and citizen control.

Hudson et al (1997, 1999b) present a 'framework for collaboration' in the form of a continuum of isolation, encounter, communication, collaboration, and integration. Isolation refers to the complete absence of joint activity, with members of different agencies never meeting, talking or writing to one another. Encounter exists where there is some interagency and interprofessional contact, but this is informal, ad hoc and marginal to the goals of the separate organisations. Communication arises where separate organisations do engage in joint working of a formal and structured nature, but this still tends to be marginal to separate organisational goals. Collaboration involves a recognition by separate agencies that joint working is central to their mainstream activities and implies a trusting relationship in which organisations are seen to be reliable partners. Finally, integration represents a point on the continuum at which the degree of collaboration is so high that the separate organisations see their separate identity as insignificant, and may be willing to contemplate the creation of a unitary organisation. Such arrangements would exhibit at least some of the following:

• joint goals;
• very close-knit and highly connected networks;
• little regard for reciprocation in relationships;
• a mutual and diffuse sense of long-term obligation;

- very high degrees of trust and respect;
- joint arrangements which are mainstream rather than marginal;
- joint arrangements encompassing both strategic and operational issues;
- some shared or single management arrangements;
- joint commissioning at both macro and micro levels,

Hudson (1999) suggests a further rung of unification. This would mean that health and social service agencies should merge rather than collaborate. The call for unification has a long history, with many advocates over many years. One recent example is the Health Select Committee, which essentially was a prediction of the failure of collaboration (DoH, 1998b, para 68):"We consider that the problems of collaboration between health and social services will not be properly resolved until there is an integrated health and social care system, whether this is within the NHS, within local government or within some new, separate organisation". An integrated structure has been in existence in Northern Ireland since 1973, and the Select Committee found much to admire in it (Ward, 2000; see also Mays, 1993). The government initially rejected the solution of integration, but the NHS Plan (DoH, 2000, p 71) argued for a "new relationship between health and social care ... a radical redesign of the whole system. In future, social services will be delivered in new settings such as GP surgeries, and social care staff will work alongside GPs and other primary and community health teams as part of a single local care network".

The vehicle for achieving this will be New Care Trusts (NCTs). This is based on an extension of the concepts of Primary Care Groups (PCGs) which were signalled in the NHS White Paper (DoH, 1997) to replace the General Practitioner Fund Holding of the Conservatives internal market (Powell, 1999). There were to be four levels of PCGs, with the top level being a Primary Care Trust (PCT). Essentially NCTs can be seen as a new fifth level of this evolution. As the NHS Plan (DoH, 2000, pp 72-3) puts it, PCTs are "providing a unique opportunity to foster close working relationships between health and social services". They are "already bringing together primary and community health services within a single organisation". By April 2004 it is expected that all PCGs will have become PCTs. The document proposed a new level of PCT that will provide for even closer integration of health and social services. NCTs will be able to commission and deliver primary and community healthcare as well as social care for older people and other client groups. Social care would be delivered under delegated authority from local councils. "These changes will remove the outdated institutional barriers between health and social services ..." (DoH, 2000, p 73).

Understanding partnerships

There is a significant evolving academic literature on the ingredients of a successful partnership. Hardy et al (1992) examine five categories of barriers to collaboration in the sphere of community care: structural, procedural, financial, professional and status, and legitimacy. For a wider range of partnerships, the Audit Commission (1998) set out a 'checklist' of 28 questions under five headings: deciding to go into partnership; getting started; operating efficiently and effectively; reviewing the partnership's success; and what partnerships can expect to achieve. Similarly, Hardy et al (2000) in their 'Partnership Assessment Tool' for health and social care agencies point to 36 elements of six principles: recognising and accepting the need for partnership; developing clarity and realism of purpose; ensuring commitment and ownership; developing and maintaining trust; creating clear and robust partnership arrangements; and monitoring, measuring and learning. In a study of partnerships to reduce health inequalities, Evans and Killoran (2000) present six categories of enabling factors: shared strategic vision; leadership and management; relations and local ownership; accountability; organisational readiness; and responsiveness to a changing environment. Ling (2000) sets out four dimensions through which partnerships might be compared: membership; links; scale and boundaries; and the context of partnership. In the USA, Mitchell and Shortell (2000) examine six dimensions of community health partnership: governance of strategic intent and reasons for organising; determining the partnership's domain and setting the strategic direction; partnership composition; resources; coordination and integration issues; and accountability.

The government has outlined some of the ingredients of successful partnership working: a clarification of the purpose of the partnership; recognition and resolution of areas of conflict; agreement on a shared approach to partnership; development of strong leadership; continuous adaptation to reflect the lessons learnt from the experience; and incentives to reward effective working across organisational (and geographical) boundaries (DoH, 1999; cf DoH, 1998b, 1998c; cf DETR, 2000).

It is clear that there is a significant degree of consensus between academics and policy makers regarding the key ingredients of a successful partnership such as shared vision, ownership and trust (see also Hudson et al, 1999a; Ling, 2000; Exworthy et al, 2001). This material is examined in terms of policy streams, building on the work of Webb and Wistow (1986) and Challis et al (1988). A successful policy is likely to have clear objectives, mechanisms which achieve those objectives, and resources to finance these objectives – the policy, process and resource streams respectively (Powell and Exworthy, 2001). Failure to connect them may lead to 'rhetorical policies', and to the realm of symbolic politics: words that succeed and policies that fail (Edelman, 1964).

Policy stream

The policy stream concerns the extent to which local goals are shared in terms of particular policies that require an interagency approach. The concern with a shared set of values and a broadly based consensus around ends and means has long been recognised (Hardy et al, 1992, pp 18, 93; Huxham, 2000). As Hudson et al (1999a, p 247) sum up, "Most approaches to collaboration take it for granted that an explicit statement of shared vision is a prerequisite to success".

The policy stream is concerned with whether there is a shared vision in terms of organisational goals and priorities. Are the partners agreed on the objectives of the partnership? More importantly, are they agreed on the ordering of organisational priorities? In other words, are health inequalities (HI) on the agenda and, if so, what is their place on the agenda in terms of other organisational imperatives such as financial balance and reducing waiting lists?

Process stream

This stream is concerned with the mechanisms or instruments to achieve the goals, and consists of three key elements: instruments, ownership, and jointness. Mechanisms should be technically and politically feasible (Exworthy and Powell, 2000). The technical dimension is concerned with 'evidence-based policy' and the philosophy of 'what works is what counts' (for example, Davies et al, 2000). This evidence is often lacking or equivocal in the field of specific initiatives to tackle HI (Exworthy and Berney, 2000). The political dimension has links with ownership. Some instruments such as income redistribution are owned at the national level. Local partners have a limited range of technical instruments, and some of these may be regarded by central government as more politically unacceptable than others. As well as ownership at the level of the partnership, it is important to consider ownership within the partnership as shown by structures of leadership and responsibility (Audit Commission, 1998). Jointness refers to the cohesion of the partnership. It has parallels with Ling's (2000) discussion of links: the 'fit' between partners. All partners are technically 'signed up', but this may hide large variations in the degree to which policies are carried out together. Jointness is influenced by past and present relationships between individuals and organisations (see below for trust).

Instruments are shown by the agreed policies of the partnership. Ownership may be seen in the remits of working parties and nominated individuals tasked with a certain policy. Finally, jointness refers to the extent to which agencies and individuals are bound together, which may be symbolised by committing resources or staking personal reputations on a policy; for example, in joint commissioning or joint appointments (see below).

Resource stream

The most obvious resource is money, and many other resources such as staff time flow from this, and carry an opportunity cost. However, it is important not to neglect other resources such as trust and information. As reducing HI must compete with other priorities, commitment of financial resources is a good test of whether stated or paper priorities (see policy stream) are backed by hard cash. In a crowded policy agenda, staff time may be crucial. In particular, the value of individuals with skills to work across boundaries termed 'partnership champions' (Audit Commission, 1998) or 'reticulists' (Challis et al, 1988) is clear. Challis et al (1988, p 137) claim that policy coordination can be bought "by offering a financial incentive to cross boundaries – 'crocks of gold'". Conflicts over resources and accountability between partners are likely, with the possibility of cost-shunting. Resource asymmetry may be at the root of power struggles (Cloke et al, 2000). Hardy et al (2000, p 16) claim that partnerships work best where each partner is perceived to have an equivalent status, irrespective of some having more of some resources than others, as these resources are not always quantifiable. "For most partnerships, building trust between partners is the most important ingredient in success" (Audit Commission, 1998, p 26; cf Hardy et al, 2000). The NHS Plan (DoH, 2000, pp 56-7) introduces a new delivery system based around the NHS as a 'high trust' organisation, "glued together by a bond of trust between staff and patient". However, trust may be a resource in short supply. Harrison and Lachmann (1996, p 10) claim that the traditional NHS was shaped by 'high trust' relationships which became corroded and replaced by low trust relationships during the quasi-market period of the 1990s. Mechanisms to build or rebuild trust remain problematic (Davies, 1999). Trust is influenced by 'embeddedness' of past formal and informal relationships (Exworthy, 1998), and this means that some partnerships may 'hit the ground running' while others may involve lengthy courtship rituals. The government views partnerships as a mechanism to reduce the transaction costs associated with information. In the quasi-markets, information was partly protected due to reasons of commercial secrecy.

Some resources may be relatively simple to quantify (Audit Commission, 1998). Pooled budgets, joint finance and joint appointments are obvious signs of the 'jointness' of the partnership, but the opportunity costs of staff attending meetings, or 'opportunity benefits' of data sharing are no less real.

Playing the game of partnership

The evolving framework can be illustrated with empirical evidence drawn from a study of how local partnerships were tackling health inequalities. Three case studies, rural, urban and 'mixed urban/suburban', were selected.

Each case study was based on a Health Authority (HA), and consisted of a partnership network which was identified through key HA staff, documentation and observation at policy meetings. The network generally comprised local authorities, NHS Trusts, Primary Care Groups (PCGs) and the voluntary sector. From the three case studies, 43 individuals were questioned about, inter alia, their definition of HI, their role in the policy process, the local factors hindering/facilitating policy implementation and experience of working in partnership with other agencies. They included public health doctors, HA managers responsible for HI and/or partnership, senior HA staff, Community Health Council Chief Officers, Local Authority (LA) policy officers, senior managers from LA departments, voluntary sector representatives, GPs or managers from PCGs, and senior managerial and clinical staff from NHS Trusts. The tape-recorded interviews were conducted in late 1999 and were later transcribed verbatim. Transcripts from initial interviews were read independently by two of the authors (ME and LB). An initial framework of predefined and emerging themes was devised for analysis (Ritchie and Spencer, 1995). The framework was applied to all transcripts using the

NUD★IST software. The framework was further refined as emerging themes were incorporated. The iterative process ensured findings were grounded in the data (Mays and Pope, 1995). Meetings were held to feed back results to the case studies and to validate the emergent findings. Revisions were made to the results accordingly.

Case study 1

Area: Rivertown
NHS family: Rural areas
Organisation: One county council, several district councils, district general hospitals and several community hospitals
Population: Distinct and dispersed communities, low wage, service and agricultural employment

Case study 2

Area: Uptown
NHS family: Maturer areas
Organisation: Three local unitary authorities, several NHS Trusts (including 2 major hospitals in the west of the district)
Population: High percentage of ethnic minority population

Case study 3

Area: Melchester
NHS family: Maturer areas
Organisation: Two unitary local authorities (contrasting politics), several NHS Trusts
Population: Pockets of deprivation/affluence reflecting local authority division

Policy stream

Many Health Improvement Programmes (HImP) faithfully echo the words of national government (see DoH, 1998a; cf Ling, 2000). For example, the Rivertown HImP stated that its aim was to improve "the health and well-being of the population whilst, at the same time, reducing inequalities in health". While this aim was fairly common to many HImPs, local areas made some choices with respect to conditions. For example, in Rivertown the key HI were identified as coronary heart disease and accidents. The Rivertown Director of Public Health (DPH) claimed that partnership working had to meet both the objectives of the individual agencies (as set by central government) *and* to aid local collaborative strategies. However, the former often crowded out local strategies:

"You just haven't been able to get [HI] onto the agenda because there have just been these other major pressures that have had to be resolved, a wealth of 'must-be-dones' which ... are not related to HI". Similarly, in Uptown social exclusion was one of the priorities of the HImP, but as a public health doctor said:"It now appears as one of the corporate priorities ... but it's not a great deal because you know that's mainly rhetoric.... Well, you know, it is very marginal to the work of the health authority". It is noticeable that several interviewees from NHS, LA and voluntary agencies felt that a shared vision was lacking as partnership agencies in Uptown held different priorities for tackling HI. In particular, the priority placed in HI by LAs was questioned. This partly reflected the large number of agencies involved in Uptown and the ways in which LA departments engaged with the HI agenda. For example, constructing cycle lanes by LAs could easily contribute to coronary heart disease strategies but the LA's contribution to, say, musculo-skeletal strategies was less easily identifiable. In Melchester, partnership working has still to transcend the myriad perspectives of stakeholders. This can be illustrated by an apparent clash between the worlds of evidence-based policy and 'realpolitik'. Several HA managers felt that a clinic on a local council estate was, *by their criteria*, an inappropriate and uneconomic use of resources. In contrast, the voluntary sector and Community Health Council (CHC), *by their criteria*, hailed the clinic as a success and viewed it as a symbol of the commitment by the HA to the community of a deprived area.

In conclusion, there seems to be only a limited development of the shared vision between partners. Vague statements about HI in the early versions of the HImP do not address the more problematic issues of where they fit on the policy agenda. Moreover, links with the process and resource streams (below) confirm the impression that HI are largely rhetorical policy or symbolic politics.

Process stream

The HImP is the prime instrument for tackling HI and developing partnerships (cf Ling, 2000). At the time of fieldwork various developments of direct relevance to HI were in their infancy. PCGs had only just come into existence and the first stages of the HImP process were nearing completion. In Melchester it was clearly stated that the HImP was an *evolving* process, with the first year seeing an action plan for development, years two and three seeing strategies and action plans on priorities and year four seeing the fully comprehensive plan emerge. Similarly, in Rivertown the HImP in the first year of its operation (1999-2000) had yet to prove an effective instrument for developing partnerships. It represented an incremental strategy that essentially rebadged much existing activity. According to a LA director: "I think possibly that there is, if you look at equality and the health improvement programme, to a large extent, the activity for the first round hasn't been driven by policy; its rather been the other way round".

Moreover, the HImP may be too ambitious, weighty and overwhelming. Interest groups ensured that it was a long 'shopping list', with little attempt to focus on the essentials, or to prioritise. As one Rivertown HA manager explained: "We have 82 action pages and 200 or 300 individual actions to try and implement in order to improve health. For each one of those we are going to have a very close monitoring of performance".

Two ideal types of policy ownership emerged from the case studies. The first may be termed a *dedicated* approach where responsibility for developing partnerships rested with a small group or key individuals. The second may be termed a *diffuse* approach where responsibility is widely devolved through the agencies. Uptown tended towards a diffuse approach. The HA's partnership work was led by a senior manager and their HI work was shared between this senior manager and the DPH. They reported to a 'partnership board' that comprised representatives from all the stakeholders. In Melchester, the DPH was, in principle, charged with responsibility for leading the HAs strategy on HI. In practice, this responsibility had been delegated to the deputy DPH. Rather than seeing this as a downgrading of HI as a priority, it was explained that this was done to allow the deputy to concentrate fully on health inequalities rather than having to divide her time between this and other areas such as waiting list pressures. Furthermore, the HA had appointed HImP facilitators in each PCG (see Resource stream). In this way the HA wished to diffuse the HImP and to ensure wide ownership.

However, the stick of central or vertical performance management concentrated the mind on central priorities and mitigated against wide ownership. A Rivertown HA manager explained its impact: "It's not that they [HA finance department staff] are against the idea of health and inequalities being important; it's because, you know, they are not measured against that – that's not how their performance is assessed". The Rivertown DPH expanded on this impact across the partnership agencies:

"[We are] still frustrated by the fact that, until our respective chief officers, boards, committees, authorities feel that this is what they are going to lose their job or seat on the social services committee or county council or whatever over, it is never going to be top of their agenda."

Informants pointed to the problems of vertical or silo performance management. Central government appeared not to be joined up, resulting in a low profile for HI for partners beyond the NHS. An Uptown senior HA manager explained that health inequalities:"is the lowest priority of those priorities and is still not being performance managed at all ... [but] it is in fact something which relates to every local authority department. It relates to Housing, it relates to Education...". Likewise, an Uptown health strategy officer reinforced this:"What [LA departments] contribute to reducing HI, which is technically a huge amount as far as I can see, is not what they are measured on". More specifically for Education departments:"what they are interested in is where their school is in the league tables. That's what gets their money, that's what drives their roles" (Uptown LA health strategy officer). One public health doctor argued that there could be little progress towards common priorities at local level until central government was more 'joined up', with compatible messages flowing down the vertical silos from the DH to the NHS and from the DETR to LAs:"It doesn't really matter what the [NHS] regional director says [about HI as a priority]. What we really want, who we really want saying it's a priority is the DETR". Even if there was agreement on broad areas, joint approaches were still hampered by different views about ownership, feasibility and time scales. As a Melchester HA manager said:

"Even if there wasn't a health angle in it then why are we putting in the HImP? But there was pressure to put in, you know, tackling unemployment. That's a route to solving poverty and deprivation, that would make people, that would improve health levels in Melchester, and undoubtedly it will in an intellectual sense of a long term in some way, but it ain't appropriate to the HImP in my view."

There was some progress towards jointness. Rivertown had appointed a HI Impact Assessment (HIIA) manager, a joint appointment between two partner agencies. In addition, the HA funded Health Improvement facilitators to work in each PCG. Finally, health strategy officers, based in each of the three LAs, were part-funded by the HA with their role partly to establish HI on the agenda of various LA departments. In Uptown, the Single Regeneration Budget (SRB) work in one LA area included health and HI as a core component. The HA had also commissioned external consultants to identify and measure the state of HI across the district. This would overcome what, for example, one NHS manager felt was a lack of meaningful local data on HI. These and other initiatives were pointing towards greater collaboration between partner agencies.

Resource stream

All HAs in the three case study areas were in budget deficit at the time of fieldwork which hindered their ability to shift significant financial resources towards the HI and partnership agenda. Tight budgets and the need to solve 'now' problems conspired to make resource shifts to long-term, more diffuse objectives without an established constituency such as HI more difficult (cf Klein, 1995 for prevention). As a Melchester HA manager stated:

> "Now if you were really, really committed to reducing variations in health, you would say, notwithstanding all these financial pressures, we are going to allocate resources to reduce health inequalities, but we don't do that. The first call on our resources it seems is to solve financial difficulties of the hospitals and trusts."

Although in Uptown a senior manager had been appointed to be responsible for partnership (which involved an ongoing financial commitment), the HImP revealed that only £115,000 of special project finances had been allocated in that year to tackling HI. The overall HA budget was several hundred million pounds. This illustrates another aspect of the dedicated versus diffuse approach. A dedicated strategy is one where all attempts to reduce HI are badged as a 'HI strategy'. On the other hand, a diffuse strategy views all policy as being influenced by reducing HI. It follows that a HA's commitment to HI cannot simply be identified through special projects, and great efforts may be made in reducing HI through mainstream activities and budgets. For example, all activities could be subject to a Health Impact Analysis or Equity Audit. However, there were few explicit mentions of these in our case studies.

Just as performance indicators came down different vertical silos, there were also silo problems with respect to finance: "It can be very difficult trying to bring together mainstream budgets in any sensible way because of the way that every government department likes to have increasingly centralised control over everything that happens" (Rivertown LA director). Moreover, central government earmarking or tagging of finances for specific initiatives effectively limited local autonomy, as explained by an Uptown senior HA manager: "But that [policy] got torpedoed by last year's funding because it all came down highly targeted, particularly the mental health modernisation fund, and meant that we had to give as much money to an area we regarded as being overfunded".

Financial difficulties were also related to the timescales of funding. Action on HI, by its very nature, is a long-term process. To ask partners to commit to such long-term strategies is problematic, if not unrealistic: "One of my concerns is that the government funding criteria, even for local government, is annual. We can't plan for three years" (Melchester HA manager). There were clearly opportunity costs of staff time in developing partnerships. As a Melchester HA manager put it:

> "I found myself in a meeting with the local police and the community safety strategy and I thought, yeh, you know, the health authority is part of an approach to community safety, but when I find myself in a two-hour meeting about bollards and closed-circuit television in the local shopping centre I think, you know, really, is this a sensible use of my time?"

Cross-funding raised some problems of accountability. In Rivertown the HA had funded speed cameras to help reduce traffic accidents which were among the highest in the country. The use of financial resources in this was questioned by some who argued that the public might prefer NHS finances being spent on traditional *health service* activity. It is possible that the use of NHS finances in this way might be offset by the collection of speeding fines, but the reciprocation to the HA had yet to be determined.

The appointment of a Health Inequality Impact Assessment manager reflected the need to collate and synthesise existing data and to collect new data on HI across partner agencies. Data on population were the prime currency for the Rivertown partnership, but were hampered by differing information systems between agencies. In particular, the performance indicators by which agencies were assessed differed for each agency and yet, ostensibly, they were addressing similar issues such as social exclusion. The Rivertown DPH asked: "How can we make that [indicators for HI and partnership] meaningful and joined up at the local level?".

Some may have been playing the game of partnership in order to reach the crocks of gold. As resources were conditional on partnership, it is possible that getting partnership money became the *end* rather than the *means*: "We've been told to go and talk to these other agencies. In their documents, they are being told that they've got to come and talk to us. And certainly from a funding point of view, you can't get the funding unless you can demonstrate a real partnership" (Rivertown HA manager). "Although we've got £2 billion of public money in [Rivertown], we'll have to make a bid to government for £200,000 because we can't actually add together our budgets. But if we go to them together then they'll give us some money" (LA Director, Rivertown).

A similar instrumental playing the game of partnership between local partners was noted. Those in control of the purse strings seemed suspicious of the motives of those who only appeared willing to participate in the partnership process when they could see a clear financial incentive to do so. As a Melchester HA manager put it:

> "I don't believe health inequalities are particularly high up the trust's agenda. And I mean they may occasionally dabble, but I mean, it is very low down their agenda and I think most of them wouldn't really recognise it apart from when they are arguing that health inequalities can lead to them to have more resources."

Similarly, the voluntary sector (very often dependent on the financial munificence of those who they are supposed to be in partnership with) felt that there was no real sharing of power (cf Cloke et al, 2000); that what we see is an illusion of equality where none exists. As a representative of the voluntary sector in Melchester noted:

> "Part of it is also the issue of power. At a very real level we don't in the voluntary sector have a say in the kinds of money there is in the NHS, or the council, nothing like it. We don't have perhaps the same explicit control over people's lives, power is something that's difficult to give up. And I mean we can make expert interventions, we can provide lots of evidence, but it doesn't always get taken on board."

Similarly in Uptown the voluntary sector perceived a confusion relating to and a degree of exclusion from partnership working.

The level of trust was influenced by previous relationships. The Melchester HImP stated that there was a well-established history of joint planning and commissioning in the area. The HA had a number of staff seconded to posts in LAs to assist them with the development of their own health-related strategies and their contributions to local action plans and cross-agency working. On the other hand, there were signs of geographical, social and political rivalries. Melchester was marked by a clear split that saw the relatively affluent west contrasted with the relatively deprived east. This split was almost exactly mirrored by the boundaries of the two local authorities, one of which, until 1997, had long been a traditional Conservative stronghold. With both councils now Labour controlled there was held to be a common purpose across the area. However, there remained well-developed resistance to many of the initiatives being proposed by the new administration. Reallocation of resources, as part of the cross-borough strategies being developed, was held to be one of the most contentious political battles to be fought.

Discussion

As Ling (2000) points out, there is no shortage of advice on how to 'do' partnership. However, this risks putting the empirical cart before the conceptual horse. Put another way, before the rungs of the ladder of partnership can be specified, it is important to be clearer about whether more than one ladder exists, and whether different ladders fit different contexts. There are a number of unresolved issues about conceptualising partnerships. To aid clarity these are presented as dualities.

Vertical versus horizontal

To what extent can horizontal partnerships exist within a vertical performance management system? Clarence and Painter (1998) argue that the government's collaborative discourse is countered by another, conflicting and contradictory discourse of central performance that drills down separate vertical silos (cf Powell, 1999; Exworthy and Berney, 2000). Similarly, at local levels there are likely to be 'lead' agencies and 'following' agencies, 'senior' and 'junior' partners, with risks of exclusion. In short, 'partnership' implies some rough level of equality (for example, Hardy et al, 2000), but vertical performance management makes the local level junior partners, and at this level some appear to be more junior than others.

Enforced versus voluntary

Can partnerships be enforced by statute? Government can remove barriers to partnership and can create a suitable environment where partnerships can flourish. However, successful partnerships are unlikely to result simply because stakeholders are told to work together. Statutory agencies have a duty of partnership, and may be subject to a range of sanctions and incentives, but voluntary agencies cannot be commanded by the government and so their participation is more dependent on incentives (see below).

Sanctions versus incentives

The NHS Plan (DoH, 2000) stresses both sanctions and incentives. The case studies suggest that as yet neither was sufficiently strong to elevate partnerships and HI towards the top of the policy agenda. As a trust manager put it, "You only do it if you really have to these days ... or if there is a whole load of money behind it of course".

Diffuse versus dedicated

Is it possible to have the 'ideal' of senior leadership *and* wide ownership (Hardy et al, 2000)? The case studies suggest that either a diffuse *or* dedicated approach was taken. In other words, there may be some trade off between seniority or leadership and wide ownership. Senior managers may have to attend meetings, because if this is delegated junior staff may have to report back and seek authority before committing to a decision. However, this may lead to the reliance on a few individual 'partnership champions', and to a conclusion that HI is 'X's' responsibility, and may become marginalised in a 'YP' (Your Problem) 'policy ghetto'. What happens if X steps under a bus?

Means versus ends

Should partnership success be seen in terms of process or outcome? It is generally claimed that partnerships should be measured in terms of outputs rather than process (Challis et al, 1988; Hardy et al, 1992). The Audit Commission (1998, p 32) suggests an ordering of outcomes before the 'health' of the partnership: "the point of forming a partnership is to improve performance, and this should principally [be] measured through the eyes of service users, citizens and other stakeholders". However, it is recognised that measurable outcomes may be long term, and be difficult to attribute to the partnership. Reduction of HI can involve a long game. Although inferior conceptually, changes in process measures can be observed in the short term, and observable 'quick wins' are perhaps necessary to keep the players interested.

Objective versus subjective

Should the health of the partnership be measured by objective measures such as meetings, joint appointments and telephone calls or in terms of the feelings of the stakeholders? While the search for objectivity may be somewhat illusory given the multiplicity of interests in partnerships, subjective measures are easily contested (giving rise to conflict and dissent) and are difficult to evaluate over time. Hudson et al (1999b) reported that respondents from HAs described their joint working with social service departments or housing departments as being more integrated than these other partners described it. Similar conclusions can be drawn from the differences in views on the current and future level of joint working evident between chief executives of health and local authorities (Patient: Citizen, 2000). As a senior HA manager in Rivertown put it: "How well do you know if you are joint working or not? I don't know if you've got an objective criteria for that but I think it [partnerships] will start to feel more comfortable and I think that will be a good step in the right direction."

Cooperation versus integration

The final issue concerns the merits of cooperation as opposed to integration. The New Care Trusts announced in the NHS Plan (DoH, 2000) are essentially an admission of failure of cooperation. Primary Care Groups and Trusts (PCG/Ts) cannot reach a sufficiently seamless service, and so integration of health and social care is required. However, does this require full integration of all health and social care, an integration of all public policy under the Department of Health, or a pragmatic response that weighs the costs and benefits of integration?

Conclusions

This chapter has sought to develop a conceptual framework by which interagency partnerships can be appraised. It is rudimentary and needs further elucidation before any attempt at operationalisation. It must be stressed that partnerships evolve over time. Partners were, in the phrase beloved by managers of failing sports teams, 'on a steep learning curve'. A Rivertown HA manager closely involved in partnership working argued that:

> "It's really about learning how to work together and learn to cooperate and about sharing a philosophy because that's something that has been missing before. The first two years of the work I was doing was more about cooperation whereas now it's about having a shared philosophy, about having a shared vision for a community.... I think that brings a subtle but effective change to the way we think about it [ie HI]."

However, it is clear that local agencies are making their own histories of partnerships in circumstances not of their own choosing. In other words, the rules of the game are laid down by the centre. It is hardly surprising that in a unitary state central government makes the rules. However, the rules are by no means clear to local stakeholders. Moreover, their interpretations of the existing rules suggest that the result of the game is unlikely to see major reductions in HI. The government's great expectations are likely to be frustrated. As the paper intentions of the 'Priorities' document of the 1970s of the need to transfer health resources to the 'Cinderella' groups achieved little in practice, reducing health inequalities appears to be a similar rhetorical priority. The emerging policy lessons appear to be that if New Labour wants to reduce HI then it requires larger carrots and sticks. Earmarked funds (such as those used for HIV/AIDS) or 'crocks of gold' may stimulate activity, but at the risk of reducing local autonomy and blurring accountability. Stronger performance management could be used to shift health inequalities up the policy agenda. Government will have to be more joined up at the centre to ensure that policy and resource streams no longer flow down separate pipes. In short, the irony may be that effective partnership working might require a more effective hierarchy.

Acknowledgement

We are grateful for the support of the Economic and Social Research Council Health Variations Programme (phase 2) (award ref no L128251039) which funded the research project upon which this chapter is based.

References

Arnstein, S. (1971) 'A ladder of participation', *Journal of the Royal Town Planning Institute*, vol 57, April, pp 176-82.

Audit Commission (1998) *A fruitful partnership: Effective partnership working*, London: Audit Commission.

Challis, L., Fuller, S., Henwood, M., Klein, R., Plowden, W., Webb, A., Whittingham, P. and Wistow, G. (1988) *Joint approaches to social policy*, Cambridge: Cambridge University Press.

Clarence, E. and Painter, C. (1998) 'Public services under New Labour: collaborative discourses and local networking', *Public Policy and Administration*, vol 13, no 1, pp 8-22.

Cloke, P., Milbourne, P. and Widdowfield, R. (2000) 'Partnership and policy networks in rural local governance', *Public Administration*, vol 78, no 1, pp 111-33.

Davies, H.T.O. (1999) 'Falling public trust in health services: implications for accountability', *Journal of Health Services Research and Policy*, vol 4, no 4, pp 193-94.

Davies, H.T.O., Nutley, S.M. and Smith, P.C. (eds) (2000) *What works?: Evidence-based policy and practice in public services*, Bristol: The Policy Press.

DETR (Department of the Environment, Transport and the Regions) (2000) *Joining it up locally*, Report of PAT Team 17, London: The Stationery Office.

DoH (Department of Health) (1997) *The new NHS*, London: The Stationery Office.

DoH (1998a) *Our healthier nation*, London: The Stationery Office.

DoH (1998b) *Partnership in action*, London: DoH.

DoH (1998c) *Health of the nation: A policy assessed*, London: The Stationery Office.

DoH (1998d) *Modernising social services*, London: The Stationery Office.

DoH (1999) *Saving lives*, London: The Stationery Office.

DoH (2000) *The NHS Plan*, London: The Stationery Office.

Edelman, M. (1964) *The symbolic use of politics*, Urbana, IL: University of Illinois Press.

Evans, D. and Killoran, A. (2000) 'Tackling health inequalities through partnership working', *Critical Public Health*, vol 10, no 2, pp 125-40.

Exworthy, M. (1998) 'Localism in the NHS quasi-market', *Environment and planning C: government and policy*, vol 16, no 4, pp 449-62.

Exworthy, M. and Berney, L. (2000) 'What counts and what works? Evaluating policies to tackle health inequalities', *Renewal*, vol 8, no 4, pp 47-55.

Exworthy, M. and Powell, M. (2000) 'Variations on a theme: New Labour, health inequalities and policy failure', in A. Hann (ed) *Analysing health policy*, Aldershot: Avebury, pp 45-62.

Exworthy, M., Powell, M. and Berney, L. (2001: forthcoming) 'Tackling health inequality', in M. Tavakoli et al (eds) *Health policy and economics*, Aldershot: Ashgate, pp 87-102.

Hardy, B., Turrell, A. and Wistow, G. (1992) *Innovations in community care management*, Aldershot: Avebury.

Hardy, B. et al (2000) *What makes a good partnership?*, Leeds: Nuffield Institute for Health.

Harrison, S. and Lackmann, P. (1996) *Towards a high trust NHS*, London: IPPR.

Health Select Committee (1998) *The relationship between health and social services*, London: The Stationery Office.

HM Treasury (1998) *Public services for the future*, London: The Stationery Office.

Hudson, B. (1999) 'Dismantling the Berlin Wall: developments at the health-social care interface', in H. Dean and R. Woods (eds) *Social Policy Review 11*, Luton: Social Policy Association.

Hudson, B., Hardy, B., Henwood, M. and Wistow, G. (1997) *Inter-agency collaboration: Final report*, Leeds: Nuffield Institute for Health.

Hudson, B., Hardy, B., Henwood, M. and Wistow, G. (1999a) 'In pursuit of inter-agency collaboration in the public sector', *Public Management*, vol 1, no 2, pp 235-60.

Hudson, B., Exworthy, M., Peckham, S. and Callaghan, G. (1999b) *Locality partnerships: The early primary care group experience*, Leeds: Nuffield Institute for Health.

Huxham, C. (2000) 'The challenge of collaborative governance', *Public Management*, vol 2, no 3, pp 337-57.

Klein, R. (1995) *The new politics of the NHS*, Harlow: Longman.

Ling, T. (2000) 'Unpacking partnership: the case of health care', in J. Clarke et al (eds) *New managerialism, new welfare?*, London: Sage Publications, pp 82-101.

Mays, N. (1993) 'What are the effects of integration in the NI health and personal social services?', *Critical Public Health*, vol 4, no 2, pp 43-8.

Mays, N. and Pope, C. (1995) 'Rigour and qualitative research', *BMJ*, vol 311, 8 July, pp 109-12.

Mitchell, S. and Shortell, S. (2000) 'The governance and management of effective community health partnerships', *The Milbank Quarterly*, vol 78, no 2, pp 241-89.

Patient: citizen (2000) 'Partnership working between local government and the NHS', Joint Supplement from *Local Government Chronicle/Health Service Journal*, June.

Powell, M. (1999) 'New Labour and the third way in the British NHS', *International Journal of Health Services*, vol 29, no 2, pp 353-70.

Powell, M. and Exworthy, M. (2001: forthcoming) 'Joined-up solutions to address health inequalities', *Public Money and Management*, vol 21, no 1, pp 21-6.

Rhodes, R. (1997) *Understanding governance*, Buckingham: Open University Press.

Ritchie, J. and Spencer, L. (1995) 'Qualitative data analysis for applied policy research', in A. Bryman and R. Burgess (eds) *Analysing qualitative data*, London: Routledge.

Ward, S. (2000) 'Barriers breached', in *Patient: citizen*, Joint Supplement from *Local Government Chronicle/Health Service Journal*, June, p 22.

Webb, A. and Wistow, G. (1986) *Planning, need and scarcity*, London: Allen and Unwin.

FOUR

Etzioni's spirit of communitarianism: community values and welfare realities in Blair's Britain

Emma Heron

Introduction

This chapter highlights the continued significance of communitarianism within the New Labour project and argues that there has been consistency within the Labour Party's social and public policy agendas in its emphasis on social and moral behaviour. Many recent policy developments emerge around an axis of rights and responsibilities, with a heightened emphasis on the restoration of moral responsibility and social pressure to behave in 'correct' and 'decent' ways. It is argued in this chapter that the sense of community and the spirit of communitarianism proposed by Etzioni are alive and well within the policy worlds of housing and regeneration, social security, criminal justice and education. Etzioni's world view of the 'common sense' behaviour of individuals within localised and morally strong communities not only resonates with Labour's policy intentions but also suggests a British future with a stronger communitarian focus and an unapologetic acceptance of the need to emphasise responsibilities over rights. The chapter aims to show the prevalence of such communitarian values and to reveal how a range of public and social policies in Britain continues to echo the spirit of American communitarianism.

American communitarianism

Communitarianism is a social and political movement originating in 1990s America but which has attracted attention and support in the UK[1]. Described as a 'flexi-philosophy' (Milne, 1994), the idea of communitarianism can be found to appeal to certain strands of the political left *and* the political right, allowing supporters to defend a variety of political territories by propounding the importance of community. All communitarians start from the same point: namely, that social values and social structures have lost their true meaning and have misled society in terms of accepted moral standards and acceptable moral values. Modern American society reflects, in both moral and civic spheres, a decline which needs to be arrested (Etzioni, 1993, 1997b). Such decline takes many forms: the rise in crime and disorder; the rise in disrespect towards others and towards the political system; the decline in family values; and poor educational achievement and low aspirations (Etzioni, 1993, 1997b), but all point to the same outcome – that society will decline further unless such problems are addressed. Communitarianism is therefore concerned with a moral agenda set within an intrinsically social context; community is unapologetically concerned with the betterment of society and all those within it.

'Social wrongs'

Communitarianism holds as a significant cause of social and moral decline the compounded effect of political extremes. The period of 1960s American liberalism, which represented for communitarians an era of appropriate challenge to assumptions and stereotypes, nevertheless left a void in constructing a new and revised social order; instead, it left society in a state of 'rulelessness' and moral neglect whereby "social anarchy and rampant moral confusion" (Etzioni, 1993, p 24) were rife and fed into a social agenda that became difficult to undo in later years. In essence, the 1960s demanded an irresponsible dominance of rights without accepting that some responsibility and duty were needed as a counterbalance. The Reagan–Thatcher decade was seen by Etzioni to be a reaction (of the wrong sort) to this continued problem of excessive liberalism (Etzioni, 1993). For communitarians, equally as damaging (but for very different reasons) was the 1980s drive for individual interest and private concern whereby the focus on independence, economic entrepreneurialism and self-interest overshadowed any social and public concern and gave no space for interests focused on concerns beyond the individual. The possessive individualism of the 1980s led to behaviours that demanded rights for the self but expected no reciprocal commitment towards others.

The past created problems that were the result of different political emphases and created a crisis that needed to be addressed. Communitarians regarded there to be a common fault line present across such disparate political eras; namely, that the relationship between the individual and society had been incorrectly interpreted. A clear result from this was a misguided view of individual and social responsibilities and rights (Etzioni, 1997b). Indeed, the 1990s represented a period reeling from this imbalance and was characterised by confusion and uncertainty about the right or wrong way to progress.

Of great concern, therefore, to Etzioni is the overall 'social deficit' found within contemporary society. Rises in crime and disorder are matched by an increased tolerance of slack moral values and weak family forms (Etzioni, 1993). Young people are leaving education with few social values and unstructured moral understanding. Equally, society has become increasingly atomised in terms of its social relations.

A clear tension exists here between the issue of rights and the issue of responsibilities; although the communitarian rhetoric concerns itself with finding a *balance* between rights and responsibilities, the agenda is very much concerned with re-emphasising responsibilities in the first instance. While communitarians argue that rights have a necessary place in society (and that without rights society would be socially unjust; see, for example, Etzioni, 1997c), their concern, therefore, is that responsibilities have not been given similar emphasis. Indeed, the only way for rights to be truly meaningful, and for society to be truly equitable, is to have them balanced with responsibilities.

Etzioni's concern about the overprotection of individual privacy illustrates the point of too heavy an emphasis on rights. Privacy, he argues, runs the risk of damaging the social and moral order if left unchecked. An individual's 'right' to privacy, he continues, can be overstated and obscure the benefits of increased social responsibility. Indeed, privacy that threatens the public good (defined as anything which holds common values and 'common sense') is legitimately questioned. Thus, defending the rights of certain sections of society to do as they wish is simply not acceptable from a wider social perspective: "... does it make sense, in the hallowed name of privacy, to allow both deadbeat fathers and students who default on their loans to draw a salary from a government agency just to avoid the use of computer cross-checks?"

(Etzioni, 1996, p 12). Examining the particular behaviour of individuals is thus legitimated in the name of responsibility over rights.

Social responsibility should increasingly come in the form of acts which communicate control, symbolise order and which are, it is believed by communitarians, truly legitimated in a society experiencing social and moral decline. Thus, for example, "... once fingerprinting is widely applied [to the issue of benefit fraud], the stigma will wane" (Etzioni, 1996, p 11). The shaming and stigmatising of individuals (including the public naming of so-called 'bad Samaritans', and face-to-face meetings between offenders and victims) is regarded as having strong merits in the rectification of imbalances between social wrongs and social 'rights' (Etzioni, 1999).

Etzioni believes that strong society is created by strong families, and that such familial strength is generated by a firmer commitment to marriage and a greater responsibility towards the upbringing of children (1993, 1997b, 1998). The trends towards longer working hours, the incentive to earn more money and the desire to aspire to the heights of career structures are symptoms of the incorrect balance of rights over responsibilities. Equally, childcare beyond the family, while necessary for some, is not the best form of care for children, and all parents should, therefore, revisit the relationship between work and home life.

Parents' responsibilities not only lie with the child at home and with the family, but also within the domain of education. Parental participation in school activities and a greater awareness of the need to encourage certain morals and values among children are each paramount if the schooling system is to help work towards creating an increasingly responsive and responsible younger generation. A concern about the young and those leaving education without the appropriate values to enter a society already characterised by moral confusion is high on the communitarian agenda (Etzioni, 1993). The young are seen as being in need of supportive education not only to help them learn right from wrong, but also to be able to give society a future of hope in terms of instilling the correct values for future generations.

'Social rights'

The key to solving the mistakes of the past and the moral confusion of the present is to look to a future based on strong community values. Communitarians regard both the ideal and reality of community as forming the basis from which the correct balance and the correct definition of rights and responsibilities are to be found.

The idea of 'community' is a relatively straightforward one for communitarians. Be it defined by geographical area (a neighbourhood) or a shared set of common experiences (workplace communities, for example), all communities have within them the potential to propound a spirit in which shared social concern can be achieved, and the ability to instil social responsibility legitimated. Community sentiment and community spirit can be classed as a 'nested hierarchy', where individuals start by helping themselves, then move 'outwards' towards helping those in their immediate (social or physical) surrounding environment (such as the family), and then outwards towards the neighbourhood and community institutions (Etzioni, 1997b). The communitarian emphasis on duty, action and responsibility is seen to lie most effectively within these 'lower' layers (Etzioni, 1993, 1997b). Indeed, bringing power, control and accountability down to the lowest possible level is one clear way in which wider social deficits can be tackled.

A particular value of community is seen as being its ability to reawaken the civic institutions that the past has come to obscure and ignore. The genuine potential of such institutions is believed to be to readdress the social concerns of contemporary society and avoid the continuing decline in values and morals. These institutions (such as family, schools and 'faith organisations') are seen to hold great power in terms of unlocking the potential for a communitarian future. Dependency on families and on local (self-selecting) communities is regarded as beneficial and actively encouraged. Indeed, the way towards a strong society is through the development of, and dependence on, the idea of family and community as the first resort:

> We correctly sense that we have particular obligations to those closest to us, above and beyond those we owe to others. This is most evident when it comes to our families.... While in some visionary future we shall all become brothers and sisters, a government that tries to ban communities from extending themselves for their own kind ... will undercut the volunteerism and charity that is distinctive of civil society and that makes America great. (Etzioni, 1997c, pp 10-11)

An emphasis on the familiar and a dependence on immediate 'layers' of community create a legitimisation of particular community values.

The 'moral culture' of the community is significant for all communitarians as it is the unspoken blueprint which determines the rights and wrongs and the behaviours and punishments necessary for a particular community. Believed to be generated from within the community itself, Etzioni suggests that moral values are consensually agreed, creating a 'community voice' which all members of the community can (and should) adhere to. When combined with the 'inner voice' that all community members possess (but may choose to ignore), the sense of 'doing the right thing' should be evident. Thus, the "moral culture can serve to significantly enhance social order while reducing the need for state intervention in social behaviour" (Etzioni, 2000, p 26). It is the community which sets its own guidelines and moral values creating, in effect, a loosely defined pressure upon all of its members. Indeed, "this social pressure is sufficient to keep most members of that community from misbehaving ... [and] to object to this mode of moral encouragement and attentiveness is to oppose the social glue that helps hold the moral order together" (Etzioni, 1998, pp 42-3).

Community spirit also encourages a belief in the positive experience of people donating time and effort. Voluntary work, the role of the voluntary sector and a sense of mutualism (whereby people help each other regardless of their own need for help; Etzioni, 2000), are regarded as necessary vehicles through which better social relations can be achieved and through which social and individual responsibility can be experienced. Thus, within the communitarian vision, social pressure, 'gentle suasion' and responsibilities towards others are seen as the appropriate and 'common sense' way forward.

Community values and institutions are also believed to be able to forge a way through the debris left by previous political eras. Described as a 'third force' taking its rightful place between 'costly government programmes' and the market (Etzioni, 1997b), reliance on community institutions and values represents a more straightforward, accountable and predictable future. For communitarians, it is wrong to rely too heavily on either the state or the market, as each runs the (proven) risk of excesses and social decay. Nevertheless, the communitarian vision of society does see a role for government and market: each has a place, but it should be of no *greater* importance than community. Making state involvement as unobtrusive as possible and ensuring any damaging side effects of such intervention are minimised, are conditions that Etzioni (1993) regards as essential if the state is not to overdominate. Significantly, the state is regarded to have certain social responsibilities, even to those who fail to contribute to the good of society: "No-one's basic humanity and membership in the community should be denied ... even if they refuse to work ..." (Etzioni, 2000, p 31), yet such protection should not suggest an overgenerous state: "The provisions to such idle or selfish people ... may be reduced and not include cash beyond some small amount" (Etzioni, 2000, pp 31-2). Overdominance of the state, including its degree of social protection, needs to be checked and balanced against community alternatives: "one can reduce social costs, public expenditures and dependency [on the state] by lowering the safety nets without removing them" (Etzioni, 1997b, p 83). Dependency on the state is reduced to a basic minimum, while dependency on community and civic institutions is encouraged and combined with independence of the individual in terms of work and general contribution. Certainly, the private sector and an emphasis on the market are regarded by Etzioni to be a significant help to an individual's ability to become independent of the state and a valued contributor to the community:

> Expanding available work through the market until unemployment is low is the most desirable outcome.... [But] surely it is better for all who seek work and are able to work to be employed than for some to have high salaries and benefits well protected, only to be highly taxed in order to pay unemployment benefits. (Etzioni, 2000, p 46)

An emphasis on the value of paid work is clear within a responsible community, illustrating Etzioni's suggestion that an additional moral dimension at a society-wide level is needed. The market is regarded as the best source of work and jobs, as well as general prosperity for the country; however, the responsibility for those who lose their jobs falls back upon state and community. 'Community jobs' are seen as a valuable force in contributing effort and work back into the community for those who cannot find paid work. Such jobs (which would be part and parcel of a workfare programme; Etzioni, 2000) would not replace existing jobs or job opportunities, but would provide both a culture of work and an opportunity for contribution and active participation. Thus, "public funds might be allocated ... to schools, hospitals ... and other community institutions, to hire people to carry out work which these institutions would otherwise not have been able to afford" (Etzioni, 1997b, p 82). The sense of social responsibility for those who are dependent on state welfare is thus clear; better to be contributing back into the community than to be receiving benefit passively.

While Etzioni (2000) holds the view that community, state and market are the three sectors that constitute the makings of a good society, he nevertheless places preference on the community whenever and wherever possible. Priority therefore is placed on the need to revisit the 'neglected partner' (Etzioni, 2000) of community, and is reflected in the drive for community institutions and the moral messages emanating from localised and morally strong communities. Thus, dependence on the 'outer' layers of the nested hierarchy, namely, the state, is more often than not seen as a process of *last* resort.

New Labour's community values

The ideal of community and the spirit of American communitarianism are each strong within New Labour philosophy[2]. The notion of community has been a consistent theme throughout the journey from opposition to newly formed government, as well as in current attempts at securing a second term.

Before Labour won the election in 1997, concern was raised about a decline in moral standards and the existence of social disintegration, with its emerging values as the Opposition clearly based around the concept of community. The Bulger murder in 1993 resulted in Blair's outspoken declaration of a lack of social cohesion (Blair, 1993), while several years on, Mandelson and Liddle's 'insider account' (1997) of New Labour's plans discussed in great length the problems of a society plagued by a culture of disengagement. The new party's version of community was to allow a practical and 'common sense' approach to social relations and be a timely corrective to social ills: "community is a robust and powerful idea ... and is at the heart of the ... economy New Labour wishes to create. It means teamwork.... It means mutuality.... It means justice.... This is [a] tough and active concept of community ..." (Mandelson and Liddle, 1997, p 19). The communitarian emphasis on rights and responsibilities, nurtured around a strong sentiment of community values, was to become an emergent theme within New Labour's rhetoric on social decline. The notion of stakeholding, for example, emphasised the responsibilities of firms and businesses to exhibit a greater social awareness, and was believed to lead to greater social cohesion between the market and wider society (Blair, 1996). The idea of a responsible 'collective conscience' underpinned by a sense of urgency in reaffirming social concern was to become a trademark of the new party. Speaking at his first conference as party leader, Blair pushed the communitarian ethos as a tool to repair the damage of society caused by Conservative policies:

They [the Tories] think we choose between self interest and the interests of society or the country as a whole. In reality, self interest demands that we work together to achieve what we cannot do alone.... Community is not some piece of nostalgia. It means what we share. It means working together, it is about how we treat each other. (Blair, 1994, pp 7-8)

The spirit of communitarianism in New Labour's Britain

Driver and Martell's (1997) suggestion that New Labour's communitarianism can best be described as morally prescriptive, conditional and conservative looks set to be confirmed. Indeed, the New Labour project continues to emphasise the sense of 'moral culture' (Etzioni, 2000; see also, Etzioni, 1995):

What gives us the power to survive in a rapidly changing environment are the habits of co-operation, the networks of support, our radius of trust.... It is there [in families, schools, congregations and communities] that we learn the grammar of togetherness, the give and take of rights and responsibilities, where we pass on our collective story, our ideals.... Without them, society is too abstract to be real. (Blair, 2000d, pp 57-8)

Order, behaviour and control

The issues of disorder, unruly or immoral behaviour and the need for social control are concerns shared by both communitarians and the New Labour government, and which unite apparently disparate social and public policies in Britain.

The perceived direct relationship between 'cutting crime and building communities' (see, for example, Home Office, 1998a), is symptomatic of the idea that community, while under threat from crime, is also a tool which can help reduce criminal activity and socially disruptive behaviours. Indeed, a threatened community is a weak community which prevents true advancement; "if you don't build strong and responsible communities then you end up with wastelands where there really is 'no such thing as society'" (Straw, 2000, p 1), whereas a strong community is representative of controlled, 'correct' and ordered behaviours necessary for social progress.

The concern about disorder and unruly behaviour and its effect on the equilibrium of the community was brought to public attention in the 1998 Crime and Disorder Act (CDA), which had a specific focus on the control of certain antisocial behaviours and an agenda of personal responsibility, prevention and punishment (Brownlee, 1998). The CDA, through its implementation of measures based around behaviour (antisocial behaviour orders (ASBOs), local child curfew schemes (LCCSs), child safety orders (CSOs), reflects a concern that behaviour and disorder are a threat to the normal workings of a decent society. Increased local partnership between local authorities, other public bodies and 'the community' within the CDA is a symbol of New Labour's (communitarian) view that the drive towards a stronger community is the joint responsibility of all, as well as a suggestion that the majority of crime is local in character (Houghton, 2000). As Home Office Minister Barbara Roche reiterated, "it is at local level where the fight against crime and disorder is won or lost" (quoted in Home Office, 2000b, p 1). ASBOs, for example, can be applied for by the police or local authority in consultation with each other and can be held against either individuals (over the age of 10) or families "... whose behaviour is anti-social (ie it causes alarm, distress or harassment to one or more people not in the same household as him/herself)" (Home Office, 1998a, p 4) [3]. Such orders are civil in nature, similar to an injunction, and are regarded as preventative, designed to put an end to 'persistent and serious' behaviour. Significantly, however, a breach of such an order becomes a *criminal* offence, with a maximum penalty of five years imprisonment (Home Office, 2000c). Thus, it can be seen that prevention and the curtailing of behaviour is regarded as a civil duty, but that an individual's decision to break this order becomes more serious in the eyes of the law:

> ASBOs are designed to deal with those persistent low level offenders ... [they] should be used swiftly where circumstances demand it, not just against the very hard cases of unacceptable behaviour.... I hope and expect this will help those communities run ragged by the anti-social behaviour of a minority. (Straw, quoted in Home Office, 2000a, pp 1-2)

The relationship between social cohesion, order and inclusion is thus one through which the Labour government wants to keep a tight reign on particular behaviours that have the potential to threaten the moral balance of the community. The CDA's concern that such disorder is a problem associated with the young suggests further that certain groups in society are a threat to that moral balance. LCCSs are regarded by the government as helping local authorities to maintain local order[4]. Such a scheme is regarded as a preventative measure against crime as it prohibits children and young people from being present (and mixing with people) in areas which *may* be conducive to crime. Indeed, as Walsh suggests, LCCSs are "... indicative of the Labour government's desire to prevent young people from congregating in public places, regardless of their criminal intent" (1999, p 142). CSOs are another example of a preventative measure based around concern with the young's potential antisocial behaviour. These again are civil (as opposed to criminal) orders which act as a control device over children whose actions would have been regarded as criminal had they been older[5]. Again, the conditions attached to CSOs (including attendance at school or the participation in extra-curricular activities such as homework clubs, being at home at certain hours or attending certain courses/sessions to address problems; Walsh, 1999) reflect a concern about the presence of potential antisocial behaviour as well as an emphasis on community institutions having a role to play in the correction of poor behaviour.

The CDA and its measures directed at both children and at general antisocial behaviour suggest concern about the threat to communities and 'respectable' members within them, as well as a belief that unruly children need 'correcting' from within the community and by community institutions when and wherever possible. Indeed, there seems to be a link made between behaviour and respectability within a communitarian context "if they [the dangerous young] refuse to submit to the discipline of society, this justifies the stick being wielded against them" (Vaughan, 2000, p 350). In essence, it is local partnership and the working of community members together that create social order:

> ... the most effective defence against antsocial behaviour is an active community. A community that pulls together is a strong community, ready and able to stand up to louts and bullies.... I want to make sure every organisation that represents local residents knows how to help tackle anti-social behaviour through working with the police or the local authority. (Charles Clarke, Home Office Minister, quoted in Home Office, 2000a, pp 1-2)

The emphasis on respect for others and the 'greater good' of community and society can be found to cross other social and public policy areas. Concern over antisocial behaviour within the housing context is strong within the New Labour agenda and it falls within the remit of the Social Exclusion Unit (SEU) to tackle such social problems and social decline. Certain behaviours adversely affecting local communities are a strong concern for the SEU's Policy Action Team on antisocial behaviour (PAT 8) (SEU, 2000); concern here is levelled at antisocial behaviour that takes place in residential areas, such as noise, the dropping of litter and rubbish, graffiti, vandalism, and unkempt gardens. Each of these, it is argued, contributes to a sense of unease within the local neighbourhood or community, and, with antisocial behaviour being a particular problem in deprived areas (and deprived areas being part of a wider picture of social decline), its control at the local level is regarded as crucial (SEU, 2000). Certainly, the PAT report suggests that poor behaviour is likely to exist at a local level, including within the family (where parental criminality, poor parental supervision and family conflict are present), at school (high truancy rates and low achievement) and within the community itself (including community disorganisation, an opportunity for crime and the availability of drugs). While the problems may lie within what Etzioni regarded as the crucial civic institutions, their solution nevertheless also lies within their bounds – a movement away from simple state intervention is typical of New Labour's 'joined-up' approach to social problems and perceived social decline.

Preventing poor behaviour within residential areas is regarded by the SEU as being possible through community initiatives. Projects which are seen to tackle the root causes of antisocial behaviour, while at the same time improving the skills of the local community (SEU, 2000), resonate strongly with Etzioni's view of the need to have 'bottom-up' regeneration which incorporates moral education and 'reskilling'. Examples of 'best practice' cited by the PAT 8 report suggest the importance of schools as a central focus within the community setting and as the central basis for children and families to tackle poor behaviour (including parent support groups, local mentoring schemes between pupils and local business people). This re-emphasises the communitarian view that poor behaviour can be best tackled through local education and community 'pressure' and 'gentle suasion' (Etzioni, 1993).

The introduction of Neighbourhood Warden schemes is another community-led, community-defined approach to the control of poor behaviour where 'community' in this context can range from a housing estate (or a particular area within one estate), to a geographical area defined by local government boundaries (DETR, 2000b). The role of wardens is regarded as one of complementing other services provided by local agencies, yet one which is integral to the make-up of local community controls. Warden schemes include tackling racial harassment within the local community and providing a 'conduit' for complaints, concerns and suggestions for improvement from local residents. Wardens are able to mediate in minor incidents of antisocial behaviour (DETR, 2000a) and at the same time create a sense of gentle and indirect pressure on communities. The support and full involvement of the local community is regarded as crucial to the successful running of warden schemes: "Schemes should be grounded in the views, needs and expectations of the local community, rather than that of external agencies…. The local community should not be limited to being involved in identifying problems but should also be involved in the solutions" (DETR, 2000b, p 4). Such a development implies the desire to move towards a grassroots, more 'bottom-up' strategy for controlling behaviour and reaching an agreement on what responsible behaviour should be within each community.

Within social security reform, the development towards a sense of 'active behaviour' (as opposed to passive receipt of welfare benefit) whereby recipients are expected to perform certain tasks or activities (including work experience, voluntary work, further training or participation in an environmental task force; Labour Party, 1997) reflects a communitarian concern that individuals – regardless of their relative misfortune – have a responsibility to contribute to society. Parallels are to be found between Blair and Etzioni's emphases on a responsible community through a modernised welfare state and active citizens (Blair, 1997, 1999b; Etzioni, 2000). The curtailment of benefit as a result of *not* behaving in correct ways for those enrolled in the New Deal (for example, the refusal to take one of the four options offered for unemployed people between the age of 18 and 24) reflects again the emphasis on particular behaviour couched in terms of contributing to the community, with a failure to do so letting down not only oneself but also the community at large; in effect, behaviours should be controlled and regulated to some extent by, and in the name of, community. The welfare context and the reform of the welfare state have very much been couched in terms of the almost 'common sense' need to improve and control behaviour to enable the community to develop.

Responsibility, contract and reciprocity

The idea of a good society, for both Etzioni and for New Labour, is heavily dependent upon a sense of social contract and a belief in the reciprocity of actions.

The emphasis on responsibility nurtured and developed by a new view of the relation between individuals, the market and the state is regarded by Straw (among others) as essential to modern social advancement[6]. Loudly echoing Etzioni, Straw argues that the Conservatism of the 1980s, which created dutiless rights (cf Selbourne, 1994) can be overcome with a better balance of social responsibility. Encouragement of *social* concern and responsibility within the private sector are needed and New Labour, he argues, has worked to rid the sector of a socially irresponsible reputation: "cynically, to argue that such companies must only be doing it [helping the unemployed back into work] to satisfy their self interest is to miss the point. Enlightened self interest, maybe, narrow profit-taking interest, no" (Straw, 1998, p 14). Equally, continues Straw, the development of the communitarian spirit of mutuality and responsibility within the community sector is significant. Reduced direct state involvement and the encouragement and celebration of volunteerism, whereby "... people doing something for each other rather than having the state doing it for them" is seen as preferable (Straw, 1998, p 15). Indeed, New Labour's interest in encouraging volunteering and "civic patriotism" (Brown, 2000), is regarded as a solid and responsible way of bridging social divides:

> If we succeed in making a more active community, I'm convinced that there will be other benefits – less anti-social behaviour; less crime; less of the corrosion of values that worries so many people – and a better understanding that every community rests on how much people give as well as what they take. (Blair, 2000c, p 6)

Thus, the responsibility of central government is to pull back and to enable private companies, community institutions and the individual citizen to work together to achieve more responsive and responsible communities. Where government is needed, partnership with other agencies is seen as the way forward: no longer should there be heavy statist intervention to the neglect of the other 'partners' (Etzioni, 2000) of community and market.

The issue of responsibility is high on the New Labour agenda and no more so than in the area of crime and disorder (Home Office, 1997). Responsibility is particularly significant for parents and children. The issue of Parenting Orders (POs)[7] within the CDA reflects the concern that although children may be disruptive and antisocial, parents need to take some responsibility for activities deemed threatening to the community. Parenting and the family are regarded as primary instruments through which individual responsibility related to crime and disorder can be inculcated (Vaughan, 2000). Certainly, this resonates strongly with Etzioni's view that parenting is a "moral act ... [which] obligates the parents of the child [and] ... to the community" (Etzioni, 1993, p 54). Vaughan argues that parental guidance through POs resembles to some degree the 19th century moral structure of the family as the private domain in which discipline and control are exerted. In the 21st century, state involvement may possibly be no less moralising but channelled more through guidance and counselling, with a view to preparing parents for parenthood and 'gentle admonition' through a "cultivation of conscience" (Vaughan, 2000, p 357).

Problematic behaviour and irresponsibility within the arena of housing and regeneration is seen by the government as needing to be tackled through community-level strategies. Responsive approaches based on local, community-led initiatives which reiterate the important balance of rights and responsibilities and the value of a strong community culture are encouraged. Prevention of poor behaviour can be tackled, for example, through a stronger sense of contract. The rewording of tenancy agreements (to ensure all involved are aware of their obligations and duties to others) within mixed social housing estates is regarded as a clear way of instilling the sense of obligation necessary for reducing poor and antisocial behaviour. Equally, the setting up of partnership agreements in which clear expectations on either side between the housing providers and the tenants reflects a social contract in which responsibilities and rights are set out clearly from the start (SEU, 2000). Rights and responsibilities within the local authority housing setting are also illustrated in the Council Tenant's Charter (DETR, 2000c). Rights (which include being given information about how the council runs its homes, being consulted on management matters, helping in the management of the estate) are somewhat 'softer' than the corresponding responsibilities. A tenant has a responsibility to abide by the rules in the tenancy agreement, to pay the rent and to be "a good neighbour and not annoy other tenants ..." (DETR, 2000c, p 1). The responsibility to act in a 'correct' way carries with it the security of tenure, whereas acting in an inappropriate way can lead to the loss of the right to housing through the removal of the tenancy.

The deliberate drive towards the responsibilities of individuals within welfare reform (DSS, 1998) reflects a concern over the need to change the culture of passivity and encourage contribution towards community and wider society from welfare benefit recipients (Heron and Dwyer, 1999). The welfare reform Green Paper (DSS, 1998) clearly emphasised the importance of a contract between the recipients and the providers of welfare, where the responsibility for provision was no longer simply assumed to lie with the state. Increased partnerships between the private sector and the government in the name of improved efficiency and equity within the welfare domain were promoted, while the emphasis on the responsibilities of the individual recipient were made very clear. The idea that welfare recipients need to take greater responsibility for their own development is manifest within the general social inclusion agenda and the drive towards increased opportunity, education and training (with a particular emphasis on paid work, Levitas, 1998). As Blair was to describe it a year after the publication of the White Paper on welfare reform, "... a welfare state that is just about 'social security' is inadequate. It is passive where we now need it to be active. It encourages dependency where we need it to encourage independence, initiative, enterprise for all" (Blair, 1999a, p 4). New Labour's emphasis on responsibilities as being of greater importance than rights within the welfare field (Lister, 2000) reflects Etzioni's moral concern about the need to reduce dependency on state welfare and encourage a sense of independence and contribution to the community. Certainly, within the welfare field, the idea of contract has had much currency: the variety of New Deal packages has seen the development of the idea of contractual agreements, whereby the loss of benefit rights is believed to be appropriate if the conditions attached to the benefit (as in the New Deal for the Young Unemployed) are broken[8]:

> The principle of rights and responsibilities – 'something for something' ... is central to the New Deal.... It is not like makework schemes which so characterised the eighties and the nineties ... it provides practical individual advice, support and training with basic and other skills. In short, it is about making people employable through a flexible programme. (Blunkett, quoted in DfEE, 2000b, p 2)

The importance of education and the schooling system is strong both for Etzioni and for New Labour. The close link made between education and the welfare state via improved opportunities to learn and train reflect a strong communitarian emphasis from the Labour government on the need for active welfare citizens. Responsible individuals taking the opportunities provided through the partnership between government, business and community sectors is the future vision of an improved and 'good society'. Blunkett's emphasis on the need for a welfare state which promotes independence and activity resonates with Etzioni, both highlighting the need for a new social contract within welfare:

> We need to examine and clarify the roles and responsibilities of the state, ensuring it supports, rather than ignores or partly replaces the roles and responsibilities of individuals and families; or in the wider context, the local community, the trade union or the employer. It is a combination of these building blocks which make up our society that form the true welfare state. (Blunkett, 2000, p 1)

The communitarian value of responsibilities over rights is highlighted also in the education White Paper (DfEE, 1997). The role of parents is encouraged by New Labour in the education of children[9]. Family learning (including the drive for family literacy) as well as the Home–School contract (which includes information about the ethos of the school, expectations about attendance, discipline and homework) suggest a degree of responsibility placed on the parent (see, for example, Blair and Waddington, 1997). Within the Home–School contract, parents are deemed to have responsibilities to ensure their children do not truant (DfEE, 2000a). An emphasis on control and possible punishment resonates with Etzioni's firm view that truancy and the problems of lack of educational interest deepen the community divides and delay the chance of progress. Additionally, the introduction of mentors to help alleviate the problems of truancy (DfEE, 2000a) resonates with Etzioni's view that the sharing of experiences and the presence of role models are a sure way to place the young back on the right track (Etzioni, 1993, 1997b).

Discussion: localism, neighbourhood and community values

The idea of community, the sense of shared meaning and collective responsibility are common within New Labour's agenda. Whether the 'community' is a particular geographical area (a 'dangerous', 'no-go' area where crime is believed to occur, or a 'rough housing estate'), or a moral community (where welfare recipients are expected to contribute to their community, or where parents are expected to ensure their children are at school), the communitarian ethos seems alive and well within Blair's Britain.

Community has come to be defined in particular ways. 'Worst estates' have a clear location with geographically bounded deprivation within them: members of these communities have their behaviour monitored in particular ways. Failure to act in a 'responsible' way can lead to harsh outcomes. Being part of the 'welfare community' demands responsibilities of everyone; on the individual to partake in welfare to work schemes, on businesses to take on recipients, and on government to provide the enabling framework. The idea of community within the welfare domain is one of honesty and sound behaviour, where the moral incentives are backed up by conditionality and coercion in order to ensure the 'correct' community is achieved (and one based around the importance of paid work). Schools are regarded as being at the centre of communities; the communitarian emphasis on education is reflected in the importance placed on the need for children to be at school and for parents, businesses and other local partnerships to reflect a positive view of education. Again, 'responsive communities' are those that accept responsibility and correct behaviour, as well as increased surveillance of those who abuse the integrative potential of educational institutions.

Discussions about social exclusion and the need for a collective sense of responsibility towards disadvantage and poverty reflect a communitarian concern about the problem of social decline[10]. The responsibilities of individuals to help themselves out of disadvantage resonate with Etzioni's view that independence and hard work within one's community setting are a sure start on the road to social improvement. As Blair recently suggested, "wherever you find a group that has managed to break free of the encircling bonds of poverty and deprivation, there you will invariably find strong families, associations, and communities of faith" (Blair, 2000d, p 58). In both Etzioni's (2000) and Blair's (1998) discussions about the Third Way, common themes are found in their view of a good society. The three pillars necessary for a good society (the state, market and community) need to be in equilibrium. To achieve this, however, community needs to be bolstered and given its rightful place. In effect, community holds the secret to the state and the market working efficiently and effectively in the modern age. The interdependence of the market and the state combined with the role and importance of community institutions is evident within New Labour's discussions about 'progressive politics' and the need to move away from 'old' views about political relations (Blair, 2000b):

> My argument to you today is that the renewal of community is the answer to the challenges of a changing world. The way we do it is to combine the old with the new, traditional British values of responsibility

and respect for others; with a new agenda of opportunity for all in a changing world. (Blair, 2000a, p 1)

The significance of community and civic institutions in achieving a sense of cohesion are each part and parcel of New Labour's third way in politics (Blair, 1998). The social exclusion debate, with its emphasis on collective and individual responsibility in achieving a better society, is very much communitarian in its values and approach: the pushing of the individual towards self-help and independent, active citizenship is a sentiment which has parallels with Etzioni, while the combined effect of business and government each contributing to the goal of social cohesion paints a policy picture which resonates with the communitarian ideal of the good society.

Throughout the communitarian vision and within the New Labour agenda, clearly defined and clearly delineated values and morals are regarded as a necessary part of a decent society. In the crime and disorder context, reparative work in the community (including face-to-face meetings between the victim and the offender; Home Office, 1998a) suggests a belief that moral justice can be achieved and that the offender will become aware of the wrong that has been done. Blunkett, in much of his rhetoric on education and employment, aims to instil what the government believes to be the correct values in children and young adults: an awareness of the balance between rights and responsibilities as the key to a successful future[11]. The importance of education for the moral training of the young is a communitarian vision which has been taken on board by the New Labour government. Raising the standard across society through communitarian means is seen by New Labour as the way to reach a better society. Thus, moral standards (through education and better training and higher expectations) as well as the raising of more 'quantifiable' standards (levels of crime and disorder, the environmental standards of a residential area) each suggests the desire to build strong communities. The betterment of society is, therefore, the responsibility of all for all. The emphasis on the family as a strong civic institution (see, for example, Home Office, 1998b) reveals a clear communitarian thread throughout (Barlow and Duncan, 1999): the family is regarded as a central lynchpin in the New Labour agenda. From role models needed to dissuade the young from slipping into crime, to the sense of pride and ownership of an area and the importance of keeping one's home neat and tidy, the family has a responsibility to steer and shape geographical and moral communities.

This chapter argues that the spirit of American communitarianism is alive and well within New Labour's social and public policy agenda. A move towards an emphasis on responsibilities is present within criminal justice, housing and regeneration, social security and education policies. The changing role of the state, with its increasing acceptance of partnership with businesses and community organisations, suggests common threads in the third way philosophy of New Labour and Etzioni in aiming for a 'good society'. Through these different policy measures, it seems that Britain under New Labour is likely to continue to move along a communitarian path.

Notes

[1] The communitarianism referred to here differs from the more 'philosophical' interpretations. For a wider discussion on these other interpretations of communitarianism, see Avineri and de-Shalit (1992).

[2] Certainly, New Labour's adoption of communitarian ideas has not been without criticisms (see, for example, Clarke, 1998; Gilbert, 1996).

[3] Orders can prohibit, for example, a person visiting a particular street or premises or from committing or encouraging acts which would "perpetuate the harassment of others in one form or another" (Home Office, 2000c, p 2).

[4] These schemes would ban children under 10 years of age from being in a public place during specified hours unless under supervision.

[5] Behaviours included here would be any that would constitute an offence if the child were older; activity as such to suggest s/he was at risk of offending; behaviour which was disruptive and harassing local residents; and finally, the breaching of a local curfew (Walsh, 1999).

[6] Indeed, this has come to typify the Third Way within New Labour (Blair, 1998; Giddens, 1998).

[7] A Parenting Order can consist of two elements: a requirement to attend counselling or guidance sessions, and requirements encouraging the exercise of control over the child (including ensuring the child attends school and avoids certain places) (Home Office, 1998a).

---

[8] The New Deal for Lone Parents (NDLP) develops the idea of a 'moral contract': although conditionality is not a characteristic of this programme, the rhetoric suggests that it is better for the individual and the family to attempt to move towards paid work and seek advice from a NDLP advisor. Concerns about the movement towards conditional citizenship and limited social rights have been voiced (see, for example, Dwyer, 2000; Lister, 1998).

[9] The emphasis of communitarians on 'the family' has not been without criticism – see Young (1990).

[10] They also reflect concern about the tensions between heightened responsibility and social inclusion (see, for example, Ellison, 1999; Powell, 2000).

[11] The communitarian ethos in schools has been given a further push recently with the 'Young Citizen's Passport': "citizenship education in schools is about ensuring that young people understand both their rights and responsibilities" (Blunkett, quoted in DfEE 2000c, p 1).

References

Avineri, S. and de-Shalit, A. (eds) (1992) *Communitarianism and liberalism*, Oxford: Oxford University Press.

Barlow, A. and Duncan, S. (1999) *New Labour's communitarianism, supporting families and the 'rationality mistake'*, Working Paper no 10, Leeds: Centre for Research on Family, Kinship and Childhood, University of Leeds.

Blair, A. and Waddington, M. (1997) 'The home-school 'contract': regulating the role of parents', *Education and the Law*, vol 9, no 4, pp 291-305.

Blair, T. (1993) Extract of speech given by Rt Hon Tony Blair MP to Wellingborough Constituency, Labour Party News Release, London: The Labour Party.

Blair, T. (1994) Speech given by the Rt Hon Tony Blair, Leader of the Labour Party, to the 1994 Labour Party Conference, Blackpool, 4 October, Labour Party News Release, London: The Labour Party.

Blair, T. (1996) Speech given by Rt Hon Tony Blair, Leader of the Labour Party, to the Singapore Business Community, 8 January, Press Release, London: The Labour Party.

Blair, T. (1997) 'Twenty-first century welfare state', Speech by the Rt Hon Tony Blair, Leader of the Labour Party, to the Social Policy and Economic Performance Conference, Rijksmuseum, Amsterdam, 24 January, London: The Labour Party.

Blair, T. (1998) *The third way. New politics for the new century*, London: Fabian Society, Fabian Pamphlet no 588.

Blair, T. (1999a) Beveridge Lecture, given by Rt Hon Tony Blair, Prime Minster, Toynbee Hall, London, 18 March, London: The Labour Party.

Blair, T. (1999b) Speech by Rt Hon Tony Blair, Prime Minster, to the Birmingham International Conference Centre, 22 June, London: The Labour Party.

Blair, T. (2000a) 'A community for all', Speech given by Rt Hon Tony Blair, Prime Minster, to the Women's Institute, 7 June, Labour Party News Release, London: The Labour Party.

Blair, T. (2000b) Speech given by the Rt Hon Tony Blair, Prime Minister, to the 2000 Labour Party Conference, Brighton, Labour Party News Release, London: The Labour Party.

Blair, T. (2000c) Speech given by Rt.Hon Tony Blair, Prime Minister, to the Active Community Convention and Awards, 2 March, London: The Labour Party.

Blair, T. (2000d) 'Traditional values for the digital age', *Responsive Community. Rights and Responsibilities*, vol 10, no 4, Fall, pp 52-8.

Blunkett, D. (2000) 'Enabling government: the welfare state in the 21st century', Keynote speech given by David Blunkett, Secretary of State for Education and Employment, to the Employment Studies Institute seminar, 11 October, (www.dfee.gov.uk/speech/egtws/shtml).

Brown, G. (2000) Speech by Gordon Brown, Chancellor of the Exchequer, at the NCVO Annual Conference, 9 February, London: The Labour Party.

Brownlee, I. (1998) 'New Labour – new penology? Punitive rhetoric and the limits of managerialism in criminal justice policy', *Journal of Law and Society*, vol 25, no 3, September, pp 313-35.

Clarke, J. (1998) 'The trouble with normal: looking for the social in social policy', Inaugural Lecture, Milton Keynes: Open University, 26 March.

DETR (Department of the Environment, Transport and the Regions) (2000a) '£7.5 million neighbourhood wardens boost for 50 deprived communities', News Release 597, 18 September, London: DETR.

DETR (2000b) *Neighbourhood Wardens Unit implementation plan guidance* (www.regeneration.detr.gov.uk/nwunit/).

DETR (2000c) *Your rights as a council tenant – The council tenant's charter* (www.housing.detr.gov.uk/local/hsg/tenchart).

DfEE (Department for Education and Employment) (1997) *Excellence in schools*, Cm 3681, London: The Stationery Office.

DfEE (2000a) 'Blunkett and Straw pledge more police sweeps as funding increases to tackle truancy', Press Release, 9 October, London: DfEE.

DfEE (2000b) 'New Deal for unemployed and "something for something" approach in schools key to an enabling government', Press Release, 29 November, London: DfEE.

DfEE (2000c) 'Young citizen's passport: Human Rights Act edition backed by David Blunkett and Jack Straw', Press Release, 13 December, London: DfEE.

Driver, S. and Martell, L. (1997) 'New Labour's communitarians', *Critical Social Policy*, vol 17, no 3, pp 27-47.

DSS (Department of Social Security) (1998) *New ambitions for our country: A new contract for welfare*, Cm 3805, London: The Stationery Office.

Dwyer, P. (2000) *Welfare rights and responsibilities: Contesting social citizenship*, Bristol: The Policy Press.

Ellison, N. (1999) 'Retreating from citizenship: New Labour and the "post-welfare" society', Paper presented at the ESRC Research Seminar into Labour and the Third Way in Public Services, Birmingham: University of Birmingham.

Etzioni, A. (1993) *The spirit of community. The reinvention of American society*, New York, NY: Touchstone Books.

Etzioni, A. (1995) 'Nation in need of community values', *The Times*, 20 February, p 9.

Etzioni, A. (1996) 'Less privacy is good for you', *Responsive Community. Rights and Responsibilities*, vol 7, no 3, Summer, pp 11-13.

Etzioni, A. (1997a) 'Education for intimacy', *Tikkun*, vol 12, no 2, March/April, pp 38-42.

Etzioni, A. (1997b) *The new golden rule. Community and morality in a democratic society*, London: Profile Books.

Etzioni, A. (1997c) 'Thou shalt not help thy kids', *Responsive Community. Rights and Responsibilities*, vol 8, no 1, Winter, pp 9-11.

Etzioni, A. (1998) 'A moral awakening without puritanism', in A. Etzioni (ed) *The essential communitarian reader*, Oxford: Rowman and Littlefield Publishers, pp 41-6.

Etzioni, A. (1999) 'Back to the pillory?', *The American Scholar*, vol 68, no 3, Summer, pp 43-50.

Etzioni, A. (2000) *The third way to a good society*, London: Demos.

Giddens, A. (1998) *The third way. The renewal of social democracy*, Cambridge: Polity Press.

Gilbert, D. (1996) 'Don't look back?', *Renewal*, vol 4, no 3, pp 24-31.

Heron, E. and Dwyer, P. (1999) 'Doing the right thing: Labour's attempt to forge a new welfare deal between the individual and the state', *Social Policy and Administration*, vol 33, no 1, March, pp 91-104.

Home Office (1997) *No more excuses*, Cm 3809, London: The Stationery Office.

Home Office (1998a) *Crime and Disorder Act 1998. Introductory guide*, London: Home Office Communication Directorate.

Home Office (1998b) *Supporting families*, London: The Stationery Office.

Home Office (2000a) 'Grassroots communities to take a stand against local louts and bullies', News Release 186/2000, 7 July, London: Home Office.

Home Office (2000b) 'Luton praised for crime cracking programmes', News Release 271/2000, 6 September, London: Home Office.

Home Office (2000c) 'New guide to help crack down on anti-social behaviour', News Release 179/2000, 28 June, London: Home Office.

Houghton, J. (2000) 'The wheel turns for policing and local government', *Local Government Studies*, vol 26, no 2, Summer, pp 117-30.

Labour Party (1997) *Getting welfare to work: A new vision for social security* ('Road to the Manifesto' Document), London: The Labour Party.

Levitas, R. (1998) *The inclusive society? Social exclusion and New Labour*, Hampshire: Macmillan.

Lister, R. (2000) 'To RIO via the third way. New Labour's "welfare" reform agenda', *Renewal*, vol 8, no 4, Autumn, pp 9-20.

Lister, R. (1998) 'From equality to social exclusion: New Labour and the welfare state', *Critical Social Policy*, vol 18, no 2, pp 215-25.

Mandelson, P. and Liddle, R. (1997) *The Blair revolution. Can New Labour deliver?*, London: Faber and Faber.

Milne, S. (1994) 'Everybody's talking about it ... communitarianism', *The Guardian*, 7 October, Section 2, p 5.

Powell, M. (2000) 'New Labour and the third way in the British welfare state: a new and distinctive approach?', *Critical Social Policy*, vol 20, no 1, pp 39-60.

Selbourne, D. (1994) *The principle of duty*, London: Sinclair-Stevenson.

SEU (Social Exclusion Unit) (2000) *Report of Policy Action Team 8: Anti-social behaviour*, National Strategy for Neighbourhood Renewal, London: The Stationery Office.

Straw, J. (1998) 'Building social cohesion, order and inclusion in a market economy', Speech given by the Home Secretary, Jack Straw, to the Nexus Conference in Mapping the Third Way, 3 July (www.netnexus.org.uk).

Straw, J. (2000) Speech given by the Rt Hon Jack Straw, Home Secretary, to the 2000 Labour Party Conference, Brighton, 24 September, Labour Party News Release, London: The Labour Party.

Vaughan, B. (2000) 'The government of youth: disorder *and* dependence?', *Social and Legal Studies*, vol 9, no 3, pp 347-66.

Walsh, C. (1999) 'Imposing order: Child Safety Orders and local child curfew schemes', *Journal of Social Welfare and Family Law*, vol 21, no 2, pp 135-49.

Young, I. (1990) 'The ideal of community and the politics of difference', in L. Nicholson (ed) *Feminism-post modernism*, London: Routledge.

FIVE

Researching consensual 'sadomasochism': perspectives on power, rights and responsibilities – the case of 'disability'

Andrea Beckmann

This chapter presents and explores selected findings from a critical criminological social research project in London's Scene of consensual sadomasochism (SM), for which I conducted unstructured, focused interviews as well as participant observations. The aim is to promote an understanding of some potentially beneficial aspects that the Scene and its practitioners offer. These are illustrated through reference to 'disabled people' that I frequently saw in the clubs and can be read as an incentive to alter the ways in which these human beings are dealt with within conventional societal contexts.

The data collected during my research not only provided information about the diversity of erotic experiments and *bodily practices* (Mauss, 1979)[1] of consensual SM that often stand in deep contrast to the cultural imperative of genital sexuality and the day-to-day wholesale presentation of sex as a consumer product, but also revealed the central importance of responsibility and rights within consensual SM that escapes traditional understandings and interpretations of these notions.

If we were to adopt the notions of responsibility and rights from liberal rights theory, we would fail to gain insights into the 'lived diversity' of the empirical world of consensual SM. The liberal perspective is limited because it advocates and presumes a legal individualism that fundamentally lacks any consideration of social context (contextuality). Traditional, conventional discourse on rights and responsibilities is thus flawed because it is inherently individualistic, antisocial, competitive, decontextualised and, fundamentally tied to the notion of formal equality.

This ascription of equal rights does not only operate in terms of veiling the *suffered inequalities* produced and reproduced by the *conditions of domination* (Foucault, 1990) inherent in capitalist consumer (I could add sexist, racist, ageist, ableist, etc) society. Importantly, and this is its most destructive effect, in practice the notion of equal rights often leads people to an uncritical state of acceptance and a feeling of false security.

In contrast, the Scene of consensual SM, provides a space for a (re)signification of 'lived bodies' through bodily practices that are accompanied by dislocated signs and symbols. The diversity of representations (discourses and narratives) thus created can further be utilised as a tool for the ongoing explorations and experiences of 'lived bodies' and their changing limits. The various possibilities of transgression and/or transcendence within the context of these bodily practices in terms of societal hierarchies (for example, class, gender, race, age) also relate to alternative patterns of discourse. On the basis of primary research this chapter will discuss the ways in which the lifeworlds of consensual SM challenge legal and scientific conceptions of sexuality and body as well as contemporary conceptions of risk and health. The chapter will also point to the selective permissiveness that appears to regulate the expression, practice and access to resources for bodies.

The research conducted aimed to explore the lived realities of consensual SM and its subjugated knowledges. One of the unexpected findings was that the Scene that developed around consensual SM annually raises funds for a charity organisation for disabled people called 'Outsiders' (with the staging of their annual Sex Maniacs Ball). While this is obviously only a minor link between consensual SM and 'disabled' people, field observations revealed something far more crucial which points to a striking difference between 'normal' clubs and Scene-clubs: the presence of disabled people as active participants. This chapter will explore reasons for this difference, which I believe to be locatable on the level of an alternative relationship to the body both in the collective space of the Scene and in the intimacy of individual consensual SM practices.

The chapter begins by introducing the reader to the lived experiences and subjugated knowledges of practitioners of consensual SM that stand in deep contrast to socio-legal and scientific concepts of 'normalisation' and that therefore allow for different perceptions of bodies. The second part of this chapter will then reflect on conventional 'naturalising' conceptions of body and their implications for those who are defined as 'disabled'. As these concepts inform decision-making processes in both the legal as well as the socio-political sphere, it is important to be aware of their limitations and potentially destructive effects. The positive implications of the differences locatable within the Scene, especially with regard to the ethics of consensual SM, are then focused on in more detail in relation to 'disabled' people in the last section of this chapter.

This chapter aims to stimulate contributions to debates that focus on or involve notions of body, health, sexuality and risk as these notions crucially impact on the way human beings relate to their bodies and on the way in which official agencies deal with them. Within this context it is important to acknowledge that contemporary life is characterised by a shift in medical care: the individual body has become a vehicle for the late-modern concern with body boundaries, individual psychology and lifestyle in general, while a whole range of agencies reinforce this new 'form of governance' (Bunton et al, 1995, p 208). As socio-legal control over bodies appears to be extended, individual and self-determined ownership of one's body appears utopian in a cultural context where bodies can be commodified and legitimately transformed so long as it serves the purposes of 'normalisation'. This development of a rational approach to risk will be at the cost of bodies that do not submit to the legitimate paths of 'normalisation'.

The Scene of consensual SM and the cultural (non) reproduction of 'disability'

In order to account for the important differences between the Scene and mainstream society, especially with regards to official agencies of state control and provision, this section will first introduce the reader to the Scene of consensual SM and then continue by focusing on specific aspects of the Scene such as the resexualisation of the 'broken body' and the empowerment of disabled people.

As with any behaviour, consensual SM bodily practices have to be learnt. The 'step' into the Scene therefore is the start of a learning process. Access to the Scene does not merely imply access to tools, outfits, setting and atmosphere, but also access to people. These 'significant others' teach new individuals specific Scene-knowledges such as the appropriate rules of conduct of consensual SM, symbols and codes (language) with Scene-specific meanings and special traits for the diverse bodily practices. Weinberg and Kamel (1983) pointed out that the ideological education of people on the Scene occupied a great deal of time in comparison to that spent on education for the practical skills that are required for this bodily practice. Diabolo, one of my interviewees, who prefers to have contact with 'Scene-people' described his understanding of the Scene:

"It's a sort of much wider, broader minded, tolerant, acceptable, more thoughtful, more sensitive social environment, generally. And the people are just nicer there and if they are not nice they don't last long. So there's a certain kind of social filter happening if the Scene is so small and related internationally, then if anybody is abusive on the Scene, they become notorious internationally, they become famous and pay a heavy social price for it. Perhaps that's the reason why we all behave so well. But there's just no comparison if you go to a SM/fetish sort of club on a Friday or a Saturday night, although everyone is drinking, you never ever come across any form of misbehaviour and yet any local pub, every pub, every club, every disco there's fights going on in the car park. I don't trust *normale* as the Germans say. And they don't trust me."

As becomes apparent through Diabolo's explanation, the Scene of consensual SM has informal control mechanisms which do not dogmatically exclude categories of people (as in mainstream society) but rather prohibit abusive actors, people who use their potential power within consensual SM bodily practice for aims other than the pleasure of the receiving part (slave, bottom, sub). The Scene of consensual SM therefore presents a counter-narrative to the medical model of the body and, equally importantly, a counter-experience, to the reductionistic, abstract and determining discourses of positivism and the recently constantly promoted 'bio-sciences'.

The medical model of the body has specific relevance for people with disabilities as Shildrick and Price state in their critical exploration and deconstruction of the 'broken body' that "... the construction and quasi-stabilisation of the disabled body is achieved through the continual procedures of both internal and external disciplinary power ..." (Shildrick and Price, 1999, p 438). However, within the Scene-clubs the cultural reproduction of 'disability' is countered as the categories of 'normalisation' that focus on the body are hindered in their operation. This special feature is created by the distinct code of conduct within the Scene of consensual SM and through the sheer limitlessness of these bodily practices that are based on fantasy. The socially constructed differences between individuals do not count in this environment and individual pleasures and limits count everything as Diabolo illustrates:

"I'm 48 years old and the SM scene is more accepting of age diversity as well as sexual diversity because they are not normal. And they don't have a normal age, there isn't a normal age to be an SMer for example. Whereas there is almost a normal age to be on a disco dance floor or in a backroom of some pub somewhere, you got to be 20 or something or at least pretend that you are. And I'm beyond all that. Yes, so there isn't ageism, there isn't sexism, as there is among the so supposed *normale.* And it's all part of people breaking free from stereotypical thinking about themselves and others."

In addition, the cultural pressure of the body beautiful is transgressed within most of the Scene clubs, with people of all ages, sizes and shapes being found there. Women and men do not hesitate to dress in skintight leather and rubber, or to turn up in nude or half-nude states. As the aim of their interactions and meetings is the exploration of fantasies and sensations, the people I encountered within the Scene-clubs displayed and lived a profound openness and appreciation towards 'difference'.

Bodies have always been the bearers of powerful socio-cultural and moral meanings. Within the discourses of modernity the 'body disabled' was asexualised. It was denied sensuality and sexuality as it was considered socio-economically and politically undesirable that these 'bodies of lack' might reproduce. As disabled people are categorised as 'other' by 'temporarily abled bodies', they are in many cases excluded from full participation in the spheres of social and sexual life. The powerful socio-cultural myths that are still being attached to disabled people play an important role in terms of impacting on others' perceptions of and behaviour towards them (see, for example, Warnemuende, 1986). The myth of the non-sexual 'body disabled' continues to underpin the socio-cultural image and the perception of disabled people as asexual.

The 'normal' social reactions towards the bodies of disabled people still appear to be influenced by Enlightenment constructions, especially with regards to traditional understandings of sexuality in terms of an imperative of genital fixation. Hearn illustrates this for the lesbian movement and club-culture in a piece entitled *A woman's right to cruise.* As a lesbian disabled woman she accuses most of the lesbian movement of 'ableism' and notes about herself and other disabled lesbians:

> ... our experience demonstrates that the reaction of severely able-bodied dykes when being cruised by one of us is likely to be embarrassment and terror. We are generally not taken seriously in these situations, since we are not supposed to have any sexual feelings whatsoever, let alone the ability to carry them out.... Different women with different

disabilities have different needs and abilities before, during and after sex. Some of us can only lie in certain positions or may have to use different parts of our bodies. (Hearn, 1988, p 50-1)

In contrast, the Scene of consensual SM that I encountered in London is open to all bodies and promotes the exploration of bodily sensations that are not at all reducible to socio-culturally promoted 'normal' bodies, positions and/or areas of the body that are ascribed to be sexual. Thus, the powerful myth of the non-sexual 'body disabled' that translates into the societal image and categorisation of disabled people as asexual does not have any relevance within the Scene. "It was a time of direct gestures, shameless discourse, and open transgression, when anatomies were shown and intermingled at will ... it was a period when bodies 'made a display of themselves'" (Foucault, 1990, p 3). This opening sequence of Foucault's *The history of sexuality*, in which he illustrates a view of the relationship towards sexual practices at the beginning of the 17th century, came immediately to my mind when I encountered the Scene of consensual SM in London. In the Fetish Scene and SM Scene, which do overlap, the exposure of bodies or body-parts and their manipulation are also the most striking features of visual encounters. The display of a diversity of interacting bodies that indulge in erotic experiments appeared like a flight from the everyday wholesale product sex.

Within the Scene the always contextual, relational and consensual exploration of bodies and their changing states lead to a different understanding of them. This new understanding effectively alters the socio-culturally sedimented and frequently internalised experience of both body and sexuality as static entities. These acquired changes of experienced meaning of body in consensual SM practice have also been a strong concern for some feminists on a theoretical level:

> We need to insist on thinking about the biological body as changing and changeable, as *transformable*.... Living the body means experiencing it *as* transformable, not only as cultural meanings/readings, but also within itself.... People with diseases, or some forms of physical disability, may well experience their bodily interiors differently from persons who are well or able-bodied: but part of that experience depends on the cultural experience of living out medical definitions of pathological functioning. In that sense at least, culture shapes our internal experiencing. (Birke, 1999, p 45)

Conceptions of embodiment and the cultural reproduction of 'disability'

My research showed that an alternative relationship to the body is cultivated in the collective space of the Scene as well as in the intimacy of individual consensual SM practices. This has specific relevance for people with 'disabilities' as consensual SM practice for example provides the possibility to explore the transformative potentials of 'lived body' (for example, tension release, relaxation and overcoming of traumatic experiences through appropriation), a possibility to experience transcendental states and further as 'disabled' people are accepted as active participants in 'play'.

In order to better understand the alternative relationship to the body which practitioners on the Scene of consensual SM seem to have developed, it is important to outline how 'normal' societal contexts and relationships produce the 'disabled body' in opposition to the 'abled body'.

The relationship we have towards our bodies is not something naturally given or idiosyncratically invented but is socio-culturally transmitted and thus political. The discourses and connected practices of the disciplinary regime of medicine produce and inscribe the embodied subject. Yet: "notions of health, of physical ability, are not absolutes, nor pre-given qualities of the human body, but function both as norms and as practices of regulation and control that produce the bodies they govern" (Shildrick and Price 1999, p 433).

The operation of *disciplinary practices* (Foucault, 1977) are at their most effective when they are functioning by means of 'self-surveillance' via an internalisation of the objectifying and reductionistic gaze of 'science' by individual human beings. "Scientific language of separate systems maintaining constancy becomes part of a wider cultural language, assumed even within accounts of the 'socially constructed body'. Thus, health is a matter of maintenance, or keeping things constant, while disease represents perturbation" (Birke, 1999, p 45).

The discourses of the Enlightenment constructed mind and body as separate units, whereby the body was perceived as being in need of control, discipline and training by the mind and external forces as "... if the body appears uncontrolled then the self is revealed as undisciplined" (Lupton, 1995, p 7).

Even within the context of contemporary consumer culture the meanings assigned to bodies during modernity did not change profoundly. The 'broken body' or the 'disabled body' is still constructed and perceived as the 'unruly body' (Foucault, 1977), as the 'grotesque body' (Bakhtin, 1984) and thus as a 'bad body' which reveals and bares the external signs of a management gone wrong. Therefore disabled people are either pitied or excluded while the differences of the body are often, on a subconscious level, interpreted as internal failures of agency. These value laden and reductionist disciplinary socio-cultural constructions of the body have fundamental importance in terms of shaping social reactions towards and the self-perceptions and/or interpretations of disabled people. Wendell argued: "For many of us who became ill or disabled as adults, reconstructing our lives depended upon forging a new identity.... This could also be described as learning to identify with a new body, as well as, for most of us, a new social role" (Wendell, 1999, p 331).

This new social role is generally a disempowered, inferior one, which is re-enforced on various levels of 'normal' social life, especially on the level of socio-political institutions that define disabled people by reference to their lack of a 'good body' and thus stigmatise them. One example of this that illustrates the re-inscription of 'disability' onto claimants bodies is the experience of claiming for Disability Living Allowance as it represents one of the crude and alienating experiences that disabled people have to deal with. 'Disability' here is continuously reproduced and reinscribed onto the body:

> ... it is in the very gestures of differentiation and individuation – as exemplified by the innumerable subdivisions of the questions posed on the DLA form – that the claimant is inserted into patterns of normalization which grossly restrict individuality. Ultimately, what the technologies of the body effect, while appearing to incite the singular, is a set of co-ordinated and managed differences.... In focusing on singular behaviour, the state sponsored model of disability promotes individual failing above any attention to environmental and social factors. The DLA pack rigidly constructs and controls the definitional parameters of what constitutes disability.... (Shildrick and Price, 1999, p 435)

Hospitalisation is another of these experiences that symbolises the bio-medical gaze on bodies that further perpetuates the operation of myths and thus contributes to the disempowerment of 'disabled bodies'.

> The power relations and forms of subjugation typified but not limited to hospitalization are organized around a certain ironic construction –

that of a form of power to which subjugated bodies give their informed
consent, because they have no other choice. Hospitalization, with or
without walls, constructs a temporal zone and social imaginary in which
regimentary repetitions produce the effect of normalization. (Singer,
1993, p 100)

'Disability' is thus constantly socio-culturally reproduced even by
institutions that were set up to help and support disabled people. In her
chapter 'Feeble monsters: making up disabled people' Evans also comments
on the reductionism and judgmental implications of the most powerful
model of disability, the medical model, which emphasises: "… individual
loss or incapacities, implying that the impairment is what limits and thus
defines the whole person. The focus is here on the failure of the individual
to adapt to society as it is, and thus the impairment is regarded as the
'cause' of disability" (Evans, 1999, p 274). Evans then refers to the social
model of disability that was put forward by the disabled people's movement
and which more adequately defines the condition of 'disability' as it:

> … places emphasis on the power of significant groups to define the
> identity of the 'other' through the lack of provision of accessible
> environments, lack of provision of sign language, subtitles on television,
> Braille and so on. So while impairment is just one limited fact about a
> given individual, an individual becomes disabled because of the failure
> of the social environment to adjust to the needs and aspirations of citizens
> with impairments…. (Evans, 1999, p 274)

As indicated in the section above, one of the interesting findings from the
practitioners of consensual SM encountered during my research is that
they do not define disabled people by their 'lack'. They have also established
and provide a socio-cultural environment that is arguably more
constructive than that of mainstream society as it enables human beings
to fulfill their aspirations in a context of openness and safety.

Contextual, relational reflexivity and consent: the 'ethics' of consensual SM

This section discusses the ethics of consensual SM that very clearly promote
informed consensual relationships that stand in contrast to socio-culturally
accepted norms.

In contrast to Western socio-cultural concepts of relationships, the bodily practices of consensual SM that I observed within the Scene are not prescriptive and objectifying (for example with regard to norms of gender) but promote and even require profound contextual reflection and relational negotiation. One of my interviewees, Bette, highlighted the difference between 'normal' clubs and consensual SM Scene-clubs with regards to individual behaviour in relationship to social constructions and expectations of gender. She mentioned one of her female friends who went for the first time to a SM club and then stated:

> "I can't believe it, these are men but they don't behave like I would expect them to behave."

> Interviewer: "So, do you think these men are more reflective in that surrounding?"

> Bette: "Oh, definitely, yes. And also because of all these negotiations."

Apart from individual self-responsibility, which appears to be increased within the Scene, Jane, another interviewee, mentioned that there is always the pressure of 'significant others'; there is "Peer pressure to behave. So people who may be not necessarily sensible and respectful will be pressured into behaving like that".

As mentioned in the introductory section, responsibility and rights within the context of the Scene escape traditional interpretations of these notions. In this context they are not defined by reference to any explicit or implicit morality, but rather through the development of a personal ethic that is necessarily contextual and relational. As such they also imply the possibility of change which parallels Foucault's (1990) notions of the *practice of the self* and *care of the self*. The framework of consensual SM bodily practices can therefore allow, and even require, far more reflection (self and contextual) about personal responsibility and rights than any 'normal' sexual encounter. This can provide a resource for acquiring a more reflective, responsible and contextual understanding of the complexity and interdependence of rights and responsibilities in human relationships that does not rely on or appeal to any universalistic code of morals.

This is particularly relevant in situations where human beings are ascribed inferior positions of power. Holland et al noted that "... controlling sexual safety can be problematic for young women if they play subordinate roles in sexual encounters" (Holland et al, 1992, p 142).

This statement again reflects the difficulty of distancing oneself within many 'normal' situations from socio-cultural constructions that position individuals and groups according to historically specific interpretations and representations such as gender, class, race, age and disability in either more powerful and/or powerless modes of being. However, it is possible to argue that within the Scene, the socialisation, code of conduct and informal control, as well as the actual bodily practices, detach 'lived bodies' from their socio-cultural position and limitations and foster an open, explorative and at the same time caring attitude towards one's self and the other.

Lara, another interviewee, discussed the difference between abuse that happens within 'normal' society and within the context of consensual SM. For her, the people that engage in consensual SM are not 'better', more responsible people as such, but there are distinct differences and risks that make the framework provided by consensual SM far more safe: "But the difference is when you're negotiating a contract and you're saying: This is what I want to do with you ...". It thus appears that the explicit negotiations about the needs, wishes and pleasures within the relative freedom of conditions of domination in the conceptual and often experienced context of consensual SM bodily practices can provide a relative safety concerning the abuse of power.

There are several levels on which the crucial importance of reflection upon limits (responsibility) and an awareness of individual possibilities of pleasure (rights) in the context of consensual SM became visible. Consensual SM requires a high level of internal reflection and external communication even before a Scene is set up, not only because of the sometimes complex techniques applied, but crucially in order to make the experience of 'play' pleasurable and safe for both parties. There is the requirement for more explicit communications and negotiations, in contrast to 'normalised' and usually unregulated relationships, that relate to the specific preferences of both parties, the setting of safe-words or safe-gestures and also to the way in which the process of 'coming down' after a Scene are handled. Even the set-up of the 'dungeons' or 'black rooms' that are used for these consensual bodily practices clearly reflect the heightened sense of care (responsibility/rights) concerning safety and health within this setting as they always contain safe sex devices like condoms and rubber gloves.

On the level of the body, the practices of consensual SM and the Scene that developed around these bodily practices, foster a *communicative body usage* (a concept developed by Frank, 1996) which not only stands in contrast to the *mirroring body usage* (Frank, 1996) that is generated and reinforced by consumer society, but also requires self-awareness in terms of responsibility and rights in terms of limits and pleasures. Preconditions for *communicative body usage* are locatable in shared narratives of the Scene, communal rituals, a Scene-specific second socialisation and, most crucially of all, in the implicit and explicit (safe-words and safe-gestures) requirement to continuously reflect upon one's own possibilities of deriving pleasure as well as the individual limits that can change.

The awareness of responsibility with regards to the limits of other and self in interdependence to the rights for pleasure that each individual on the Scene expressed, is acquired through a learning process on the Scene and also informally controlled and reinforced within the Scene. If, for example a 'top' does not 'play' safely no one will 'play' with this person again. If people who are traditionally labelled 'male' behave according to the socio-cultural behaviour patterns and rules established by conventional society they will soon find themselves outside the Scene and this, although only operating on an informal basis, appears to have profound effects in terms of behaviour changes. Jane confirmed that responsibility and safe sex are important issues in the Scene, more so than in mainstream society, so that:

> "... it's a lot better, I mean, I [would] much rather go to a party that is an SM party than a 'normal' party because, you know, that if somebody harasses you that's considered unacceptable and it's going to be dealt with. People are much more responsible usually about sex and there's a lot more emphasis on safe sex."

In addition, the Scene of consensual SM provides a space for counter-practices as it disconnects the fundamental philosophical pattern of the Western world which ties sexuality to subjectivity and truth which, in effect, permanently shapes human beings' relationships to themselves.

In order to fully appreciate the respect and empathy for both limits and pleasures that a lot of the 'tops' had in relation to their 'bottoms', it is crucial to not only be aware of the profound interdependence of 'play' but further to know about the golden rule of consensual SM that states, 'A good top has to be a bottom first' which will generate empathy on an experiential level for being in positions that are characterised by a lack of control. Lara notes:

"You know, I'm too strong a personality to come off as a bottom. You know, I've started off as a bottom because I believed that's what you're supposed to do. That's the best way to do it and I think I'm right but then I decided that I've learnt enough and I didn't really enjoy that position, mostly because I didn't.... It's very hard to find someone who's skilled, and they have to be skilled not just in the physical thing but in the emotional safety, you know, that's also what Pat Califia and SAMOIS [a lesbian feminist support group in San Francisco] stressed, was emotional safety and what happens afterwards."

As the pleasure and safety of the partners engaged in consensual SM 'play' are existentially interdependent, a 'good top' will not only rely on the previously negotiated safe-word or gesture but continuously care for and monitor the 'bottom'. According to Anthony:

"... if you are a 'top' you have to be aware of how your 'bottom' is feeling at every single stage. A 'top' has to take responsibility, like a 'bottom' has also to take responsibility. A 'top' has to be aware of how exactly his 'bottom' is feeling. Is he okay, can he breath okay ... is he mentally okay.... Sometimes a 'bottom' might say: 'Yes, I'm okay'. But they might not be okay as well. So it must be like a unit, you must have a sixth sense. You have to pick up on body language, breathing. And you might say: 'Well, actually, I don't think you're okay.'"

'Play' with formerly painful and threatening situations within the context of consensual SM appears to have therapeutic effects on some practitioners. Traumatic experiences can sometimes be relived or re-experienced within this trusting and safe context whereby the experiential transformation of traumatic experiences does allow for a process of re-memorising and increases, according to my observations, self-confidence and assertiveness in many practitioners. Former abuse experiences can thus at times be transformed through erotic practices in combination with trust and emotional safety. Lara suggested that:

"... a lot of things that we work out sexually do have to do with childhood that those fantasies that are the most taboo and the most exciting often have to do with things that have happened to us that we haven't resolved or ways that we have learnt to deal with things that are abuse by eroticising it."

Interviewer: "Like overcoming the pain through eroticism?"

Lara: "Yeh. The psychic pain, it might not even have been physical pain, but, you know, there's a lot of things that you can work out."

The ethics of the self are therefore necessarily contingent, local, specific, never complete and experimental. The shared 'pleasures in limits' (rights and responsibilities) of consensual SM practitioners concerning bodily integrity and/or harm are contextual and relational and based on respect, acquired trust and explicit negotiations and do not depend on 'regimes of truth' but crucially on the reflexive awareness of the partners engaged.

Conclusions

This chapter has argued that the stereotypes about disabled people that saturate 'normal' societal contexts are generated by the reductionistic discourses of liberalism that can undermine the possibility of empowerment, while perpetuating the likelihood of their abuse.

While professionals concerned with the problems facing disabled people demand appropriate sex education not only in terms of promoting disease or pregnancy prevention strategies and to prevent the sexual abuse of people with disabilities, the Scene of consensual SM actually appears to offer many of the most important elements that the professionals list (Sobsey and Mansell, 1990, p 52-3):

• individually tailored and focused on the learning of enhanced communication skills (especially also in terms of verbalising feelings);
• reaching beyond the biological and addressing the socio-emotional aspects of sexuality;
• assertiveness training, choice-making and personal rights education versus aiming for generalised compliance;
• emphasising an awareness of the range of lifestyles available while helping the students to choose among these versus an education that isolates and desexualises people with disabilities.

An adaptation of some of the most crucial elements within the counter-culture of consensual SM within 'normal' societal contexts, especially with regard to the delivery of services to people with disabilities would allow them to explore and live their capacities in a much more constructive way than is the case now.

> Disabled people are held to be a homogenous group of people who are
> more similar to each other than to anyone else through the unifying
> factor of a shared nature; and therefore, whose situation, behaviour,
> actions, thoughts and needs are simply expressions of the truth of a
> deeper biological pathology. (Evans, 1999, p 275)

The repertoires of representation and representational practices that were
and are used to mark bodily difference and signify the 'disabled body' as
'other' always appear to desexualise the difference thus constructed. This
subordinates the disabled body to its opposite of abled body, and further
implies a belief in disabled bodies' innate primitivism which, through the
representational strategy of *naturalisation* (Hall, 1997) depoliticises the
constructed absolute 'difference'. This practice is counteracted within
the framework and practices of consensual SM, where nothing is taken
for granted or expected in terms of socio-cultural constructions ascribed
to human beings, but where exploration and communication are fostered.

With regard to the expression of sexuality this is crucial for disabled
people, who are often desexualised due to a cultural heritage that only
acknowledges and legitimises genital sexuality. In contrast to this
reductionism Foucault's *The history of sexuality* suggests the ethical task "...
of detaching ourselves from those forces which would subordinate human
existence [bios] to biological life [zoe]" (Foucault, 1990, p 262).

Especially in times where the threat of HIV infections have led to a
public promotion of safe sex, a re-determination of the 'body sexual'
should be promoted which would particularly help disabled people as:

> ... the ideology of safe sex encourages a reorganization of the body
> away from the erotic priorities with which it has already been inscribed.
> Specifically, safe sex advocates indulgence in numerous forms of non-
> genital contact and the re-engagement of parts of the body marginalized
> by an economy of genital primacy.... The success of this strategy will
> thus depend not only on promulgating these techniques, but also on
> circulating a discourse that allows individuals to reconsider their bodies
> in a more liberatory and strategic way. (Singer, 1993, p 122)

What is seen as constituting – and is 'naturalised' as the 'truth of sexuality'
and as the 'truth of the body' – is often the contradictory result of complex
discourses and strategies of 'normalisation'. This chapter has attempted
to demonstrate the need to "... dissolve devalued identities and theorize
new constructions of embodiment. In contesting the universal signification

of the living body our aim should be to acknowledge the plurality of possible constructions and the multiple differences which exceed imposed normativities" (Shildrick and Price, 1999, p 439).

The imposed normativities restrict human beings' freedom of expression and their ability to relate openly to themselves and others, and should not be incorporated in policies that aim to help, support and enable them. This is especially crucial for disabled people. One suggestion that could alter the status quo is mentioned by Shildrick and Price: "... one strategy recently advocated in disablement politics is to push the 'healthy' majority to a recognition that they are merely temporarily able bodies" (Shildrick and Price, 1999, p 440). They recognise that this notion was intended only to point to the material precariousness of 'health', but suggest extending it in order to provide a "... thoroughgoing critique of health/ill-health, able-bodied/disabled that a post-structuralist approach would demand" (Shildrick and Price, 1999, p 440).

To sum up the main concerns and suggestions of this chapter, I would like to underline the importance of challenging the cultural reproduction of 'disability' that is reflected in both the formal processes of gaining access to resources, and in the non-promotion of alternative forms of sexualities to disabled people as well as for 'temporarily abled bodies'. Yet, for example, it can be argued that:

> Every minority sexual behaviour has been mythologized and distorted. There is a paucity of accurate, explicit, nonjudgemental information about sex in modern America. This is one way sexual behaviour is controlled. If people don't know a particular technique or lifestyle exists, they aren't likely to try it. (Califia, 1996, p 231)[2]

The benefits of such developments might not be "... tangible in the new managerialist sense" (Clarke et al, 1994, p 179). Yet, as Clarke rightly pointed out in his critique of public service managerialism, it is not quantitative appreciation but qualitative appreciation by the individuals and social groups provided with public services and facilities that should be decisive in guiding access to leisure provisions.

Notes

[1] I consider this term more adequate in describing and understanding the empirical world of consensual SM I encountered in London, than the value laden and in contemporary consumer society, arguably meaningless term 'sexuality'.

[2] I would like to underline that apart from a continuous proliferation of meaningless 'sex' the same holds true for the UK in particular in terms of disabled people.

References

Aggleton, P., Davies, P. and Graham H. (eds) (1992) *AIDS: Rights, risk and reason*, London: The Falmer Press.

Bakhtin, M. (1984) *Rabelais and his world*, Bloomington: Indiana University Press. Birke, L. (1999) 'Bodies and biology', in J. Price and M. Shildrick (eds) *Feminist theory and the body*, Edinburgh: Edinburgh University Press.

Birke, L. (1999) 'Bodies and biology', in J. Price and M. Shildrick (eds) *Feminist theory and the body*, Edinburgh: Edinburgh University Press.

Bunton, R., Nettleton, S. and Burrows, R. (eds) (1995) *The sociology of health promotion*, London: Routledge.

Califia, P. (1996) 'Feminism and sadomasochism', in S. Jackson and S. Scott (eds) *Feminism and sexuality*, Edinburgh: Edinburgh University Press.

Clarke, J., Cochrane, A. and McLaughlin, E. (eds) (1994) *Managing social policy*, London: Sage Publications.

Evans, J. (1999) 'Feeble monsters: making up disabled people', in J. Evans and S. Hall, (eds) *Visual culture: The reader*, London: Sage Publications.

Evans, J. and Hall, S. (eds) (1999) *Visual culture: The reader*, London: Sage Publications.

Foucault, M. (1977) *Discipline and punish*, London: Allen Lane.

Foucault, M. (1990) *The history of sexuality*, London: Penguin Books.

Frank, A. (1996) 'For a sociology of the body: an analytical review', in B.S. Turner (ed) *The body and society*, London: Sage Publications.

Hall, S. (ed) (1997) *Representation. Cultural representations and signifying practices*, London: Sage Publications.

Hearn, K. (1988) 'A woman's right to cruise', in C. McEwen and S. O'Sullivan (eds) *Out the other side*, London: Virago Press.

Holland, J., Ramazanoglu, C., Scott, S., Sharpe, S. and Thomson, R. (1992) 'Pressure, resistance, empowerment: young women and the negotiation of safer sex', in P. Aggleton, P. Davies and H. Graham (eds) *AIDS: Rights, risk and reason*, London: The Falmer Press.

Jackson, S. and Scott, S. (eds) (1998) *Feminism and sexuality*, Edinburgh: Edinburgh University Press.

Lupton, D. (1995) *The imperative of health. Public health and the regulated body*, London: Sage Publications.

Mauss, M. (1979) *Sociology and psychology*, London: Routledge and Kegan Paul.

McEwen, C. and O'Sullivan, S. (eds) (1988) *Out the other side*, London: Virago Press.

Price, J. and Shildrick, M. (eds) (1999) *Feminist theory and the body*, Edinburgh: Edinburgh University Press.

Singer, L. (1993) *Erotic welfare: Sexual theory and politics in the age of epidemic*, London: Routledge.

Shildrick, M. and Price, J. (1999) 'Breaking the boundaries of the broken body', in J. Price and M. Shildrick (eds) *Feminist theory and the body*, Edinburgh: Edinburgh University Press.

Sobsey, D. and Mansell, S. (1990) 'The prevention of sexual abuse of people with developmental disabilities', in *Developmental Disabilities Bulletin*, vol 18, no 2, p 51-66.

Turner, B.S. (ed) (1996) *The body and society*, London: Sage Publications.

Warnemuende, R. (1986) 'Misconceptions and attitudes about disability and the need for awareness', *Journal of Applied Rehabilitation Counselling*, vol 17, no 1, p 50-1.

Weinberg, T. and Kamel, G.W. (1983) *S and M: Studies in sadomasochism*, New York, NY: Prometheus Books.

Wendell, S. (1999) 'Feminism, disability, and the transcendence of the body', in J. Price and M. Shildrick (eds) (1999) *Feminist theory and the body*, Edinburgh: Edinburgh University Press.

Part Two:
International developments

The chapters in this section have one feature in common: they all address the issue of pressures for change and the actual or potential transformations of social policy in various international contexts. Whether considering a specific policy area, a range of national or regional social policy systems, or the implications of changing work patterns, the chapters all point to the central importance of international comparison for contemporary social policy analysis.

John Dixon's chapter (Chapter Six) provides a wide range of information on marketisation pressures and changes in social security systems right across the globe. Dixon provides a clear and incisive analytical framework for understanding these changes, and indeed, for evaluating the ideological context of the changes being made. In short, the chapter not only reviews the changes in social security policy towards the marketised and away from the publicly-funded, but also provides a fascinating discussion of the ethical and practical governance questions that such changes bring with them.

Turning to Nick Manning's chapter (Chapter Seven), again we are provided with a wide-ranging survey of social policy issues, this time in the countries of Central and Eastern Europe. The pressures on social policy here are at least twofold: these countries are struggling to transform their previous welfare regimes to the constraints and challenges of an aggressively capitalist world economy, while at the same time struggling to deal with fundamental problems of poverty and social exclusion which appear to have become worse since the transition from communist control. Manning shows that the central problem for such countries is that of rising social costs for welfare, plus a mix of poorly organised and poorly performing economies which show little potential for being able to pay such costs in the short to medium term. The role of international actors, especially the UN in this case, in supporting such transition countries to cope with their economic and social welfare problems, appears vital in such circumstances.

Christian Aspalter (Chapter Eight) provides a rather different survey of social policy developments, this time in a quite different international context: looking at the systems of Taiwan, Hong Kong and mainland

China. Little has been written in comparative or even single country social policy literature about the systems of such countries, so the material here presented is very valuable for those wishing to broaden the range of comparative study. What Aspalter shows is how politics has been central to the previous development of social policy in his selected systems, and how, indeed, politics remains the central factor. The difference now, however, is that the political systems of Taiwan, Hong Kong and mainland China are being forced to cope with a variety of new pressures for change – economic, cultural and administrative, for example – without completely restructuring their political and governmental systems.

Zoë Irving's chapter (Chapter Nine) moves our attention from current policy systems and change to look at the significance for future social policy shifts of changes in labour market forms and work patterns. Irving uses OECD data to focus attention on a crucial feature of labour markets internationally – their gendered characteristics. The chapter reviews the patterning of such changes in different countries, links these patterns to different types of welfare system, and suggests that developments in male part-time work rather than women's work patterns may generate a challenge to the use of the 'male model' as the basis for welfare regimes in the future.

SIX

Global perspectives on the market reform of social security: protecting the public interest in perpetuity

John Dixon

Introduction

A spectre of marketisation is haunting mandatory social security around the world. There has been a profound shift over the last 20 years in the ideology underpinning statutory social security provision from collective to individual responsibility (Dixon, 1999; Dixon and Hyde, 2001)[1]. The objectives of this chapter are threefold: first, to identify the driving forces behind the global push for the marketisation of statutory social security; second, to provide a global perspective on the market provision of mandatory social security; and third, to explore the challenges facing governments that see marketisation to be at least a part of the panacea for their perceived social security ailments.

The market's global push to appropriate social security

The driving forces behind the global push for the marketisation of statutory social security come from public social security being perceived as a significant cause of budget deficits, which are considered a major barrier to economic growth, although this is seen by some as a smokescreen to hide the resultant redistribution of power and resources away from workers to capitalists that inevitably follows marketisation (Dixon and Hyde, 2001).

To some analysts the explanation for the observed increased in market-oriented statutory social security reform across a diversity of jurisdictions is the product of unsustainable fiscal pressures that have been engendered by the state's prior permissive commitment to public provision. This major cause of public expenditure growth over the last 30 or so years is a consequence of the juxtaposition of three factors (Cantillon, 1990; Carter and Shipman, 1996; Dornbusch, 1997; Glennerster and Hills, 1998; Gustafsson and Klevmarken, 1988; Hagemann and Nicoletti, 1989; ILO, 1989; Jordan, 1996; MacKeller and Bird, 1997; Rosa, 1982a, 1982b; Simanis, 1989). The first is population ageing associated with the post-war baby-boom, increasing life expectancy, and declining fertility rates. The second is a slowing down of economic growth. The third is the emergence of intractable unemployment levels. Addressing this escalating public social security cost burden in the face of a diminishing workforce constitutes the supreme challenge. The prophets of doom, with their rhetoric of crisis and their "doom-laden tracts" (Littlewood, 1998, p 1), assert (with a certainty that belies the complexities of the constellation of political, economic, demographic and social dimensions that impact on public social security policy) that without radical market-oriented reform its future is bleak. Peters (1995, p 272) captures the spirit of these prophecies with his comments on the United States' situation: "The massive debts, the unprecedented unfunded [social security] liabilities, and the unsustainable taxes that future generations will have to pay is nothing less than fiscal child abuse".

In the Austrian setting, Prinz (1995, p 17) puts this potential intergenerational conflict argument another way: "inequities between the baby-boom and after baby-boom cohorts could indeed threaten the implicit [social security] generational contract". In this view, the central aim of public social security restructuring in favour of the market is to reduce the burden of existing expenditures, thereby averting a fiscal crisis of the state.

An equally influential explanation proffered by other analysts is that the drive towards market-oriented social security reform, whether in developed, developing or post-socialist countries, needs to be understood in the context of a global political movement that aims to redistribute power and resources away from workers and their organisations to capitalists and their organisations (Mishra, 1990; Deacon et al, 1997; Byrne, 1999). This goal has been pursued through a variety of labour strategies, including the promotion of work incentives through reductions in public social security protection. Essentially, it is argued, these measures have aimed to bring about productive relations which are unfettered by the demands of organised labour and which are conducive to highly profitable investments. This perspective gains credibility from the views expressed by the international financial institutions that the privatised provision of social security is a integral part of any national economic restructuring strategy aimed at stimulating economic development in a globalised competitive environment (for example, World Bank, 1994).

Both the unsustainable fiscal pressures explanation and the global political movement explanation for the drive towards market-oriented social security reform share a common belief that the global public social security reform agenda has been informed and justified by a distinctive set of neo-conservatism political ideas and social values. These ideas and values, according to Mishra (1990, p 14), "... broadly represents the response of capital, suggested the return to a pure form of capitalism – the rigour and discipline of the market place – including unemployment as natural and inevitable in a market society, privatisation, a lean even if not mean social welfare system, and reliance on non-government sectors for meeting social needs". They are being inculcated into social security reforms provisions, according to Martin (1993, p 6), by a global neo-liberal alliance of "... economists, accountants or lawyers ... the big banks and management consultancies; the World Bank and the IMF; regional financial institutions, such as the Inter-American Development Bank (IADB) and the European Bank for Reconstruction and Development; and bilateral agencies, notably the United States Agency for International Development (USAID)".

Essentially, the argument is that many market-oriented public social security reforms that have been introduced in different countries over the last 20 years are seen to be part of a cohesive welfare restructuring initiative that draws its ideological inspiration from the Radical Right. An examination, elsewhere, of the main welfare ideologies that have influenced contemporary statutory social security provision suggests that the market is not the exclusive preserve of the Radical Right (Hyde and Dixon, 2001).

The promises of marketisation

Governments of both developed and developing countries are increasingly using market reform to shift responsibility for social security provision on to individuals, though this is perhaps more an acknowledgement of state failure than an acceptance of the rhetoric of market supremacy. In developed countries, market reform has its advocates because public social security systems are perceived to be heading rapidly towards financial crisis: the precommitment of future generations to unsustainable forced transfers, especially those needed to support an ageing population. The alluring long-term policy vision, if not promise, for any reforming government intent on introducing market provision is that of improved efficiency and the imposition of limits on penal tax and contribution burdens imposed on future generations by what are seen as short-sighted, and wasteful politico-administrative groups (see, for example, Shapiro, 1998; Tanner, 1996). In less developed countries, market reform has its advocates because it offers the hope, if not the promise, of enhanced economic performance: increased domestic savings; enhanced domestic capital market efficiency, depth and liquidity; and reduced labour-market distortions (World Bank, 1994).

Market reform ideologues advance the proposition that individuals should, in their self-interest, fend for themselves in the face of life's risks (Culpitt, 1999). They should not depend on governments for 'cradle-to-grave' statutory protection that bloats public social security budgets. Those who are genuinely unable to support themselves through labour and capital market participation, the deserving poor, should only have access to a residual public welfare safety net. Those who miss, or fall through, that welfare safety net, the undeserving poor, are expected to fend for themselves as best they can by means of informal family and community provision. This brings into focus a rebalancing of the equity and efficiency dimensions of social security.

At the ideological heart of market reform is the myth of the idealised and stylised marketplace (Engler, 1995), characterised by 'perfect competition', posited by its adherents as being morally right and economically efficient as an impersonal distributor of a society's resources. It is as if private managerial authority is, without doubt, legitimate, while government authority is a malevolent burden (Rowlands, 1990, p 267). Harris and Seldon (1979, p 23) captured the spirit of this malevolence in the British setting when they remarked "The welfare state has gradually changed from the expression of compassion to an instrument of political repression unequalled in British history and in other Western industrial societies".

Of the market reform agenda, Cerny (cited in Kouzmin et al, 1997, p 19) has observed "The central policy objective has been to shift public policy from the 'social goal' to the 'economic goal'; from the 'welfare state' to the 'competitive state'". Advocates of the market provision of mandatory social security, with their penchant for economic perspectives and actuarial predictions (see, for example, Estrin et al, 1994; Ippolito, 1986; Kotlikoff, 1989; Reichlin and Siconolfi, 1996), are disdainful of a subjective, value-laden discourse on social justice. This is particularly the case if that discourse is framed by the notions of a 'civil society', conceived of as embracing all citizens within a social fabric, based on a generalised and reified conjunction of citizenship rights and obligations that places stress on equality, positive freedom ('freedom to') and social cohesion, and of collective state responsibility, as envisaged by Marshall (1950, 1964, 1965), Titmuss (1973) and Williams (1989). They prefer their social justice discourse to be framed by the notions of a 'contractual society', conceived of as a "complex network of interaction, bargaining and compromise which interpose and counterpose interlocking, but separate, networks of individual obligations" (Culpitt, 1999, p 81). This society is based on the elusive multiplicity of individual needs that places stress on enterprise, individual (and ultimately family and charity) responsibility, negative freedom ('freedom from'), personal choice, dignity based on contractual relationships, fair returns and economic efficiency (see, for example, Bell et al, 1994; Friedman, 1962; Himmelfarb, 1995; Marsland, 1996; Murray, 1990, 1994; Velthoven and Winden, 1985).

Thus, market provision advocates prefer to conceptualise social security as a set of purely technical issues, which allows efficiency considerations to be stressed and kept separated from the (downplayed) equity considerations (see, for example, Reichlin and Siconolfi, 1996; Ippolito, 1986; Kotlikoff, 1989; but see also Culpitt, 1999; Gustafsson and Klevmarken, 1988; LeGrand, 1990; Self, 1993; Taylor, 1990; Taylor-Gooby, 1999). It is as if the economic efficiency of social security systems is all that matters. Kingson and Williamson (1996, p 30), however, make the pertinent observation:

> There is a disturbing tendency in public discourse to reduce social security discussions to mere accounting exercises on the financial costs of the programme, overlooking its value as a source of national social cohesion and as an expression of the obligations of all to each member of the national community, especially those at greatest risk.

The mandated market provision of social security: a global perspective

Since Chile's bold experiment in the early 1980s, marketisation has acquired a cult status, feeding on the popular and political reactions to what is seen as the uneconomic excesses of the state welfare paternalism.

This applies in a variety of ideological settings, from China to Chile (Midgley and Tang, 2001: forthcoming). The market provision of statutory social security benefits has become a replacement for, or a complement to, public provision in 33 countries by the late 1990s (US, SSA, 1999; Dixon, 1999).

The market provision of statutory social security provision spread rapidly in the 1980s and 1990s, particularly in Latin America, and has begun to make inroads into Western and post-socialist Europe, but, as yet, its appeal in both Asia and Africa is quite limited (US, SSA, 1999; Dixon, 1999). It has taken a variety of forms, involving varying degrees of competition in the marketised mandated private social security industry.

Complementary benefit privatisation

This occurs when governments oblige individuals to purchase (with or without employer contributions) approved benefits (whether defined-benefit or defined-contribution in form) from approved market providers *to supplement the publicly provided primary benefits.*

Central here is the use of approved market providers including independent non-profit 'social partner' organisations (typically industry-based, and administered by trade unions and/or employer organisations) operating under collective agreements as regulated monopolies to provide mandatory complementary benefits in relation to long-term contingencies. Such provision first occurred in Finland and the United Kingdom (1961) and France (1960s) and, somewhat later, in Bolivia (1972), Ivory Coast (1976), Switzerland (1985), Liechtenstein (late 1980s), Australia (1988), Venezuela (1990), Mexico (1992), Argentina (1994), Denmark (1998), and Hong Kong (1998). Such mandated market provision typically covers all the long-term contingencies on a defined-contribution basis financed by employer and employee contributions, though there are some variations in terms of the contingencies, contributions and finance.

Coverage privatisation

This occurs when government privatises the existing public provision of primary social security benefits and takes two forms: *coverage contracting-out* and *mandatory market provision.*

Coverage contracting-out occurs when contracting-out of public provision is permitted by individuals who have purchased (with or without employer contributions) approved benefits (whether defined-benefit or defined-contribution in form) from approved market providers.

Contracting out public old-age, disability and survivor programme coverage by contributors to approved occupational plans that provided equivalent (typically defined-contribution) benefits was first permitted in Greece and Malaysia (1951), then India (1952), Singapore (1953), Japan (1954), Sri Lanka (1958), followed by the United Kingdom (1961), Fiji (1966), Zambia (1973), the Solomon Islands (1976), Papua New Guinea (1980) and Vanuatu (1987).

The contracting-out of public social security programme coverage by contributors to approved personal plans began in Chile (1981), with respect to its sickness and maternity insurance programmes. This approach was subsequently adopted in the United Kingdom (1988), with respect to its public old-age, disability and survivor insurance programmes; in Peru (1991), with respect to both its public old-age, disability and survivor insurance programmes and its public sickness and maternity programmes; and then in Argentina (1994) and Colombia (1994), both with respect to their public old-age, disability and survivor programmes. Colombia (1995) also permits contracting out of its public healthcare insurance programme into individual healthcare plans.

Mandatory market provision occurs when individuals are obliged to purchase (with or without employer contributions) approved benefits (whether defined-benefit or defined-contribution in form) from approved market providers to replace publicly provided primary benefits. Replacing the public provision of long-term contingency social insurance programmes with mandatory personal (defined-contribution) programmes first began in the early 1980s in Chile (1981) and, a decade later, in Peru (1991), then Uruguay (1996), Bolivia and Mexico (1997), El Salvador and Hungary (1998), and Poland (1999). Mandatory personal (defined-contribution) programmes have also been used to replace mandatory employer-liability measures in Afghanistan (1987), for its employment-injury programmes, and in Colombia (1991), for its unemployment programme.

Coverage marketisation

This occurs when government creates a market for the provision of new social security benefits, by obliging individuals to purchase (with or without employer contributions) approved benefits (whether defined-benefit or defined-contribution in form) from approved market providers *in lieu of the public provision of such benefits.* Guatemala (1991) established a mandatory personal (defined-contribution) programme to provide its only form of unemployment provision.

The mandated market provision of social security: a contested policy discourse

The market provision of statutory social security has blossomed over the last two decades, particularly in Latin America and increasingly elsewhere, under pressure exerted by international agencies, notably the World Bank (see, for example, Beattie and McGillivray, 1995; Commander and Jackman, 1993; Estrin et al, 1994; Hagemann and Nicoletti, 1989; World Bank, 1994; but also Deacon et al, 1997). Such provision draws its legitimacy from the spirit of liberalism, the apparent virtues of the marketplace, and the erosion of public confidence in traditional forms of public provision based on public administration, if not public financing (Weimer and Vining, 1992; Kooiman, 1993; Hult and Walcott, 1990). This is a view that promotes the new orthodoxy of anti-statism (Freeden, 1978) and justifies the call, with almost missionary zeal, for radical systemic surgery, however politically unpalatable that may be in the short term.

Market provision advocates the call for a shift in responsibility for statutory social security provision away from public sector (where it reflects community solidarity, through the acceptance of collective responsibility by means of risk pooling, and seeks to enhance social cohesion, integration and inclusion) to marketplace (where it reflects individual responsibility, through the medium of work and savings, and seeks to enhance choice and produce enforceable contractual rights, promote efficiency, and depoliticise policy decision making). Preferred provision is typically in the form of mandated occupational or personal defined-contribution programmes, thereby divesting government of at least part of its social security obligations, if not responsibilities. This paradigmatic policy shift moves the social security discourse away from issues of social justice, social inclusion and equality of opportunity towards issues related to the technical realignment of boundaries that demarcate public–private responsibilities for social security, especially with respect to its funding.

That the marketplace can deliver adequate social security protection more cost efficiently than the public sector is axiomatic to market reform advocates. The premises upon which this proposition rests are, however, tenuous.

The first is that adequate social security protection can be provided, without risk pooling and without the inflation (or wage) indexing of the final benefit provided, by making a long period of contribution payment obligatory as necessary for the accumulation of savings needed to purchase the annuity, or to finance the instalment payments, which achieve the minimally acceptable rates of income replacement[2]. Furthermore, for any given contribution regime, the maximisation of accumulated savings requires:

• the shortest periods of time out of covered employment by covered employees, due to, for example, child bearing and caring or unemployment;
• the highest possible rate of interest payable on savings, which means achieving the highest the rate of return that is compatible with the market providers' long-term financial solvency;
• the smallest possible administrative costs, which means achieving the lowest rate of profit on the capital invested by market providers (notably the approved commercial carriers) that will keep that investment in the marketised mandatory social security industry; and
• the smallest possible proportion of outstanding (uncollected) contributions, which means maximising the appropriate authority and diligence exercised by the market providers.

Furthermore it assumes:

• that a capital market infrastructure exists, or can be created, to allow the market providers to invest profitably the mandatory contributions they collect;
• that market providers can deliver the required statutory social security outputs (typically defined contribution benefits to a designated population upon the occurrence of a designated social security contingency) more cost efficiently than a public agency;
• that the enabling market environment established by government for the market provision of statutory social security is and remains a competitive or, at the very least, contestable market; and
• that market providers can be disciplined by state-sanctioned incentives and disincentives to achieve articulated public social security policy goals.

However, cynics might be tempted to conclude, as Wright (1992, p 1031) does, that "welfare and profit-maximisation are not good bedfellows", or as Silburn (1998, p 244) does, that "the mantra of the unregulated free market forces may act as little more than ideological cover for sectional advantage and, at the extreme, of unbridled corporate greed". Indeed, there would seem to be many cynics in countries with mandated market provision. In Chile, a survey conducted in 1987 by the *Centro de Estudios Públicos* (1987), revealed that over 50% of those interviewed believed that the state would provide them with a better pension. In New Zealand, a referendum conducted in 1997 to consider a proposal for mandated market retirement income provision to replace the existing public universal retirement income provision led to its rejection by over 93% of the electorate (Else and St John, 1998). In Hong Kong, a December 1999 survey conducted by the City University of Hong Kong revealed that most respondents believed that the Mandatory Provident Fund system would not provide adequate financial resources for their retirement (Ngan, 1999).

Reflecting on market provision of social security, Maydell (1994, p 506) ponders thus: "... one question that should be asked is whether [such] a system will guarantee the safety of the long-term capital investment for old age and whether it can achieve a measure of equality between the weak and the strong ".

At risk are the working poor and near-poor, who confront the prospect of paying contributions they can ill afford for a promised and remote benefit of uncertain, or even unknown, value, with their fallback being a residualist welfare safety net, informal family provision, or charity.

The mandated market provision of social security: protecting the public interest

The state's mandating of market provision, which places constraints on the principle of caveat emptor, obliges it to ensure that market providers conducts their affairs in the 'public interest' (Martin, 1993; Mitnick, 1980; Ward, 1983) and for the 'common good', which, however defined, must reflect a society's shared values about social cohesion and identity (Elster, 1991; Plant, 1991; Schubert, 1960) and which must thus be a matter of public policy. The fiduciary principle of the 'public interest' holds that the state has a duty to serve and enhance the well-being of all its citizens: citizenship rights and obligations must be expounded clearly; social assets must be conserved and enhanced; the vulnerable must be protected; and diversity must be recognised and acknowledged (Brown, 1994). Determining the public interest involves a delicate balancing act. On one side is private interest 'autonomy' promoting positive freedom, or 'freedom to'. On the other side is public interest 'control' constraining positive freedom to promote negative freedom, or 'freedom from' (see also Dahl, 1982; Goodin, 1982).

Where the marketplace, with its egoistical assumptions and individualistic presumptions, has become the dominant ideology and the centrepiece of the marketising state, governments have a duty, as a matter of public policy, to define an appropriate enabling market environment for the market provision of mandatory social security that ensures that market providers contribute to the 'common good' by achieving articulated public social security policy goals. In so doing the state needs to address an array of fundamental social security policy issues, including:

- the appropriate degree of population coverage (eg whether mandatory market coverage should not be expected for employees in particular industries (for example, agriculture and fishing), occupational groups (for example, domestic servants) or employee categories (for example, low-wage earners), or for the self-employed;
- the appropriate forms of benefits (for example, whether defined-contribution or defined-benefit programmes should be mandated, or whether lump-sum benefits only should permitted);
- the appropriate contribution rates to be charged (for example, whether contribution floors and ceilings should be set, or whether contribution rates, including minimum or maximum rates, should be specified);
- the appropriate public financial support (if any) to be provided (for example, whether taxation benefits, minimum benefit guarantees or targeted or general subsidies should be provided); and
- the appropriate degree of market competition or contestability in the marketised mandated sector.

The policy responses to these fundamental policy issues determines who should pay for designated benefits from designated market providers, operating in a competitive or contestable market, in the event of designated social security contingencies, whether in the distant or the near future. Whether this will avoid the unintended recourse by beneficiaries or by market providers to public financial support in the future is, ultimately, dependent on the socio-political governance mechanism put in place by government.

This balancing act raises a policy dilemma for government: should it limit any market-driven ownership concentration in the mandated private social security industry, especially when it involves foreign corporations, in order to ensure the survival of the market's automatic disciplining mechanism, which constrains the rent seeking behaviour of oligopolists and monopolists. The ownership concentration experience in Chile, where three market providers hold over 80% of the market (Borzutzky, 2001: forthcoming), and Hong Kong where four market providers hold about 60% of the market (Ngan, 1999) is, if replicated elsewhere, a significant challenge to those required to regulate mandatory private provision.

The socio-political governance issues

The public interest can only be protected by regulatory compliance of market providers of mandatory social security provision within the context of a socio-political governance mechanism. Kooiman (1999, p 70; see also Kooiman, 1993; Peters and Pierre, 1998; Rhodes, 1997) defines this mechanism as "All those interactive arrangements in which public as well as private actors participate aimed at solving societal problems or creating societal opportunities and attending to the institutions within which these governing activities take place". Kooiman (1999, pp 83-4) goes on to distinguish between three regulatory modes: self-regulation (where the regulated are their own regulators, perhaps by state delegation or default); co-governing (where the regulated voluntarily cede some autonomy to the state, in return for agreed common rights and acceptable common obligations); and hierarchical governing (where the regulated are subject to a set of state-imposed rights and obligations). Governance involves the design and implementation of regulatory regimes embodying both structural regulations and conduct regulations (Jessop, 1997; Majone, 1994; Wright, 1992). Structural regulations determine the characteristics of acceptable market providers. Conduct regulations determine what are the acceptable forms of institutional behaviour and private governance practices in the marketised mandatory social security industry.

The achievement of public social security policy goals in a market environment requires a socio-political governance mechanism that coordinates, steers, influences and balances pluralist interactions (Gilbert and Gilbert, 1989; Wright, 1994; Rose, 1996), with the civil service acting as the trustee of the public interest (Ott and Goodman, 1998). There have, of course, long been debates about the governability of modern societies (see Foucault, 1991; Maynetz, 1993; Willke, 1990), about whether any governance mechanism can ever be, and remain, focused on the public interest (Edelman, 1964; Lowi, 1969; Peltzman, 1976; Schubert, 1960), and about the causes of regulatory failure (Donohue, 1989; Gormley, 1994).

The central socio-political governance challenges emerge due to market providers' desire to serve private interest goals, as defined by their 'owners', which feeds their drive for efficiency, almost regardless of social cost. This stands in stark contrast to the public sector's desire to serve often competing public policy goals, as defined by politicians, which feeds its drive to protect and promote the public interest, almost regardless of efficiencies forgone.

Thus the key governance questions are:

1. What is the best way of creating an enabling market environment that will foster adequately profitable but socially and politically acceptable market provision of statutory social security, in both the distant and the near future?
2. What multilevel political, administrative and regulatory structures, culture and processes are needed to protect the 'public interest' in a marketised statutory social security environment?
3. How should sub-optimal provision by market providers be dealt with in a market environment?

Whether public interests become subservient to private interests depends crucially on whether the state is willing and able to design, implement and administer a set of regulatory arrangements that require market providers to deliver their promised social security outputs when contracted to do so. This raises further governance policy issues. What administrative and financial constraints (if any) should be placed on market providers, such as, institutional management constraints; portfolio management constraints; and public acceptability (reporting and disclosure) requirements? What about the statutory record-keeping requirements, the statutory right-of-access by contributors and beneficiaries to information stored by private providers; the statutory guarantee of confidentiality of such information; and the probity (auditing) requirements? What are the statutory sanctions (at the corporate and responsible-individual level) available to government in the event of institutions acting contrary to the current and future public interests? Finally, what are the statutory winding-up provisions in the event of market providers being unable (even unwilling) to meet their financial obligations to permit the effective socio-political governance of the following risks?:

• *Investment risks*, which relate to contracted market providers' inability to provide their promised or expected benefits because they achieve a lower rate of return than anticipated on accumulated contributions collected, the financial cost of which is carried by beneficiaries under defined-contribution programmes and by market providers under defined-benefit programmes.
• *Corporate risks*, which relate to contracted market providers' inability to provide their promised or expected benefits because of organisational termination, which may result from corporate bankruptcy, or from deliberate boardroom business strategy decisions, the financial cost of which would be carried by beneficiaries, if market providers can legally abdicate their full contractual obligations because of organisational termination.

The design features of regulatory regimes (their requirements, structures, culture and processes) determine the degree of risk of governance failure due to two factors (Bernstein, 1955; Majone, 1994; Thompson et al, 1998; Wright, 1992):

• *asymmetrical information flows* when the regulated market providers distort or withhold from regulators the information they needed to regulate effectively (say, information on financial product commission rates, management incentive and bonus payments, actual administrative costs, actual profit margins, proposed or likely business rationalisation measures, corporate mergers or takeovers) to achieve their private interest ends; and
• *agency capture* when the regulated market providers manipulate the regulators (by, perhaps, strategic agenda-setting or compromise bargaining at the political or administrative levels) to achieve their private interest ends.

It has been argued that a regulatory regime for a mandated private social security industry should therefore have the following features (Doyal and Gough, 1991; Drover and Kerans, 1993; Gunningham and Sinclaire, 1999; Lamour, 1997; Le Grand and Robinson, 1984; Rees et al, 1993; Taylor-Gooby, 1999). First, it should ensure an appropriate degree of market competition or contestability in the mandated private social security industry. Second, it should not impose excessive cost on the regulated market providers and so encourage compliance avoidance. Third, it should be flexible enough to allow the regulated market providers to respond to the challenges of complexity, diversity and the dynamics of modern society. Fourth, it should place the private and the public sectors within a cooperative continuum rather than a conflictual dichotomy, both working towards the achievement of mutually beneficial public policy outcomes. Fifth, it should be transparent, not only to engender public trust, so essential in an environment where the assessment of investment and corporate risks is problematic, but also to foster coordination and cooperation between the community-at-large, the regulated market providers and the public regulators. Sixth, it should acknowledge participation as a precondition for human action and interaction, and thus involve contributors directly or indirectly in strategically important decision making. Finally, it should foster equitable outcomes. These socio-political governance imperatives are central to the building and maintaining of public trust and confidence in, and support for, marketised mandated provision of social security.

That there is a need for a regulatory regime that ensures that the interests of future beneficiaries do not become incongruous, incompatible or even subservient to the private interest goals of market providers is clear. There is, however, little reason to be confident that the state can resist the appropriation of the public interest by the marketplace, for any socio-political governance failure may well encourage the spectre of government subsidies. Pressures would build for government subsidies to be paid to market providers of mandated defined-contribution programmes if their achieved levels of accumulated savings (or equivalent annuities) are so inadequate, or so much below community expectations, as to be fiscally and politically unacceptable. Similar pressures would build up if the profitability (or financial viability) of market providers of mandated defined-benefit programmes was threatened.

Conclusion

The shift from public provision of mandatory social security (which reflects a collective responsibility that enhances social cohesion, integration and inclusion) to market provision (which reflects an individual responsibility that enhances choice and produces enforceable contractual rights) has moved the global social security policy discourse away from issues of social justice, social inclusion and equality of opportunity towards technical issues related to the demarcation of public and private financial responsibilities. These marketisation pressures have blossomed, especially over the last two decades, one result of which is the market provision of statutory social security benefits in 33 countries by the late 1990s.

The daunting challenges facing governments intent on marketising their statutory social security systems are threefold. First, they must decide who must pay for what form of social security protection from what sort of market provider, in what sort of market environment, in the event of a which social security contingencies, and whether in the distant or the near future. Second, they must design a set of regulatory arrangements that can protect the public interest in perpetuity in an environment where private interest goals can easily come into conflict with public interest goals. Finally, they must resist calls for government subsidies to support the 'economic rent' (Tullock and Eller, 1994) or excessive profit expectations of market providers.

The policy dream that market provision of mandatory social security will allow governments to reduce fiscal deficits or even to limit or reduce future tax burdens, could, however, become part of a public interest nightmare. This would be so especially if governments were to create, by statute, mandatory private insurance markets to facilitate the reduction of public expenditure on, or the abandonment of government responsibility for, other public programmes that address other insurable social risks. These might include old age, disability, unemployment, sickness, and non-compulsory education provision.

Notes

[1] Statutory social security provision relating to old age, disability, death, sickness, maternity, employment injury and death, unemployment, and children and families by the state can be by public provision, by mandated joint provision with private sector, or by mandating market provision by the private sector, whether on an occupational basis (necessitating employee and/or employer contributions) or a personal basis (necessitating only individual contributions), whether delivered by commercial-for-profit, by commercial mutual-aid, or by independent non-profit ("social partner") organisations (typically, industry-based and administered by trade unions and/or employer organisations), and whether on a defined-contribution (money purchase) basis (under which there is a statutory definition of the contributions to be collected, but not future benefits to be provided) or on a defined-benefit basis (under which there is a statutory definition of the future benefits to be provided for the payment of prescribed contributions).

[2] Illustratively, a 30-year continuous contribution period must elapse before covered employees can accumulate enough savings to achieve an income replacement rate of 25%, assuming a combined employer and employee contribution rate of 10%, a growth in employee earnings of 7% a year and an real investment return of 8% a year (Hewitt Assoc and GML Consulting, 1995, p 5).

References

Beattie, R. and McGillivray, W. (1995) 'A risky strategy: reflections on the World Bank report averting the old age crisis', *International Social Security Review*, vol 48, pp 5-22.

Bell, M., Butler, E., Marsland, D. and Pirie, M. (1994) *The end of the welfare state*, London: Adam Smith Institute.

Bernstein, M..H. (1955) *Regulating business by independent commission*, Princeton, NJ: University of Princeton Press.

Borzutzky, S. (2001: forthcoming) 'Chile's pioneering privatisation', in J. Dixon and Hyde, M. (eds) *The marketisation of social security*, Westport, CT: Quorum.

Brown, P. (1994) *Restoring the public trust*, Boston, MA: Beacon Press.

Byrne, D. (1999) *Social exclusion*, Buckingham: Open University Press.

Cantillon, B. (1990) 'Socio-demographic changes and social security', *International Social Security Review*, vol 43, no 4, pp 399-425.

Carter, M..N. and Shipman, W. G. (1996) 'The coming global pension crisis', *Foreign Affairs*, vol 75, no 6, pp S1-S16.

Centro de Estudios Públicos (1987) 'Estudio social y de opinión pública en la población de Santiago', *Documento de Trabajo*, vol 83.

Commander, S. and Jackman, R. (1993) 'Providing social benefits in Russia: redefining the roles of firms and government', Policy Research Working Paper 1184, Washington, DC: World Bank.

Culpitt, I. (1999) *Social policy and risk*, London: Sage Publications.

Deacon, B. with Hulse, M. and Stubbs, P. (1997) *Global social policy. International organisations and the future of welfare*, London: Sage Publications.

Dahl, R. (1982) *Dilemmas of plural democracy*, New Haven, CT: Yale University Press.

Dixon, J. and Hyde, M. (eds) (2001) *The marketisation of social security*, Westport, CT: Quorum.

Dixon. J. (1999) *Social security in global perspective*, Westport, CT: Praeger.

Donahue, R. (1989) *The privatisation decision: public ends, private means*, New York, NY: Basic Books.

Dornbusch, R. (1997) 'Japan's pension crisis: growth the only way out', *Business Week*, vol 35, no 11, 27 January, p 18.

Doyal, L. and Gough, I. (1991) *A theory of human need*, London: Macmillan.

Drover, G. and Kerans, P. (eds) (1993) *New approaches to welfare theory*, London: Edward Elgar.

Edelman, M. (1964) *The symbolic uses of politics*, Urbana, IL: University of Illinois Press.

Else, A. and St John, S. (1998) *A super future?*, Auckland, New Zealand: Tandem Press.

Elster, J. (1991) *The cement of society: A study of social order*, Cambridge: Cambridge University Press.

Engler, A. (1995) *Apostles of greed: Capitalism and the myth of the market*, London: Pluto Press.

Esping-Andersen, G. (1990) *The three worlds of welfare capitalism*, Cambridge: Polity Press.

Estrin, S., Shaffer, M. and Singh, I. (1994) 'The provision of social benefits in state-owned, privatised and private firms in Poland', Paper presented at the Workshop on Enterprise Adjustment in Eastern Europe, World Bank, Policy Research Department, Washington, DC, 22-23 September (distributed by the World Bank).

Foucault, M (1991) 'Governmentality', in G. Burchaell, C. Gordon and P. Miller (eds) *The Foucault effect: Studies in governability*, London: Harvester Wheatsheaf.

Freeden, M. (1978) *The new liberalism: An ideology of social reform*, Oxford: Clarendon Press.

Friedman, M. (1962) *Capitalism and freedom*, Chicago, IL: University of Chicago Press.

Gilbert, N. and Gilbert, B. (1989) *The enabling state*, Oxford: Oxford University Press

Glennerster, H. and Hills, J. (eds) (1998) *The state of welfare: The economics of social spending*, Oxford: Oxford University Press.

Goodin, R.E. (1982) 'Freedom and the welfare state: theoretical foundations', *Journal of Social Policy*, vol 11, no 2, pp 149-76.

Gormley, W.T. Jr (1994) 'Privatisation revisited', *Policy Studies Review*, vol 13, nos 3/4, pp 215-34.

Gunningham, N. and Sinclaire, D. (1999) 'Regulatory pluralism: designing policy mixes for environmental protection', *Law & Policy*, vol 21, no 1, January, pp 49-76.

Gustafsson, B.A. and Klevmarken, N.A. (1988) *The political economy of social security*, Amsterdam: Elsevier.

Hagemann, R.P. and Nicoletti, G. (1989) 'Population ageing: economic effects and some implications for financing public pensions', *OECD Economic Studies*, vol 12, Spring, pp 59-110.

Harris, R. and Selden, A. (1979) *Over-ruled on welfare: The increasing desire for choice in education and medicine and its frustration by representative government*, Hobart Papers 13, London: Institute of Economic Affairs.

Hewitt Associates and GML Consulting (1995) *Report of the consultancy on the mandatory provident fund system*, Hong Kong: Hewitt Associates and GML Consulting for the Hong Kong Government.

Himmelfarb, G. (1995) *The de-moralisation of society: From victorian virtues to moral values*, London: Institute of Economic Affairs.

Hult, K. and Walcott, C. (1990) *Governing public organisations*, Brooks/Cole Publishing Company.

Hyde, M. and Dixon, J. (2001: forthcoming) 'Welfare ideology, the market and social security: towards a typology of market-oriented reform', *Policy Studies Review*.

ILO (International Labor Office) (1989) *Social security protection in old-age*, Geneva: ILO.

Ippolito, R.A. (1986) *Pensions, economics and public policy*, Homewood, IL: Dow Jones..

Jessop, B. (1997) 'Capitalism and its future: remarks on regulation, government and governance', *Review of International Political Economy*, vol 4, no 3, pp 561-607.

Jordan, B. (1996) *A theory of poverty and social exclusion*, Cambridge: Polity Press.

Kingson, E.R. and Williamson, J. (1996) 'Undermining social security's basic objective', *Challenge*, vol 39, no 6, pp 28-30.

Kooiman, J. (1993) *Modern governance: New government-society interactions*, Beverly Hills, CA: Sage Publications.

Kooiman, J. (1999) 'Socio-political governance: overview, reflection and design', *Public Management*, vol 1, no 1, pp 67-92.

Kotlikoff, L.J. (1989) 'On the contribution of economics to the evaluation and formation of social security policy', *American Economic Review*, vol 79, no 2, pp 184-90.

Kouzmin, A., Leivesley, R. and Korac-Kakabadse, N. (1997) 'From managerialism and economic rationalism: towards "reinventing" economic ideology and administrative diversity', *Administrative Theory and Praxis*, vol 19, no 1, pp 19-46.

Lamour, P. (1997) 'Models of governance and public administration', *International Review of Administrative Science*, vol 63, no 3, pp 383-94.

LeGrand, J. (1990) 'Equity versus efficiency: the elusive trade-off', *Ethics*, vol 100, no 4, pp 554-68.

Le Grand, J. and Robinson, R. (1984) *Privatisation and the welfare state*, London: Macmillan.

Littlewood, M. (1998) *How to create a competitive market in pensions*, Choice in Welfare, 45, London: Institute of Economic Affairs Health and Welfare Unit.

Lowi, T. (1969) *The end of liberalism*, New York, NY: Norton.

MacKeller, L. and Bird, R. (1997) 'Global population ageing, social security and economic growth: some results from a 2-region model', Paper presented at a Project LINK meeting, New York, March.

Majone, G. (1994) 'The rise of the regulatory state in Europe', *West European Politics*, vol 17, no 3, pp 77-101.

Marshall, T.H. (1950) *Social class and citizenship*, Cambridge: Cambridge University Press.

Marshall, T.H. (1964) 'Citizenship and social class', in T.H. Marshall (ed) *Class, citizenship and social development*, Garden City, NY: Doubleday.

Marshall, T.H. (1965) 'The right to welfare', *Sociological Review*, vol 13, no 3, pp 261-72.

Marsland, D. (1996) *Welfare or welfare state? Contradictions and dilemmas in social policy*, London: Macmillan.

Martin, B. (1993) *In the public interest? Privatisation and public sector reform*, London: Zed.

Maydell, B. von (1994) 'Perspectives on the future of social security', *International Labour Review*, vol 133, no 4, pp 251-10.

Maynetz, R. (1993) 'Governing failure and the problem of governability: some comments on a theoretical paradigm', in J. Kooiman (ed) *Modern governance: New government-society interactions*, London: Sage Publications.

Midgley, J. and Tang, K. (2001: forthcoming) 'Individualism, collectivism and the marketisation of social security', *Policy Studies Review*.

Mishra, R. (1990) *The welfare state in capitalist society: Policies of retrenchment and maintenance in Europe, North America and Australia*, London: Harvester Wheatsheaf.

Mitnick, B.M. (1980) *The political economy of regulation*, New York, NY: Columbia University Press.

Murray, C. (1990) *The emerging British underclass*, London: Institute of Economic Affairs.

Murray, C. (1994) *Underclass: The crisis deepens*, London: Institute of Economic Affairs.

Ngan, R. (1999) 'The mandatory provident fund scheme in Hong Kong', Unpublished paper, Department of Applied Social Studies, City University of Hong Kong.

Ott, J.S. and Goodman, D, (1998) 'Government reform or alternative bureaucracy? Thickening, tides and the future of governing', *Public Administration Review*, vol 58, no 6, pp 540-5.

Peltzman, S. (1976) 'Towards a general theory of regulation', *Journal of Law and Economics*, vol 19, August, pp 211-40

Peters, P.G. (1995) 'Pensions and reform', *Vital Speeches of the Day*, vol 61, no 9, 15 February, pp 272-6.

Peters, B.G. and Pierre, J. (1998) 'Governance without government? Rethinking public administration', *Journal of Public Administration Research and Theory*, vol 8, no 3, pp 223-43.

Plant, R. (1991) *Modern political thought*, Oxford: Basil Blackwell.

Prinz, C. (1995) 'Population ageing and intergenerational equity in the Austrian pension system: a long-term analysis of cohorts born in the twentieth century', Paper presented at the European Population Conference, Session IV(3), Vienna.

Rees, S., Rodley, G. and Stilwell, F.J.B. (eds) (1993) *Beyond the market: Alternatives to economic rationalism*, Sydney, Australia: Pluto Press.

Reichlin, P. and Siconolfi, P. (1996) 'The role of social security in an economy with asymmetrical information and financial intermediaries', *Journal of Public Economics*, vol 60, no 2, pp 153-75.

Rhodes, R.A.W. (1997) *Understanding governance: Policy networks, governance, reflexivity and accountability*, Buckingham: Open University Press.

Rosa, J.-J. (ed) (1982a) *The world crisis in social security*, San Fransisco, CA: Institute for Contemporary Studies.

Rosa, J.-J. (1982b) 'France', in J.-J. Rosa (ed) *The world crisis in social security*, San Fransisco, CA: Institute for Contemporary Studies.

Rose, N. (1996) 'The death of the social? Re-figuring the territory of government', *Economy and Society*, vol 25, no 3, pp 327-56.

Rowlands, D. (1990) 'Privatisation and managerial ideology', in A. Kouzmin and N. Scott (eds) *Dynamics in Australian public management: Selected essays*, Melbourne, Australia: Macmillan.

Schubert, G. (1960) *The public interest*, New York, NY: Free Press.

Self, P. (1993) *Government by the market? The politics of public choice*, London: Macmillan.

Shapiro, D. (1998) 'The moral case for social security privatisation', *Social Security Privatisation*, vol 14 (http://www.socialsecurity.org/pubs/ssps/ssp-14es.html).

Silburn, R (1998) 'United Kingdom', in J. Dixon and D. Macarov (eds) *Poverty: A persistent global reality*, London: Routledge.

Simanis, J.G. (1989) 'National expenditures on social security and health in selected countries', *Social Security Bulletin*, vol 52, no 12, pp 18-26.

Tanner, M. (1996) 'It's time to privatise social security', *Challenge*, vol 39, no 6, pp 19-20.

Taylor, I. (ed) (1990) *The social effects of free market policies: An international text*, London: Harvester Wheatsheaf.

Taylor-Gooby, P. (1999) 'Markets and motives: implications for welfare', *Journal of Social Policy*, vol 28, no 1, pp 97-114

Thompson, M., Rayner, S. and Ney, S. (1998) 'Risk and governance part II: policy in a complex and plurally perceived world', *Government and Opposition*, vol 33, no 3, pp 330-54.

Titmuss, R. (1973) *The gift relationship*, Harmondsworth: Penguin.

Tullock, G. and Eller, K. (1994) *Rent seeking*, London: Edward Elgar.

US, Social Security Administration (1999) *Social security programmes throughout the world – 1999*, Washington, DC: US Government Printing Office.

Velthoven, B. van and Winden, F.A.A.M. van (1985) 'Towards a political-economic theory of social security', *European Economic Review*, vol 27, pp 263-89.

Ward, E.J. (1983) *An exploration of the public interest concept: Towards and enhanced theoretical and practical understanding*, Ann Arbor, MI: UMI Dissertation Information Service.

Weimer, D.L. and Vining, A.R. (1992) *Policy analysis: Concepts and practice*, Englewood Cliffs, NJ: Prentice Hall.

Williams, F. (1989) *Social policy: A critical introduction*, Cambridge: Polity Press.

Willke, H. (1990) 'Disenchantment of the state: outline of a systems theoretical argumentation', in Th. Ellwein, R. Mayntz and F. Scharpf (eds) *Yearbook in government and public administration*, Baden-Baden: Nomos.

World Bank (1994) *Averting the old age crisis*, New York, NY: Oxford University Press.

Wright, V. (1992) 'The administrative system and market regulation in western Europe: continuities, exceptionalism and convergence', *Rivista Trimestrale di Diritto Publico*, vol 4, pp 1026-41.

Wright, V. (1994) 'Reshaping the state: the implications for public administration', *Western European Politics*, vol 17, no 3, pp 102-37.

SEVEN

Copenhagen +5: what should be done about the transition in Eastern Europe?[1]

Nick Manning

This chapter is based on an analysis and set of recommendations that were commissioned in 2000 by the UN Department of Economic and Social Affairs (UNDESA) for a review of the social situation in Central and Eastern Europe in the preparations for the UN World Summit for Social Development scheduled for June, 2000 in Geneva. They were presented to a joint meeting of the UNDESA and the Inter-Parliamentary Union in St Petersburg in March, 2000, and subsequently to a joint session of the UN Development Programme (UNDP) and Council of Europe in the Geneva meetings.

The chapter examines a number of areas in which social costs have risen sharply, such as poverty and health, and makes suggestions as to policy initiatives that the UN might recommend as ways of addressing these issues. The chapter deliberately links analysis and policy recommendations. A similar exercise has recently been published by the Institute for Public Policy Research (Eatwell et al, 2000).

The Copenhagen +5 process

Social policy has been given a more central place in UN deliberations since the World Social Summit in Copenhagen in 1995. At the end of that series of meetings 117 countries jointly supported the 10 commitments that were adopted covering three core issues of poverty, employment, and social development. In addition, there was a commitment to review the progress that countries were making towards these social goals every five years, with the first review due in Geneva in 2000. Other major UN meetings, such as Beijing on Women, Cairo on Population, and Rio on the Environment, have had a similar commitment to regular review.

The 10 commitments covered both specific areas of social need as well as more general issues about developing and sustaining the mechanisms for these needs to be met. In the process leading up to the 2000 review, the UN Economic and Social Council invited countries to report on the progress that they had made in meeting the Copenhagen commitments. By December 1999, 74 countries had reported on poverty reduction and employment in some detail, and in addition had discussed the extent to which the social integration of vulnerable groups such as older people was improving. In the summary of these reports, the UN Preparatory Committee put particular emphasis on the mobilisation of resources for social policy, both state and non-state, and the development of the capacity for developing social policy in terms of good governance and civil society initiatives.

Within the UN system, such discussions are not apolitical. Not only do different countries try to influence the kind of policy aims and mechanisms recommended, but also within different branches of the UN, different emphases can be found between, for example, UNDESA and UNDP. Thus the support of or opposition to targeting of benefits, or the balance between state, market and community led services can be marked, and intense debates develop around these issues. With the rapidly changing social and governmental situation within different countries of Central and Eastern Europe, such debates about the best way forward, and the balance between realism and aspiration, have been particularly sharp. The analysis and suggestions contained in this chapter have in general been widely supported in debates within the UN.

The transition in Eastern Europe

In the 10 years since the fall of the Berlin wall, and the revolutions in Central and Eastern Europe and the Former Soviet Union, there has been a significant rise in social costs. In the very early stages, in many countries, it was recognised that social costs were likely to rise, and structures were extended or put in place to deal with this – for example, benefit for unemployment. However, both financial and administrative incapacity rapidly revealed the limitations of this early social protection, and entitlements and benefits were widely cut back. Since that time, social costs have been relatively neglected on the assumption that priority should be given to economic liberalisation, and building the institutions of representative democracy.

The very first commitment made at the 1995 Copenhagen Summit was towards creating an enabling environment for social development. Research on policy developments in the social sphere in the transition countries reveals incoherent policy debates at the national level, combined with policy ignorance at the level of real policy actors – civil servants, trade unionists, and local business leaders (Collier et al, 1999). Economic and institutional improvement has been sluggish, in turn undermining both the resilience of households and communities in the face of rapid change and the resources available for social intervention. This has given rise to a marked deterioration of human security in the region. Problems such as poverty, inequality, poor health and social exclusion have multiplied. Since 1995, however, there has also been an increasingly uneven spread of such problems, so that it is more and more difficult to generalise across all 27 countries. Consequently measures to halt and reverse this deterioration need to be disaggregated into groups of countries facing broadly similar difficulties.

Social needs can be divided into two types. Those related to the physical survival of individuals and households include deprivation of food, goods and services, shelter, and health care. In the short run, even physical survival in the region has not been secured for many people. In the longer run, social needs of a second type include those related to the reproduction and survival of the society on which such individuals and households depend, such as education and community participation. The social costs of the transition include increases in both of these types of social need, and also the limited capacity of governments, communities and markets to deal with them.

Poverty

Income poverty in the region has grown rapidly, from 14 million people in 1988 to 140 million by the late 1990s (EBRD, 1999; UNICEF, 1999a). However there are difficulties in measuring its extent. Most international studies use income as a proxy for the household's capacity to acquire essential goods and services. In the United Nations system, it is generally held to be necessary for individuals to have at least four US dollars per day at purchasing power parity to avoid poverty. On this measure, poverty rates in the region have grown and continue to be high, for example 31%

in Russia and the Ukraine, over 50 % in the Central Asian countries, and 24% in Poland (Ruminska-Zimny, 1997).

There are two important limitations to the use of this measure. First, we know from studies in Ireland and Sweden that only 50% of households with income poverty are deprived, and only 50% of deprived households have income poverty. This is particularly the case for rural areas (Callan et al, 1993; Halleröd, 1995; Ovcharova, 1997). Households have alternative sources of 'command-over-resources', not captured by income measures. In the transition countries these alternatives are much greater: non-monetised exchange networks, or barter, including casual work; self-provisioning, especially of food; and stocks of existing goods, such as housing, with low or subsidised utility prices. Some work in the region has therefore used physical measures of stunted growth or malnutrition to identify poverty (Ismail and Micklewright, 1997). Second, the meaning of poverty is sensitive to social or cultural criteria. Poverty can be argued to be that level of deprivation at which a household feels excluded from normal community life. This may mean that where deprivation is widespread it is less likely to be excluding. Thus work using either the social or physical alternatives to money income to measure poverty has suggested a lower level of poverty across the region (Manning et al, 2000).

These alternative criteria also have significance for the type of policy measures that should be adopted to combat poverty. It is important, therefore, that regular panel data on deprivation should be collected across the region. Data should include health, shelter, food, and education access measures, and vulnerable groups should be monitored – large families, disabled and older people.

Which countries have high poverty rates?

Income poverty rates are not consistent across the region. This is only partly the result of a reduction in economic activity. Other reasons include a rapid growth in exceptionally high levels of inequality, the economic insecurity of particular groups and household structures, and the falling of real wage levels, including delays in wage payment. Those countries waiting to join the EU have typically low rates, even by West European standards, certainly less than 10%. By contrast, Central Asia and the Caucasus countries have rates in excess of 50% and in the extreme touching 80% for Azerbaijan and Tajikistan (Ruminska-Zimny, 1997). In between, and significant by virtue of the population size, are Russia and Ukraine where poverty rates are around one third of the population.

Even in more affluent countries income poverty is only loosely related to deprivation; in this region the relationship is very tenuous, yet most estimates of poverty are still dependent on measured income. This is one reason why the Russian financial meltdown in August 1998 has not been as devastating as had been expected, with a rise in the proportion of the population in poverty from 22 to 30% (EBRD, 1999). Poverty reduction thus needs to be developed in a way relevant to the regional context. Poverty reduction strategies have not been put in place in all countries in the region. These could be developed in the context of the establishment of a bank of best practice from projects where poverty reduction has worked, collected by UN affiliated social policy research centres. For example, an equivalent commitment to universal access to primary health care, and primary education, such as a commitment to 'primary economic security' might be promulgated.

Who is poor?

There are three important groups in poverty. The first are the working poor, for whom the decline in money wages in real terms has brought poverty. Second, children in particular have suffered a growth in poverty more acutely than any other group across the region. Families with several children are particularly likely to be poor. This finding is robust, since it turns up in all studies using a variety of different measures and surveys across the region. Children have suffered more than any other social group in the region from the social costs of the transition (UNICEF, 1999b).

The third group are pensioners. However, the continued existence of relatively generous retirement rules, retained partly, as in many industrial countries, to massage unemployment figures, has meant that pensioners have suffered less than children. Indeed a pension remains a significant additional income stream into many households in the region – more significant than secondary employment (Manning, 1998b). The balance between different groups, especially pensioners and children has been widely discussed. While pensioner poverty is widespread, between a quarter and a third of individuals have pensions, which have maintained their purchasing power over the 1990s. Pensions reform has been implemented or discussed right across the region; partial privatisation has led to multi-tiered pensions.; and the relationship of pension rates to wages is one of the most significant drivers of both public expenditure and poverty rates. In Poland, Slovenia and Lithuania, pensions have improved in relation to average wages, but in Romania, Bulgaria and Azerbaijan they have fallen.

A further question relates to whether the poor are occasional or permanent sufferers. Most of the data across the region are cross-sectional. However, there is a panel of data for Russia that covers the middle years of the 1990s. Russia lies somewhere between the lower Central European and the very high Central Asian and Caucasus poverty rates. In Russia the poor are not permanently in poverty – about a quarter of the poor, or perhaps 10 % of the total population, appear to be locked into this state, with the rest cycling in and out (Lokshin and Popkin, 1999).

Targeting is a key issue in discussions across the region concerning measures directed at poverty. Some believe that it is the only option in the face of shortage of resources, and because it is a common strategy in the industrial world. However, the administrative capacity to operate targeting is relatively weak, and where based on income it can be misleading; others have shown empirically that it does not work and suggest that categorical targeting, or categorical universalism, is the alternative. Universal and taxable child benefits are a good example of a semi-targeted mechanism (Falkingham, 1997). Similarly, access to other basic services will reduce non-income deprivation. One implication is that categorical targeting to vulnerable groups should be encouraged, but with careful monitoring of the results. Targeted support for children through child benefits should be a high priority, together with a comparative review of pensions reform across the region to identify the impact of reform on poverty.

Employment

Rapid growth in poverty has resulted from a number of changes. The decline, and in Russia non-payment, of real wages is pre-eminent. Even before the transition, the rate of economic growth in the 1980s was almost at a standstill, compared for example with China at 9%, or Vietnam at 6%. Since the early 1990s, GDP has fallen by between a third and a half across the region, although a few countries have now recovered to the level of the 1980s – particularly the EU pre-accession group, and notably Poland. In addition there has been a substantial growth in inequality. This is conventionally measured with the Gini coefficient by ranking the population by income and measuring the distortion away from perfect equality. The measure varies between perfect equality (zero) and perfect inequality (one), and for Western Europe is typically around 0.3. Gini coefficients across the region have grown rapidly, by a quarter to a half in Central Europe, and to more than double in Russia (UNDP, 1999). A further and less visible change has occurred in relation to the tradition in some countries for enterprises to provide goods and services that contributed significantly to household income. The slow and uneven withdrawal of such 'occupational welfare' has exacerbated deprivation. Finally, of course, open unemployment, and hidden unemployment caused by 'administrative leave', and other forms of short-time working, have grown substantially and unevenly across the region.

A major mechanism for exclusion in industrial society is unemployment. Paid work is not only the key means by which citizens can create income, but it is health-enhancing and provides access to a range of other goods, services and relationships. Before 1989, work was a right under state socialist constitutions, and unemployment did not officially exist. By the early 1990s, unemployment was anticipated, even welcomed, as a sign that the new market mechanisms, including the labour market, were developing. At first, relatively generous benefit schemes were devised in anticipation of reasonably rapid adjustment to these, after which economic growth was expected to take off, as has happened in China. Unfortunately economic growth did not take off and the whole region plunged into a very deep industrial recession.

Unemployment was allowed to rise rapidly in some countries, but kept very low in others. For example, by the mid-1990s the official rate had exceeded 15% in Poland, Hungary and Slovakia, but was barely above 4% in Russia and Ukraine (although ILO estimates would put the latter at nearer 9%) (UNICEF, 1999a). In the latter case, the motive was explicitly one of restraining social and political unrest by encouraging citizens to keep registered at work, even when there was little to do, and to retain many of the benefits that were traditionally provided through the Russian enterprise.

The variation between countries is mirrored by disagreements between analysts as to the significant changes that have developed within the labour markets of Eastern Europe. Broadly, there are some who suggest that labour market adjustment is moving along nicely, and that fairly soon economic growth will take off (has taken off in Poland, they would argue), creating the possibility even that a Russian boom might be coming (Layard and Parker, 1996). Transition social costs will prove to be temporary, and worth paying in this view.

Others however are more pessimistic. Regional pockets of high unemployment exist in Poland and are widespread in Russia. The August

1998 financial meltdown in Russia, and the continuing political uncertainty and economic corruption, do not suggest a boom is around the corner, but rather mass unemployment: the 'dead souls' hidden within the registered employed might soon emerge (Standing, 1996).

Survey evidence suggests that policy capacity in the area of employment is poor, and that the hopes for an effective trade union movement have failed (Vickerstaff et al, 1998). Significant social policy development will come in part from the interests of workers and management being articulated and negotiated in public. There is a need to strengthen both employees' and employers' organisations to create effective social partners, and for education towards both trade unions' and employers' good practice.

In all industrial countries most people get jobs through friends and contacts. Survey evidence suggests the same pattern in this region (Clarke, 1999). The labour market has split into sectors with highly flexible movement, and sectors where turnover and performance are sluggish. Employment services in the region have not been effective at providing training to open up movement between these sectors. Nevertheless, employment services are relevant to a substantial minority. Employment-led growth and public works have not been promoted sufficiently. Job creation, if necessary through public works, and through the non-profit sector, is essential, together with training that should be designed to open up and connect separate sectors of the labour market.

Health

The health of the population, in terms of both morbidity and mortality, is a crucial measure of the impact of changing social costs. If rapid social change occurs it does not necessarily bring health hazards. Rapid economic growth in China has brought a marked increase in life expectancy: for men it is now around 68 years. By comparison, Russian male life expectancy in particular has plummeted to a mere 58 years – fully 10 years less than in China. Of any single statistic about the costs that the transition has unleashed, this is the most telling. Across the region nearly 10 million 'missing' men have died prematurely in middle age of stress and cardiovascular problems. Suicide rates for men are typically three times Western European rates (UNDP, 1999).

Demographic variations between countries were marked before 1990, and these have grown in the 1990s. While marriage rates across the region were uniformly high, the divorce rate was more varied: very high in the Baltics and Western CIS, but much lower elsewhere. Fertility levels were in general relatively low, but again much higher in some countries, particularly Central Asia. Changes have not been uniform. While fertility has dropped everywhere, leading to a slow convergence of rates across the region, divorce rates have changed at different rates. For example, divorce rates soared in the Baltics and to a lesser extent Russia, whereas they have steadily declined in Central Asia (UNICEF, 1999a).

One consequence of falling fertility and volatile divorce rates is that the percentage of births to teenage mothers, and the percentage of those mothers who are unmarried, has changed dramatically. Thus in 1989 14% of Czech births were to teenagers, but only 5% in Azerbaijan. By 1997 the situation had been reversed, with the Azerbaijan rate doubling to 11% and the Czech rate almost halving to 8%. In addition, the percentage of those teenagers bearing children outside marriage has varied enormously: doubling to around two thirds in Hungary, Slovenia, Estonia and Bulgaria; but still only around 20% in Croatia, Ukraine, and Azerbaijan (UNICEF, 1999a). This dramatic shift has been caused by both absolute and relative changes: not only have total teenage births fallen in Central Europe, and grown in Central Asia, but the relative share of teenage births has been affected by the collapse in fertility among older women. Thus the fall in fertility and varied divorce rate has not been equally shared between women of different ages. Teenage fertility has not dropped nearly so fast as for older women, and with the generally early age of marriage across the region, and volatile divorce rate, there is concern for the vulnerability of young mothers, over a period when state support for families has weakened considerably (UINCEF, 1999b).

Reproductive health has been worsening for the most part. Maternal mortality has grown in Russia and Central Asia particularly, as have birth complications, and although infant mortality rates are on the whole stable they remain relatively high. Low birth weight, stillborn and congenital abnormality rates have grown in all countries. Abortion rates remain very high by West European standards, and there has been a marked rise in sexually transmitted diseases. The health of children is a key issue, both because they are particularly vulnerable to their situation and because problems developed here will create problems and costs for social policy for years to come. The rise in child poverty, the rise in rates of institutionalisation, and the relatively high levels of fertility for teenage mothers, especially unmarried mothers, are not encouraging developments (Bradbury and Jäntti, 1999). A comprehensive programme of reproductive health is a priority, while children's health and social care needs to be given a clear policy focus, for example through separate ministerial responsibility.

Demographic effects of health costs extend beyond falling life expectancy. Birth rates have also fallen right across the region, by between a quarter and a third in most countries. In combination, shorter lives and fewer babies mean that for two thirds of the region population growth has gone into reverse – an unprecedented shift in peacetime (Manning and Davidova, 2001).

Infectious diseases have re-emerged and in some cases reached epidemic proportions: polio, diphtheria, tuberculosis. This will lead to further death, and/or disability in future years, even if the immediate pattern of stress-induced death and infertility passes. This in part will be due to the ineffectiveness of primary health care, particularly immunisation. However, we know from the history of these diseases in 19th century Europe, that they are also returning as a result of poverty and poor nutrition. Self-reported levels of poor health in Russia, for example, are between 50% and 100% higher than typical for Western Europe, and closely correlated with material deprivation (Bobak et al, 1998). The proportion of money allocated to food in household budgets has jumped. There are also unhygienic water supplies, even in Moscow, by far the most affluent part of Russia, where 80% of people boil drinking water 'just in case' (Manning, 1998a). Access to primary care remains therefore a significant priority, with a target of 100% access.

Behavioural aspects of health status include both people's loss of perceived control over their daily life chances, and risky behaviour. These cannot be changed through medical or technical intervention alone. Alcoholism for example has been a contributory factor to a number of problems. We know this because of the dramatic improvement in health, mortality and violence when Gorbachev's anti-alcohol campaign took effect in the mid-1980s (Manning, 1992). Since then alcohol has reappeared as a public health problem, contributing to middle-age mortality, domestic violence, and is also strongly associated with tobacco use which has also mushroomed across the region. Without community involvement control over alcohol consumption will be difficult, and best practice on how this can be achieved needs to be documented and shared.

Public expenditure on health care, particularly public and primary care, for which the previous regime had been renowned, has fallen back, and is well below the percentage of GDP spent on health in Western Europe. As many as a quarter of poor people who need to purchase medicines are unable to (UNDP, 1999). States are spending too little of their resources on health, even within their difficult funding situation. Apart from the state, the main groups driving health policy in industrial societies are the medical professions and commercial health concerns but both are weak in the region. Salaries for medical staff have been seriously eroded, and commercial interests are still developing. International comparisons suggest that there should be an increase in state spending on health to a target of at least 5% of GNP, so that medical salaries and infrastructure can be upgraded, together with the rigorous regulation of neophyte commercial health companies.

Social integration

Social integration, or the reduction of social exclusion, is not simply a matter of poverty reduction, but also covers inequalities on a number of 'horizontal' dimensions, such as gender and ethnicity. Exclusion also connotes a 'relational' quality, by which is meant a severance of social relations and hostile stereotyping between groups, in addition to the mere ranking of some quantity. Exclusion can thus occur horizontally as well as vertically, across gender, employment, ethnicity, age and other dimensions. Nevertheless, the rapid rise in income inequality across the region has driven deep splits into these societies, and a reduction in general inequality is essential. Ratios between the top and bottom income deciles show large variation across the region, from 3.0 in the Czech Republic, 5.8 in the Ukraine, to 10.4 in Russia (Flemming, and Micklewright, 1999). In Russia the Gini coefficient reached close to 0.5 at its worst. A crucial reason for this is the variation in minimum wages. In many countries the minimum wage drives access to many social benefits, but the level varies widely. For example it is only 8-12% of the average wage in Russia, Moldova, Belarus, Armenia and Kyrgyzstan. But in Latvia, Hungary, Romania and Slovakia it is around 30%, and 50% in Lithuania and Slovenia (UNDP, 1999). Clearly, in many countries the minimum wage is too low, and should be reviewed in a regional context. A minimum wage target of, for example, 30% of average wage could be adopted.

Commitment to social integration and gender equality at Copenhagen in 1995 implied mechanisms for the empowerment of marginalised groups. Recent research in public health has identified a strong link between the sense of control that citizens feel over their lives and their health status. Indeed it is the loss of such a sense of control that has contributed to the cardiovascular epidemic in middle-aged Russian men (Bobak et al, 1998).

One of the expected gains from the transition was the real democratic involvement of citizens in public life. This has not, however, translated into the empowerment of all, particularly the empowerment of women or children. We can identify three sources of empowerment. First is the involvement of people in informal social networks. These were well developed as survival strategies in pre-transition state socialist societies, and there is evidence to show that they continue to be an essential, indeed more essential, survival strategy in the 1990s. Unfortunately, extremely poor people find it difficult to sustain such networks, and in part may be in difficulty due to impoverished survival networks. For example, in all industrial societies, including Eastern Europe, getting a job is in the majority of cases achieved informally through social networks (Clarke, 1999). Where these are weak or ruptured, individuals will be vulnerable.

A second kind of empowerment is involvement in civil society activities, such as community groups and social movements. Evidence here is mixed. Across the region, informal groups and movements initially mushroomed in the early days and months of the transition. However, as the euphoria of freedom subsided, and the reality of economic survival grew, there has been a general decline in such activity. Some of the activists also transferred their allegiance to formal political institutions and processes, in those countries where regular party political processes emerged (Lang-Pickvance et al, 1998). Now single-issue groups, such as women's groups, are emerging. These however are very varied between countries. The development of such groups depends crucially on the resources available rather than an objective level of need – indeed as a rule these are inversely related between countries (UNICEF, 1999b).

A third form of empowerment is political involvement. One of the chief aims of the transition has been political participation. The reality has been mixed. At the national level some groups, particularly women, have suffered very sharp declines in participation. Under the old system, a third of elected positions were held by women but now this has dropped to between 1% and 20%, with around 5% being typical for ministerial positions. This compares poorly with the OECD average of 17%. At the local level women have fared better with typically around 20 % of elected positions (UNICEF, 1999b). The active encouragement for women to enter politics would help to place social policy on government agendas.

Empowerment can seem a rather nebulous concept, for which particular interventions are difficult to specify. Empowering communities and individuals means enhancing both the formal and informal sources of power and control that already exist. Self-help has de facto become necessary, although civil society has been dismissed as weak in the region.

At the same time survey evidence suggests that the level of informal networks of friends, families and acquaintances is exceptionally high, and has provided, more often through women, the 'strength of weak ties' through which communities and households have survived the transition years (Granovetter, 1973). This has recently come to be described as 'social capital' (Putnam, 1993; EBRD, 1999). Local services should build on these networks and foster them as a significant resource. The very poor also appear to be relatively excluded from these networks, and local social services need to work with civil society associations to track and identify those households with poor networks.

At Copenhagen in 1995, commitment five highlighted equality and equity between men and women. Social costs fall unevenly on men and women, and support systems at state, community and household level also vary by gender. Women have suffered from unemployment, and from the steady reduction of childcare and family support that had traditionally enabled them to attain a relatively high economic activity rate. Across the region female economic activity rates have fallen in all but one or two countries (notably Romania). Of course, male activity rates have also fallen; nevertheless the relative gap between activity rates of men and women has on the whole risen, particularly in the Baltics, Russia and Bulgaria. The exceptions have been Belarus, Azerbaijan and Tajikistan (UNICEF, 1999b).

Even though women's activity rates have fallen, unemployment has also unambiguously affected women more than men, which means in total that the number of women working has declined significantly. While some of this has been the result of industrial restructuring there is also evidence that direct discrimination has grown around the ideology that women should return to their domestic responsibilities. For those in work, the gap between men's and women's wages has not been growing, but nevertheless remains between 10% and 30%. The relatively high levels of skill and education in the region have tended to mitigate tendencies for the wages gap to widen, generated by the concentration of women in lower-paid sectors, especially state-funded education, health and welfare.

Within Western welfare states, the women's movement has played a key role in the 20th century in drawing attention to unmet social need, and has been a major force for innovation and reform in social policy in recent years. Such a movement in the transition countries is slowly developing, and there are many women's groups springing up across the region. For example, violence towards women is a particular problem, against which women's grassroots organisations have emerged. This violence includes markedly higher homicide rates in general, growing domestic violence related to household stress and alcoholism, and a rapid growth in the sex trade stimulated by poverty (UNICEF, 1999b). These groups need resources to develop, and should attract state funding. But empowerment also brings its burdens. Women were said to suffer from a double burden of paid and domestic work under the old system. Their survival skills, through the use of rich and diverse social networks to supplement meagre household resources, have become in effect a third burden to shoulder in the transition years, in addition to which, for those getting involved in grassroots and civic actions, there is now effectively a fourth burden. Since time-budget studies indicate that men continue to do far less household work than women (Pascall and Manning, 2000), and since resources for children and families, such as cash transfers, maternal/ parental leave and pre-school provision have been eroded, there should be vigorous efforts to encourage men to undertake a larger share of this work, to enable women to find the time for community-oriented actions.

Enabling social development

The EBRD (European Bank for Reconstruction and Development) estimates the progress that different countries are making in terms of a 'transition indicator' which includes economic factors such as price liberalisation, privatisation, financial reform, and restructuring. The index suggests that the countries across the region are moving into different clusters. Central Europe (at 3.4) is the most advanced, followed by the Baltics (3.2), Western CIS (2.4) and Central Asia (2.2) (EBRD, 1999). Similarly we can note that in the EU pre-accession countries, Poland, Estonia, Slovenia, Hungary and the Czech Republic, economic output has recovered to, or exceeded that of 1989, and growth continues to rise. This pattern does not necessarily mean that there are not still significant social costs in these countries. A rising tide does not necessarily lift all boats. There are significant pockets of rural poverty and unemployment, for example, in Poland, where GDP has overtaken the level of the late 1980s. Nevertheless steady economic growth does provide employment and income for most households, helps to contain poverty, and very importantly provides the turnover through which governments can raise the taxation essential to the public support of social services.

At the other end of the economic scale is a group of countries where the economic consequences of the transition have been disastrous. For these there has been a continuing collapse in industrial output, on which the majority of the population had previously been dependent, and a steady rise in poverty and poor health. They comprise the countries of the Former Soviet Union, apart from the Baltics: Russia, Ukraine, Moldova, the Central Asian Republics, and the Caucusus. There have been moments, for example before the August 1998 Russian financial crisis, when recovery seemed finally under way in these countries. The situation after 1998 is mixed. Some commentators have argued that the underlying recovery was not greatly affected, since a great deal of local economic activity is now demonetised and undertaken through barter (Gustafson, 1999). For example, inflation in Russia was only 3% in the second quarter of 1999, and the World Bank has observed that short-run economic performance has been better than feared (World Bank, 1999). Others, however, especially from the point of view of the capital cities, see this event as marking a further weakening of these economies within the global economic system.

Social policies can be provided, regulated or financed by the state. Alternatively, NGOs or enterprises in civil society can substitute for the state, or households can provide for themselves directly or through the market. Whether the state provides or not, it has an inescapable function for clear and transparent regulation of appropriate actions, even in family life where the welfare of children, or domestic violence, is concerned. Across the region, state withdrawal of provision has been confused with state withdrawal of finance, and regulation.

While economic growth is essential for containing social costs and paying for services, the capacity of governments independently affects the possibilities for social intervention. One measure of this capacity is the proportions of GDP that governments are able to tax and spend. Tax burdens in the industrial world have not fallen over the 1990s. There is no particular reason for the transition countries to pursue such a goal. Tax burdens have however moved sharply away from capital towards labour. Tax collection efficiency is also relatively poor in some countries, and can be very varied regionally, which is particularly the case in Russia. Efficient and non-corrupt tax collection costs money, particularly in terms of well-paid civil servants. Taxation is also more tolerable to the general public when there is transparency about government expenditure. However, since the transition a significant proportion of economic activity in the region has developed outside the formal and taxable economy. Around one third of the employed work in Bulgaria is in the hidden or informal economy; 30% of GDP in Croatia is similarly hidden; 10% in the Ukraine; 19% in Russia; 13% in Estonia (UNDP, 1999). This economic activity, while essential to the survival of households across the region, must also become more regularised and subject to tax, since this sector of the economy includes some of the wealthiest in the region.

Although there has been a widespread desire for a less oppressive state throughout the region, there continues to be steady public support for the provision of public services such as health and social care, education, and poverty relief (Rose, 1998). However, government expenditure as a proportion of GDP has not been uniform. We can group countries by the level of expenditure, and by the stability of expenditure over the 1990s. For almost all countries, there was some decline on the proportion of GDP spent by governments. The desire to reduce state intervention in general, and to reduce responsibility for such services as housing, education and health care, resulted in a steady decline in the early 1990s. After the initial fall, however, there has been a levelling out of expenditure for most countries at between 40% and 50% of GDP. But for others, the decline was precipitate and much steeper: in Central Asia and the Caucasus all but one government now spends less than 20% of GDP. Such low levels mean that social intervention is poorly funded. By contrast, governments of Central Europe and the Western CIS are generally spending over 40% of their GDP. For a small number, typically in the Baltics, government spending as a proportion of GDP is creeping back up to pre-transition levels (UNICEF, 1999a).

In the past, the role of enterprises in making social provision for their staff was fairly significant: one third of all the Soviet state's social infrastructure belonged to enterprises. In theory in a market economy, oriented towards efficiency, enterprises will find themselves unable to maintain their social objectives and will have no financial interest in doing so. However, enterprise welfare has not been divested to the extent expected; indeed some private firms are recreating the provision of social benefits. While this is also to be found in the West (most US citizens for example have health insurance through their employers), there has been no systematic articulation of the division between enterprise, private and local government provision. This pattern varies widely between regions and localities, and enterprise, private and local government provision should thus be monitored and coordinated at the local level.

Regional variation

It is essential to recognise that the rise in social costs has not been even across the region, nor has the capacity and willingness of governments and communities to deal with it. Moreover, some costs are more significant or intractable than others. Recommendations for measures to tackle social costs cannot thus be uniform. The region is beginning to diversify into blocks of countries manifesting some common regional characteristics, in contrast to neighbouring blocks. For Russia this process is also apparent within the country. Of course this is not a neat process, out of which we can easily identify new uniformities appropriate to the development of new policy measures. The clustering of countries varies with the relevant issues and has been constantly evolving over the 1990s. Nevertheless there are commonalities. For example, the poverty rate is clearly clustered: in Central Europe (Hungary, Czech Republic, Slovakia and Slovenia) it is relatively low; in Poland, the Baltics, Russia and the Slavic it has been well into double figures, but not in the majority, despite the August 1998 financial crisis in Russia. As for many of the patterns we have seen, however, the Caucasus and the Central Asian Republics are in a qualitatively different situation, with a majority of the population in poverty, and physical damage, for example to children's development, being noticeable.

How can we usefully group these countries? There is no doubt that their economic situation is highly varied. The pre-accession group are marked by a return to growth, less poverty (although not necessarily low unemployment), lower rates of teenage pregnancy, and lower rates of infectious diseases. We might characterise this group as the *recovery group* in which economic growth has returned, governments have the capacity to tax and spend for social intervention, and social costs have been contained. At the other end of the scale are the Central Asian and Caucasus countries (and regions of Russia in Northern Caucasus). These are typically exhibiting very high rates of poverty, growing levels of infectious diseases, extremely low levels of government expenditure as a proportion of GDP, a return to traditional patterns of marriage, and economies that for the most part have failed to return to a pattern of growth. This might be called the *disintegrating group*. In between these two extremes are a variety of countries struggling with different problems. We can separate two types. Those in which *conflict* has disrupted economic and social life to such an extent that it is difficult to identify a stable trend in terms of social costs and their amelioration. We might include the Balkans and Caucasus areas here. Finally there are those countries in which economic growth has yet to materialise, where as a consequence a large section of the population is suffering, but in which there is every potential for a better future in terms of available raw materials and levels of education.

This group is *struggling* and may or may not join the EU pre-accession pattern in the future. The pre-eminent case is, of course, Russia, highly significant for the region as a whole because of its overwhelming size.

Where countries are large, internal regional differentiation is growing fast. This is most obvious in the case of the biggest country, Russia. This country is so big that it is more appropriate for us to remember the huge regional variations within it, and consider that some of its regions should perhaps more appropriately be classified with other groups: the Northern Caucasus with the rest of the Caucasus regions, for example; or Moscow with the EU pre-accession group. The regional impact of the August 1998 financial crisis was quite varied: 30% of the regions retained their industrial production levels, while 15 % suffered further industrial loss of around 20-30% (UNDP, 1999). It is misleading to think of social issues in relation to the country as a whole, since very sharp differences are manifest between the different regions. For example, per capita income varies between three typical levels. At the top is Moscow with seven times the income of most other regions. In between are a small number of areas, such as St Petersburg, the North, Siberia, and the Far East, which have per capita incomes that are double most of the other regions, but still only about one third of Moscow's. Unemployment is similarly varied – very low in Moscow at around 4%, and St Petersburg at 9%, but between 10-20% for the rest of the country (Manning et al, 2000). This is compounded by the Russian government's manifest divestment of its social responsibilities from central to local government. This decentralisation was foreshadowed in the 1993 constitution and has been driven by the inability and unwillingness of central government to raise funds and redistribute them in relation to the varying needs of the regions.

Global participation means joining the EU for some countries, but social policy issues are almost absent from the accession process, and in general the development of social policy at the EU level is weak. EU law is good for equal opportunities, the movement of labour, and social security harmonisation, but is not strongly related to children and families (Pascall and Manning, 2001). While EU accession countries will be able to use EU funding to engage in European social policy debates, within the three other regional social policy environments regional social policy mechanisms should be set up to encourage appropriate and relevant debates within and between pertinent groups and organisations.

Conclusion

Suggested measures for effective intervention in the region depend on a realistic analysis of how things can change. Specifying the ideal, whether from a liberal or collectivist position, may at best be ineffective or at worst damaging. Historical experience suggests that welfare innovation occurs as a result of the following kinds of processes:

• elite fear of political instability;
• realisation by business that its interests can gain from social welfare;
• middle-class desires for collective consumption;
• popular opposition to or support for policies;
• humanitarian concerns.

While humanitarian concern may motivate reformers, little has been achieved without the additional operation of one or more of the other four factors, and in all cases nothing can be achieved unless these are articulated into feasible policies, often in terms of an internally consistent welfare state regime. Recent detailed research on Russian social policy actors, including business leaders, politicians, civil servants and trade unionists suggests widespread ignorance about social policy options (Manning et al, 2000). Policy development has been weak. Consistent policy development might be stimulated by a network of UN affiliated social policy research centres or high-quality think tanks. These could raise the quality of policy debate and involve business or middle-class representatives, trade unions, and community groups.

However, the most striking development in the region is the rapid differentiation that has occurred. The single welfare regime derived from Soviet state socialism that was quite clearly identifiable across the region up to the late 1980s is beginning to diversify into different regimes. This has resulted from the different economic fortunes, and different political trajectories, that are emerging. Although the EU accession countries will not be closely constrained in respect of their social policy developments, they have all moved towards a mixed economy of welfare, with private and public provision of key sectors such as pensions and health care, and a reduction in family benefits. However, this is not social democracy, and unless they come to be classified as a new regime type, these countries probably will join the ranks of social corporatism in Europe.

By contrast the Central Asian countries are enormously constrained by their weak economies, resulting in limited state capacities; with the resurgence of traditional cultural and family traditions, their relatively progressive social policies of the Soviet era have been eroded to the greatest extent in the region, and social issues have emerged that are more familiar within the less developed countries, such as child malnutrition. Russia remains an uncertain case. The economy now appears to be making another rapid recovery, just as it did in 1997 prior to the 1998 financial crash. If the recovery is more sustained this time, then with economic growth might come the possibility of social investment and a new attempt to build social integration, probably around nationalistic sentiments. Whether this would be a distinct welfare regime, and what its key components might be is as yet unknown. Perhaps the UN review at Copenhagen +10 will be an opportunity to reconsider Russia's social development.

Note

[1] I would like to acknowledge the support of UNICEF, UNDESA and the Council of Europe for supporting various stages of the work from which this chapter has been drawn.

References

Bobak, M., Chenet, L., Hertzman, C., Leon, D., McKee, M., Marmot, M., Pikhart, H., Rose, R. and Shkolnikov, V. (1998) *Surveying the health of Russians*, Studies in Public Policy, no 299, Strathclyde: Centre for the Study of Public Policy.

Bradbury, B. and Jäntti, M. (1999) *Child poverty across industrialized nations*, Innocenti Occasional papers, Economic and Social Policy Series, no 71, Florence: UNICEF, ICDC.

Callan, T., Nolan, B. and Whelan, C.T. (1993) 'Resources, deprivation and the measurement of poverty', *Journal of Social Policy*, vol 22, no 2, pp 141-72.

Clarke, S. (1999) *New forms of employment and household survival strategies in Russia*, Warwick: Centre for Comparative Labour Studies.

Collier, I., Roggemann, H., Scholz, O. and Tomann, H. (eds) (1999) *Welfare states in transition, east and west*, London: Macmillan.

Eatwell, J., Ellman, M., Karlsson, M., Nuit, D.M. and Shapiro, J. (2000) *Hard budgets, soft states. Social policy choices in Central and Eastern Europe*, London: Institute for Public Policy Research.

EBRD (European Bank for Reconstruction and Development) (1999) *Transition Report 1999*, London: EBRD.

Falkingham, J. (1997) 'Public transfers and targetting in Kyrgyzstan', in J. Falkingham et al, *Household welfare in central Asia*, London: Macmillan, pp 163-82.

Flemming, J. and Micklewright, J. (1999) *Income distribution, economic systems and transition*, Florence: UNICEF Innocenti Occasional Papers, Economic and Social Policy Series, no 70, Florence: UNICEF, ICDC.

Granovetter, M.S. (1973) 'The strength of weak ties', *American Journal of Sociology*, vol 78, pp 1360-80.

Gustafson, T. (1999) *Capitalism Russian-style*, Cambridge: Cambridge University Press.

Halleröd, B. (1995) 'The truly poor: direct and indirect consensual measurement of poverty in Sweden', *Journal of European Social Policy*, vol 5, no 2, pp 111-30.

Ismail, S. and Micklewright, J. (1997) *Living standards and public policy in central Asia: What can be learned from child anthropometry?*, Innocenti Occasional Papers, Economic and Social Policy Series, no 63, Florence: UNICEF, ICDC.

Lang-Pickvance, K., Manning, N. and Pickvance, C. (1998) *Environmental and housing movements, grassroots experience in Hungary, Russia and Estonia*, Aldershot: Avebury.

Layard, R. and Parker, J. (1996) *The coming Russian Boom, a guide to new markets and politics*, New York, NY: Free Press.

Lokshin, M. and Popkin, B.M. (1999) 'The emerging underclass in the Russian Federation: income dynamics, 1992-1996', *Economic Development and Cultural Change*, no 4, pp 803-29.

Manning, N. (1992) 'Social policy in the Soviet Union and its successors', in B. Deacon et al, *The new Eastern Europe: Past, present and future for social policy*, London: Sage Publications, pp 31-66.

Manning, N. (1998a) 'Patterns of environmental movements in Eastern Europe', *Environmental Politics*, vol 7, no 2, pp 100-34.

Manning, N. (1998b) 'Social policy, labour markets, unemployment, and household strategies in Russia', *International Journal of Manpower*, vol 19, nos 1-2, pp 48-67.

Manning, N., Shkaratan, O. and Tikhonova, N. (2000) *Work and welfare in the new Russia*, Aldershot: Ashgate.

Manning, N. and Davidova, N. (2001) 'Russia – from transition to crisis', in P. Alcock and G. Craig (eds) *International social policy*, London: Macmillan.

Ovcharova, L. (1997) 'The definition and measurement of poverty in Russia' (www./fac/soc/complabstuds/russia/russint.htm).

Pascall, G. and Manning, N. (2000) 'Gender and social policy: comparing welfare states in Central and Eastern Europe and the former Soviet Union', *Journal of European Social Policy*, vol 10, no 3, pp 240-66.

Pascall, G. and Manning, N. (2001: forthcoming) 'The social dimension: gender and poverty in an expanding Europe', in M. Ingham and H. Ingham (eds) *EU expansion to the East*, Basingstoke: Palgrave.

Putnam, R.D. (1993) *Making democracy work*, Princeton, NJ: Princeton University Press.

Rose, R. (1998) *Getting things done with social capital: New Russia Barometer VII*, Studies in Public Policy, no 303, Strathclyde: Centre for the Study of Public Policy.

Ruminska-Zimny, E. (1997) 'Human poverty in transition economies: regional overview for HDR 1997', UNDP.

Standing, G. (1996) *Russian unemployment and enterprise restructuring, reviving dead souls*, Basingstoke: Macmillan.

UNDP (United Nations Development Programme) (1999) *Human Development Report for Central and Eastern Europe and the CIS*, New York, NY: UNDP.

UNICEF (United Nations Children's Emergency Fund) (1999a) *TransMONEE 4.0*, Florence: UNICEF.

UNICEF (1999b) *Women in transition*, Regional Monitoring Report no 6, Florence: UNICEF.

Vickerstaff, S., Thirkell, J. and Petkov, K. (1998) *The transformation of labour relations: Restructuring and privatisation in Eastern Europe and Russia*, Oxford: Oxford University Press.

World Bank (1999) *Country brief: Russian Federation*, Washington: World Bank.

EIGHT

Politics and its impact on social policy in Taiwan, Hong Kong and mainland China

Christian Aspalter

This chapter discusses the politics of social policy making in East Asia. The three polities covered by the study are chosen not for their political or cultural proximity but for the differences in their political and social systems. What emerges from this chapter is that despite significant political linkages in the past, current political and social policy developments seem to be moving along quite distinct and different pathways in each system. After giving a description of the development of political institutions in each, the chapter analyses the impact of politics on social policy making in each, that is, the course of welfare state development, and examines the basic design of the different welfare state systems and their overall development since 1945. Then the chapter proceeds to discuss the overall impact of various political determinants on social policy making, and closes by projecting the past development of these welfare states into the future.

The Taiwanese political system

After the outbreak of the Chinese civil war in the late 1940s, the Nationalist forces under Chiang Kai-shek lost control over the mainland and had to retreat to Taiwan which was situated far enough away from the Fujian coast so that it could not be taken by the Communist forces. After the retreat, President Chiang Kai-shek, proclaimed martial law that had been lifted four decades later, on 15 July 1987. During the days of the civil war with the Communists, the Nationalist government promulgated a new constitution, on 1 January 1947. In 1948, the government amended the constitution in order to give the president the power of proclaiming martial law. This amendment came to be known as the Temporary Provisions. Another amendment in 1966 gave the president the power of calling for elections for the National Assembly and the Legislative Yuan, the two houses of the parliament, in order to fill vacancies caused by natural deaths of those MPs who had become quasi lifetime parliamentarians after general elections had been set out with the promulgation of the Temporary Provisions. New elections for all of the Legislative Yuan and National Assembly seats had been held in 1991 and 1992 respectively. Finally, in 1992, as a result of a judicial decision of the Council of Great Justice, the last of the lifetime parliamentarians had to retire.

Owing to the provisions in the 1947 constitution, the Republic of China (Taiwan) could in practice be either a cabinet system or a presidential system (Zhao, 1996). When the president simultaneously holds the leading posts of the party and the military, and the party of the president has a majority in both chambers of the parliament, then, the government system clearly is a presidential one. If not, the form of government in Taiwan may represent more that of a cabinet system.

For most of the post-war period, the Taiwanese government represented a presidential system of government. The president appointed the prime minister and the ministers of the executive branch of government, the Executive Yuan (TC, Articles 55-56). Since 2000, the Legislative Yuan is dominated for the first time by a party that is not the president's. The cabinet, thus, has become more independent of the president since now it is backed by a coalition of parties in the parliament, and not the party of the president alone. Until the late 1960s, the party was the prime policy maker in Taiwanese politics. Only after 1969 did the Kuomintang (KMT) gradually take on the role of a policy coordinator, and passed the role of policy maker to the cabinet (Jiang and Wu, 1992, p 84).

Kuomintang (KMT), the China Nationalist Party, dominated Taiwanese politics from 1945 to 2000. Under martial law, KMT prohibited the formation of new political parties. Opposition leaders were punished with long-term prison sentences and the death penalty. Political murder was an instrument that was often applied to suppress the opposition movement: opposition politicians were killed, and their family members were also systematically killed and maimed (cf Lu, 1997; Aspalter, 2001a: forthcoming). In the light of growing international isolation, the ruling KMT finally gave in to the pressures emerging from the opposition movement. Chiang Kai-shek's son, President Chiang Ching-kuo, reformed the party, for the first time incorporating KMT members into the rank and file of the party who had been born in Taiwan (Tien, 1992, 1996, p

10; Dickson, 1996). The old ruling KMT elite, the Mainlanders, who were born on the mainland and fled to Taiwan with Chiang Kai-shek in 1949, heavily opposed the diffusion of power. However, their opposition was in vain. The designated predecessor of Chiang Ching-kuo was Taiwan born Lee Teng-hui who turned the KMT into a Taiwanese-dominated party. The New Party (NP) was formed by Mainlanders within the KMT in 1993 and became the third party to play a significant role in Taiwan's politics (Huang, 1996; Lin and Zhang, 1998).

Since the late 1980s, electoral competition had been intensified, as the Democratic Progressive Party (DPP) began to win its first big victories in local elections. In 1989, the DPP candidate You Ching became County Commissioner in Taipei county, Taiwan's largest constituency. In 1994, Chen Shui-bian was the first opposition leader to become mayor in Taipei. In the 1997 county commissioner and city mayor elections, the DPP for the first time won more votes in island-wide[1] election than the ruling KMT. The KMT only won in eight counties out of 23 counties and cities, lost most of its power bases, and the victory of the DPP in national elections was merely a matter of time. In March 2000, former KMT Provincial Governor, James Soong, established the People First Party (PFP), having come in second behind Taiwan's new President Chen Shui-bian from the DPP in the year 2000 Presidential Elections. The new cabinet under Chen Shui-bian is headed by a KMT prime minister and is composed of politicians coming from all major sections of the political spectrum.

Besides the political opposition movement of the Democratic Progressive Party, there were also a series of important social movements that challenged the authority of the state and pushed for the improvement of social welfare. Between 1980 and 1986, the consumers' movement, various environmental protection movements, the women's movement and the student movement spearheaded the new wave of social movements. In 1987, there were three new social movements that posed a strong challenge to the ruling KMT, namely the labour movement, the farmers' movement and the veterans' welfare protest movement (Hsiao, 1992, pp 153-4, 1991, p 138). Subsequently, a series of social welfare movements demanded the expansion of existing social welfare programmes as well as the introduction of new social legislation

The political system of Hong Kong

At the time of the Second World War, Hong Kong had a population of some 1.6 million. This had reduced to only slightly more than 600,000 in 1945. When the number of residents surged to two million in the first five years after the war, the living conditions of ordinary people deteriorated. The population situation became more settled by the 1960s but Hong Kong's population continued to grow at a speed of a million per decade. In 1967, social unrest reached its post-war peak. The government at that time feared that this social unrest steered by Communist forces in Hong Kong could also lead to a transfer of the Cultural Revolution from mainland China too. However, the streets of Hong Kong soon became peaceful again. In the early 1980s, the issue of the 99-year lease held by Britain on Hong Kong led to negotiations between British and Chinese authorities over the future of this British crown colony (Ngan, 1986, p 90; Aspalter, 2001d: forthcoming). On 19 December 1984, the Joint Declaration was signed in which the date and the basic conditions were laid down for the handover of Hong Kong to China on 1 July 1997. Hong Kong is now a Special Administrative Region (SAR) directly under the authority of the Central People's Government of the People's Republic of China.

Under the new constitution, the Basic Law, it is stipulated that the socialist system and policies of the People's Republic of China (PRC) shall not be practised in Hong Kong for 50 years following the handover. The Joint Declaration states that Hong Kong has 'executive, legislative and independent judicial power'. Hong Kong was ensured a high degree of autonomy, with the exception of foreign and defence affairs, (HKJD, 1984, Articles 1-5). In accordance with Article 31 of the PRC Constitution, Hong Kong constitutes a Special Administrative Region (SAR). The new form of political entity has come to be known as the 'one country, two system' formula. In fact, with respect to economic and social affairs Hong Kong represents a sort of country of its own inside the People's Republic of China. The Basic Law, the constitution of Hong Kong SAR, provides that the Chief Executive of Hong Kong SAR shall be selected by election, or through consultations held locally, and be appointed by the Central People's Government in Beijing. The Chief Executive may appoint principal executive authorities, members of the Legislative Council and public figures to become members of the Executive Council that assists the Chief Executive in policy making (CPRC, 2000, Article 31; CHKG, 45/1, 54, 55/1).

Power within the Legislative Council (Legco) has shifted since 1997, however. Before 1997, liberal, pro-democratic forces – which captured a secure majority of seats in the Legco in the 1991 and 1995 elections – dominated the legislature. After 1997, their significance in policy making has been highly curtailed since amendments to government bills must now be passed by a majority of both the 30 MPs elected by geographical constituencies and the MPs not elected by geographic constituencies (that is, elected by functional constituencies or appointed by the Chief Executive). In the September 2000 Legislative Council election, there were 24 members elected by geographic constituencies and six members appointed by the Chief Executive. In 2004, there will be no appointed members, and the number of geographically elected members will increase accordingly. Conservatives, most of them business representatives, hold a majority of functional membership seats. Their significance has increased, since only 16 functional members are enough to reject amendments of the Legislative Council to bills proposed by the government (Lo and Yu, 1996, p 99; HKE, 2000; Miners, 1998, pp 152-3; CHK2, 2000).

In the 1970s, new political organisations were formed in Hong Kong that could rely on the support of the masses, such as the People's Council on Public Housing Policy and the Society for Community Organisation. In the early 1980s a new set of political organisations were founded, most of which were liberal and pro-democratic political in their orientation. Since the second half of the 1980s, a series of new liberal, pro-democratic political parties have also been formed: the Hong Kong Association for the Promotion of Democracy and People's Livelihood (ADPL) in 1986; the Hong Kong Democratic Foundation in 1989; and the United Democrats of Hong Kong in 1990 being the most influential. The Democratic Party was formed in 1994, and is today the leading democratic party in Hong Kong. The democratic movement of the 1980s represented the newly emerging educated middle class. The conservative Liberal Party was established in 1993. The pro-China camp also gained momentum with the formation of the Association for Betterment of Hong Kong in 1990. Together with members of the Hong Kong Citizen Forum this party formed the influential Democratic Alliance for Betterment of Hong Kong (DAB) in 1992 that was supported by left-wing trade unions. The DAB thus represents middle and working class interests with pro-Chinese government political orientations (Leung, 1998, pp 87-90; Lam and Lee, 1993, pp 64, 69-73; Li and Newman, 1997, pp 216-18).

The franchise of Hong Kong's Urban Council elections between 1952 and 1981 was highly limited since only less than 1% of the population had the right to vote. In 1982, the Hong Kong government first introduced universal suffrage for district level elections. The newly founded political organisations of the early 1980s were only loosely organised opinion and discussion groups. In the late 1980s, the democratic movement succeeded in pushing the government towards reform. The three most important pressure groups of the democratic movement were the Hong Kong Affairs Society, the Meeting Point and the Hong Kong Association for the Promotion of Democracy and People's Livelihood (Lam and Lee, 1993, p 67; Leung, 1990, p 58). The first-ever popular elections to the Legislative Council were held in 1991. However, only 18 of the total 60 members of the Legislative Council were elected from geographical constituencies. The United Democrats of Hong Kong gained 12 seats (with 45.1% of votes), the Meeting Point two seats, the ADPL and a pro-democratic independent one seat each in the geographical constituencies. Thus, pro-democratic forces gained 89% of geographically elected seats. In the 1995 Legislative Council elections, the pro-democrats won 16 out of 20 seats, still holding 80% of geographically elected seats. The Democratic Party obtained 12 seats with 42.3% of votes (Li and Newman, 1997, pp 220-3).

Hong Kong's major social movements preceded the democratic movement in urging the colonial government to change its policies and to introduce reforms. The first significant movement of concern to the government was the labour movement. The heydays of the labour movements after the Second World War only lasted until 1953. Then, the level of strikes fell significantly and by 1968, the level of labour strikes dropped a second time. In 1967, the Communist-controlled Federation of Trade Unions (FTU) together with other pro-Communist organisations set up 'struggle committees' in the light of the Cultural Revolution on the mainland. These committees launched and coordinated a territory-wide anti-colonial struggle. In the beginning, the struggle committees organised large-scale industrial actions, such as. a joint strike (from 10-15 June), a general strike (24-28 June), and a trade suspension (29 June-2 July). After the government had proved to be resilient to these strike actions, the struggle committees resorted to extreme measures, such as terrorism and bombing attacks. However, the struggle of the anti-colonial movement ultimately ended in failure since the public strongly opposed these measures (Leung, 1996, pp 145-53).

The political system of mainland China

Mao Zedong defeated the Kuomintang in the Chinese civil war and became the first chairman of the People's Republic of China. Due to the failure of a national programme for initiating industrial growth, the Great

Leap Forward of 1958, Mao was replaced as head of the state, but kept his position as party chairman. In 1959, his interim successor, Liu Shaoqi, became head of state. Then, having been heavily criticised during the Cultural Revolution (1966-69), Liu was purged from power in 1968. Mao Zedong, returned to power and managed to consolidate his power position as chairman of the CPC and head of state. In 1976, after the death of Mao Zedong and Zhou Enlai (the long-term prime minister), Hua Guofeng became chairman of the CPC and prime minister. In December 1978, the policy of promoting class struggle had been replaced by the four modernisation policies of Zhou Enlai[2] that promoted an open-door policy with regard to foreign economies, and the creation of a 'socialist market economy'. Political achievements abroad, notably the diplomatic recognition of the PRC by the United States, and improvements in the economic situation strengthened the power base of Deng Xiaoping, who was now the unquestioned leader of Communist China. In March 1993, Jiang Zemin became president of the PRC. Five years later, Zhu Rongji, a political reformer, became prime minister (Shinn and Worden, 2000; Meisner, 1999; Hsu, 1999).

In 1954, the Constitution of the People's Republic of China had been promulgated by the National People's Congress, the highest Organ of the State. Formally, the National People's Congress exercises the legislative power of the state. However, apart from the early period of the PRC, the National People's Congress did not make use of all of its constitutionally granted powers. In China, constitutional provisions are valid if they fit the party line. It is for this reason that the provisions of the PRC Constitution are more suggestions than binding legislation. Nonetheless, these provisions contain a lot of the policy intentions of the Communist Party of China.

The state was rather weak and, in fact, only really an executive organ of the CPC. Due to the lack of legislation by the National People's Congress, the country was essentially ruled by ordinances of the State. When the president of the People's Republic of China can count on the support of the Politburo (the Standing Committee of the CPC) and the People's Liberation Army, the powers of the state are united in one person. The State Council, also referred to as the Central People's Government, is the highest administrative organ of the state. It adopts administrative measures, enacts administrative rules and regulations, and issues decisions and orders (CPRC, Articles 80, 89). The prime minister is responsible for and directs the work of the State Council. Two ministries under the State Council are a Ministry of Health and a Ministry of Labour and Social Welfare.

The locus of power in the political arena of the PRC is neither the National Peoples Congress, nor the State Council, but the Communist Party of China, and especially the Politburo of the CPC. Whereas, in the beginning, the party was under the charismatic leadership of party chairman Mao Zedong, charismatic leadership weakened and was replaced by a more institutionalised leadership in the years following 1959 (cf Walker, 1955, p 27; Domes, 1975, pp 334-7).

According to the preamble of the constitution, a broad patriotic front was formed under the leadership of the CPC to support socialism and reunify the motherland. This front included another eight democratic parties, which are still legal political parties today (CNT, 2000; CPRC, 2000). With regard to the Communist Party of China, it needs to be pointed out that a new power bloc emerged inside the CPC in 1961. This new dominant leadership was centred on a group of moderate politicians under the leadership of Liu Shaoqi and Deng Xiaoping. This party faction stood in opposition to party Chairman Mao Zedong, Minister of Defence Lin Biao, and their followers. These two groups were in disagreement about the methods of achieving Communism. From 1961 to 1965, the group around Liu and Deng managed to strengthen party organisation and party discipline, set up realistic economic planning instruments, and decentralise decision making. Thus, in the early 1960s, Mao found himself on the political sidelines and in semi-seclusion. Subsequently, Mao set out with the help of the People's Liberation Army to regain control over the state and party apparatus. With the Cultural Revolution Mao launched a mass assault on the CPC and the state bureaucracies. By mid-1965, he had regained control of the party. By mid-1966, the Great Proletarian Cultural Revolution was set in motion, the first mass action that was directed against the CPC apparatus itself (Hsu, 1999; Meisner, 1999; Shinn and Worden, 2000; Harding, 1990).

The Chinese polity does not rely on elections to alter its leadership. This function is carried out by the Politburo of the CPC instead. The National People's Congress (NPC) is composed of deputies elected for a five-year term by the provinces, autonomous regions, the municipalities directly under the control of the central government, and the People's Liberation Army. In addition, the minority nationalities of China are entitled to appropriate representation in the NPC. The NPC elects the president and the vice president of the PRC, whose term of office is the same as that of the National People's Congress, and they are not allowed to serve more than two consecutive terms (CPRC, 2000, Articles 59, 60, 62/4, 65/2, 65/3, 79).

In May 1986, Chinese students first called for the introduction of democracy. Fang Lizhi, the student leader, became a hero to students and intellectuals. Subsequently, students assumed the leadership of China's new reform movement. The government tried to downplay the student movement and to brand students as hooligans. In May 1989, at the 70th anniversary of the 4 May Democracy Movement, students began to occupy Tiananmen Square in the centre of Beijing. On 13 May, workers joined the students in a hunger strike. By the end of May, however, Deng Xiaoping had declared martial law and ordered the forcible clearance of Tiananmen Square on 3 June which ended in a massacre of many protesters. The Tiananmen pro-democracy demonstrations of May 1989 was a major test for the survival of the government. However, thousands of students had died. Zhao Ziyang (party secretary general since 1987) who supported the students was removed from power. Li Peng, the new prime minister from 1987 to 1998, played an active role in suppressing the democracy movement (Yee, 2000; Hsu, 1999; Tien and Chu, 2000). The student movement of 1986, however, did not alter the regime or the course of national development chosen by the new Chinese leadership after 1978.

Social policy in Taiwan, Hong Kong and mainland China

Social policy development in Taiwan

The Taiwanese welfare state first began to evolve in the 1950s. Between 1950 and 1958, the government tested the implementation of a national labour insurance scheme by introducing it on a voluntary basis first under the auspices of the Provincial Government. The new Labour Insurance scheme covered a wide range of social risks, such as maternity, injury and illness, disability, old age, and death, but benefits were meagre. On 21 July 1958, the Legislative Yuan passed the Labour Insurance Act and transformed Labour Insurance into a statutory insurance scheme, also making it a national scheme. In the 1960s and 1970s, the government continuously extended the coverage of the Labour Insurance system (BLI, 1997; CLA, 1997; Chan, 1985, p 326).

On the eve of the lifting of martial law, KMT decided to incorporate farmers into the social insurance system. This was the first step towards universal integration of the population into Taiwan's welfare state programmes that by then was exclusively designed for core groups of vital interest to the KMT regime, that is, military personnel, government officials and teachers (Aspalter, 2001a: forthcoming; cf also Ku, 1995, p 52). The Farmers' Health Insurance Law was implemented in 1989. In 1990 and 1991, the government introduced for the first time health insurance schemes that were designed for groups other than their specific KMT clientele, that is, low-income families, and handicapped persons respectively.

In 1987, the then premier minister Yu Kuo-hua declared the government's intention to introduce a national health insurance scheme by the year 2000. Under pressure, the target was soon altered to 1995. On 19 July 1994 the parliament passed the Health Insurance Law so that the National Health Insurance Scheme (NHI) could start on 1 March 1995 (Ku, 1995, p 52; Hwang and Hill, 1997, p 89). The NHI is the first Taiwanese insurance scheme that incorporates virtually the entire population. Nonetheless, the redistributive effects of the new NHI are rather limited since there exist different brackets of the insured with different rates of contribution (cf Chen, 1995; NHIB, 2000). A new unemployment benefit scheme started to operate on 1 January 1999. Following election promises, the government is about to introduce a national pension scheme. The implementation of the National Pension Plan, however, has been delayed by the lack of funds and the earthquake in September 1999. The current prime minister, Tang Fei, noted that the pension system would be introduced as soon as possible and before 2004. In the meantime, President Chen Shui-bian introduced an old age allowance system for the elderly of NT 3,000 (approximately 90 US dollars) a month (BLI, 1997; Low, 2000; Sung, 2000; Lin, 2000).

The politics of social policy in Taiwan

After the Nationalist Chinese government moved to Taiwan, it hurried to implement policies aimed at ameliorating the social and economic well-being of the people, notably land reform and the labour insurance scheme. The government, however, did not want to endanger economic development by any financial commitment of the state in the field of social security and social welfare. Thus, it worked out a compromise between its conservative, anti-welfare stance and the need to legitimise its rule, a need which significantly increased after expulsion from the United Nations (1971), and the loss of diplomatic recognition by the United States of America (1978).

Welfare state development in Taiwan could rely on both the constitutional provisions for social insurance and the government's full commitment to these provisions. Since the constitution was designed after Sun Yat-sen's Three Principles of People, constitutional provisions regarding the development of a welfare state were taken very seriously (Aspalter, 2001a: forthcoming). A common explanation for the persisting lack of welfare state institutions in Taiwan, is the lack of power of government institutions (see, for example, Chan, 1998; Cheng, 2001: forthcoming). This explanation represents more an excuse than a real explanation since the Republic of China government has otherwise shown that, wherever and whenever it wanted, it had all the means for implementing its policies, for example land reform and economic policy (see Aspalter, 2001c: forthcoming). The necessary powers to implement comprehensive welfare state policies had been (intentionally) split between a large number of ministries and councils: for example the Ministry of Interior, the Ministry of Defence (insurance for military servicemen), the Ministry of Examination (insurance for government employees), the Ministry of Economic Affairs (pension system), the Council of Labour Affairs (labour and unemployment insurance), Department of Health (NHI), and Council for Agriculture (insurance for farmers and fishermen).

Until the lifting of martial law in 1987, the welfare state, with the exception of the Labour Insurance scheme and social assistance to the very poor, focused on occupational groups that were of special importance to the ruling KMT regime. These were soldiers, government employees, public and private school teachers, as well as their spouses and family members. Only with the coming of democracy from 1987 did KMT extend existing welfare state arrangements to farmers, the poor, the handicapped and the rest of the population. Today, Taiwan is one of the most developed democracies in East Asia and has a unique record of social welfare. The formation of a great number of social welfare movements has pushed the government to implement still more social legislation and social welfare programmes for their particular needs (cf Hsiao, 2001: forthcoming). Party competition and electoral competition between candidates in national and local elections has been another important factor behind welfare state development since the mid-1980s (cf Aspalter, 2001b: forthcoming).

Social policy development in Hong Kong

The Hong Kong welfare system is based on the one hand on non-contributory social security systems, and on the other on social welfare services run by non-governmental organisations (NGOs) financed by the government. A non-contributory social security system exists which is aimed at the provision of basic and special needs for the elderly, the sick, the disabled, single parent families, the unemployed and people with low incomes. The two largest schemes providing social security are the Comprehensive Social Security Assistance Scheme (CSSAS) and the Social Security Allowance Scheme (SSAS). Today, the Social Security Assistance Scheme offers aid to all the above social groups. The CSSAS is a means-tested assistance scheme. In 1971, the Public Assistance Scheme (replaced by the CSSAS in 1993), covered food costs only, but it then raised its benefit levels and increased its range of benefits. The second large social security scheme, the Social Security Allowance Scheme (SSAS) (known as Special Needs Allowance before 1993) grants monthly allowances to the elderly and the disabled exclusively. Recipients of the Comprehensive Social Security Assistance Scheme cannot apply for allowances of the SSAS (HKGOV, 1984, p 205, 1994, p 254, 1996a, p 2; 1996b, pp 12-16).

Hong Kong's non-contributory social security system alone cannot cope with the needs of people, however. Therefore, the state has relied mainly on the private and voluntary sectors to provide social services. Until the mid-1960s, the local branches of international welfare organisations brought in overseas relief for the needy. However, since absolute poverty had largely disappeared by the mid-1960s, voluntary welfare organisations took up new roles in Hong Kong's welfare provision. Instead of bringing in overseas relief, they began to act as 'agents' of the government in providing social services.

In 1973, the White Paper on Social Welfare (HKGOV, 1973) initiated close cooperation between the government and non-governmental welfare organisations in provision of welfare services. This year brought a change towards greater participation by the NGOs in running social services and a close partnership between the government and NGOs in the planning, provision and development of social welfare and rehabilitation services (HKCSS, 1996). In the mid-1960s, the key source of income of voluntary welfare organisations was overseas donations, which counted for up to 50% of total NGO revenues. After 1973, the NGOs became the most important supplier of social services, especially in the field of services for young people and the elderly, through a system in which government subventions provided most of financial resources needed by the NGOs (Chow, 1994, p 325). However, by 1987 up to 70% of these agencies relied solely on public funding (HKCSS, 1987). The increased importance of NGOs stemmed from the rising needs of the people. The demand for social services grew owing to changes in the age structure of the population, a decreasing participation of the elderly in the labour force, and the abandonment of traditional family structures as the basis for welfare.

The politics of social policy in Hong Kong

The colonial government of Hong Kong, except during the second half of 1967, never experienced a threat to its rule. Although the first two decades after the Second World War were the most devastating with regard to social conditions, it was in this period that the government's efforts in the field of social policy were least. Only after the 1967 riots, which raised the possibility that the Cultural Revolution might spill over from mainland China, did the government began to implement social security systems for the most needy and to cooperate with NGOs to secure the provision of social services. With the governance of Governor MacLehose from 1971 to 1982 (Chan, 1996), the government saw a vital interest in promoting new social policies, such as new social security schemes, the extension of the subvention system to NGOs, and expanded governmental efforts in health, education and housing. In this period the colonial government implemented a specifically Hong Kong type of welfare state, that is, a residual type relying heavily on non-contributory social security schemes and social welfare provision secured by a partnership between NGOs and the government. Though being very residual in the beginning, the welfare state in Hong Kong gradually developed into an 'expanded residual welfare state'.

With the rise of the new middle class and social pressure groups, such as social workers, in the 1970s, the government was continuously pressed to extend the existing welfare system further. In the 1980s, first new political organisations and then political parties joined the social pressure groups in demanding new social welfare schemes and services. Then, in the early 1990s, additional factors added to the pressure on the government to increase its welfare efforts, and subsequently to spend more money on social welfare. This was the rise of new powerful political parties in favour of social welfare, and a lack of government legitimacy that became increasingly evident since people were calling for the introduction of democracy. The rise of pro-democratic political parties that won 89% and 80% respectively of total votes in certain constituencies in the 1991 and 1995 Legislative Council elections, as well as the rise of working-class and middle-class pro-China political parties, pressured the government to rethink its stand on social policy. Previously, it had shared the view of the business elite in Hong Kong which tried to prevent any governmental commitment to social policy. After the handover of Hong Kong, the position of conservative forces in policy making was strengthened again, and that of the pro-democratic, pro-welfare forces weakened.

Social policy development in mainland China

The Chinese welfare system is a welfare state with regard to public provision, either provided by subsidies or regulated by state programmes, legislation or policies (cf Chan and Tsui, 1997, p 177). In 1950, the Government Administrative Council announced the Labour Insurance Regulations (LIR) that covered benefits for sick and disabled workers, as well as retirement benefits. The Labour Insurance Scheme covered a wide range of risks, such as occupational and non-occupational injury, disability, death, maternity benefits, and birth allowances. The financing of the welfare system was left entirely to the companies themselves, whether they were state owned, cooperatively owned, or privately owned. In 1956 and 1957, the government extended the coverage of the Labour Insurance Scheme a great deal: membership rose consequently from 24 million members in 1956 to 45 million in 1958. Today, the scheme covers 95 million workers and 30 million retirees (Dixon, 1981, pp 27-43; Guo, 2000).

By the late 1970s, social welfare had expanded to cover 78% of urban wage earners, but this represented only 19% of China's total labour force, which lived mainly in the countryside. In 1978, out of 95 million workers who were entitled to pensions, 74.5 million were former state sector workers and 20.5 million collective workers. After 1978, the government began to increase social welfare spending on pensions, health services and housing. In 1979, the government also introduced the 'One Child per Couple' policy (promoting the motto: 'Smaller families, richer life') that had significant effects on the age structures in the great cities where the policy had been implemented much more vigorously (Selden and You, 1997, pp 1658-60; Lee, 1993, pp 33, 35; Dixon, 1981, p 30; Kang, 2000; Chow, 1999, pp 25-6). In the early 1980s, China began to reform its pension system by upgrading retirement schemes from enterprise level to local or provincial government level. By the late 1980s, approximately 80% of all townships and counties across China have implemented pooled pension funds. In 1995, the Chinese pension system adopted a two-tier system, that is, a defined benefit system financed by pay-as-you-go taxes, and a system that relies on contributions of both employers and employees in state owned enterprises (Lee, 1993, pp 39-40; Feldstein, 1998, pp 3, 6).

By 1978, the Chinese welfare state comprised a wide range of programmes aimed at enhancing the social security of the people, such as pensions, birth control allowances, health insurance, housing benefits, and social assistance (Yeung, 1986, p 8; Lee, 1993, p 35). The great social reforms since 1978 transformed the formerly work–unit-centred social security system into a society-centred social security system. Before the 1980s, the Chinese state bore all the financial burden of the social security system. Thereafter, the state, the work units and the employees share the expenses for social security. Old age insurance, unemployment and health insurance have become the cornerstones of the new Chinese welfare state. However, the dualism between the countryside and the cities continues to disadvantage farmers in comparison to city dwellers (CIRD and CASS, 1998, pp 49-50; Chi and Zhu, 1998, p 61; cf Zhu, 2000; Zhang, 2000).

The politics of social policy in mainland China

The Communist Party of China (CPC) began as early as the civil war to implement a comprehensive social security system in Manchuria. The long experience in participating in policy making in China (since 1921) in combination with the pro-welfare communist ideology enabled the CPC to quickly establish an extensive social security system. The Communists won the support of the farmers by promoting land reform, and the support of labourers by focusing on industrial development and social welfare provisions. In the 1950s, the Communists tried to realise Marxist theories and to create a socialist state. Land had been confiscated and industries nationalised. Common farmers and workers were in the centre of the Communist Party's concern. However, the power struggle within the CPC summarised above led to the outbreak of the Cultural Revolution which attacked local, provincial Communist elites and their authorities. As a consequence, government, party and labour union organisations were significantly weakened. In 1969, the administration of the pension system was put into the hands of enterprises on an ad hoc basis (Lee, 1993, p 39). Hence, the understanding of the development of the Chinese welfare state is tied to the understanding of state institutions and its structures (cf Chen, 1996, p 278). Only in the early 1980s did the state begin to relocate the management of the pension system and other social security systems to higher administrative levels.

The Chinese welfare state was and still is characterised by a great dualism between the welfare rights of people living in the cities and those living in the countryside. Since about 80% of China's population resides in the cities, the welfare state was especially designed for the workers and employees in the cities who might have represented an acute danger for the Communist regime in times of social discontent. State intervention aimed at the welfare of city dwellers helped to sustain the legitimacy of the state and the power of enterprises over the work force (Wong and Mok, 1995, p 16). The consequent increase in legitimacy significantly decreased the likelihood of social uprisings, and increased the support of the long-term ruling government of the Communist Party of China.

The future of social policy in Taiwan, Hong Kong and mainland China

Taiwan

In Taiwan, the government has promised to set up a national pension system and a means-tested, monthly old age allowance system for those not eligible for pensions under the new system (which began to operate in July 2000). Furthermore, we may expect major changes to come with regard to the National Health Insurance system that is chronically underfunded and needs to be reformed. Since the two major political parties of Taiwan, KMT and the DPP, both pursue conservative fiscal policies, we may expect a hefty increase in contributory social security systems and a continuous emphasis on means-tested social assistance schemes in the years to come. The impact of elections – and election promises – is likely to lead to the implementation of new social policies, which will continue to expand welfare state programmes in the years to come.

Hong Kong

There have been no strong labour or welfare movements in Hong Kong. For decades, company bosses formed the only powerful political interest group. In addition, Hong Kong is a society where a fully-fledged democracy has not existed for a long period of time, and it is a society where the middle class does not profit from welfare arrangements and, hence, opposes the extension of public welfare for the lower strata of society. Therefore, it seems to be the fate of the welfare state in Hong Kong to be residualised and comparatively weak in the foreseeable future. Hong Kong's welfare system has, however, evolved into an 'expanded residual' type of welfare state due to enormous extensions in social security and social service provision over the past three decades. Bearing the political changes of the 1990s in mind, one may conclude that the future of Hong Kong's welfare state is one with a constantly increasing welfare budget, while new welfare state schemes are not to be expected in the near future.

Mainland China

In the last two decades, economic reforms have forced state enterprises to lay off millions[3] of workers and employees. In 1986, the government installed unemployment insurance for state-owned enterprises. In addition, more than 100 million peasants have left their farms and are now working in individual enterprises in both the cities and the rural areas (Hu, 1997, p 51; Chow, 1995, p 27). Between 1984 and 1994, the state started to reform and unify the pension system and to set up an unemployment insurance scheme and experimental schemes for unifying maternity insurance schemes (which formerly operated at company level). Since 1994, the Chinese welfare state experienced a period of fast reform in the field of pensions and recently also health care (Hu, 1997, pp 47-54; Zhu, 2000). The major tasks for future social policy in China are two. The first is to incorporate those who are not covered by social security schemes, that is, farmers and their dependants, as well as workers and entrepreneurs in the booming small and medium-sized enterprises. The second is to continue the unificiation of social security schemes.

Notes

[1] The two largest cities, Taipei and Kaohsiung, voted one year later, in 1998, when the DPP lost the mayorship of Taipei to the KMT, and the KMT lost that of Kaoshiung to the DPP.

[2] In 1975, Zhou Enlai outlined a programme of what has come to be known as the Four Modernisations for the four sectors of agriculture, industry, national defence, and science and technology.

[3] In the year 1998 alone, two million workers were laid off. In 1997, the official unemployment rate was 4%, that is, eight million unemployed workers (cf Biffl, 1998).

References

Aspalter, C. (2001a: forthcoming) *Democratization and welfare state development in Taiwan*, Aldershot: Ashgate.

Aspalter, C. (2001b: forthcoming) 'On the road to a Taiwanese welfare state: political parties capitalizing on the issue of social welfare', in C. Aspalter (ed) *Understanding modern Taiwan, essays in economics, politics and social policy*, Aldershot: Ashgate.

Aspalter, C. (2001c: forthcoming) 'The Taiwanese economic miracle: from sugar cane to high-technology', in C. Aspalter (ed) *Understanding modern Taiwan, essays in economics, politics and social policy*, Aldershot: Ashgate.

Aspalter, C. (2001d: forthcoming) 'The Hong Kong way of social welfare: an NGO-based welfare system', in C. Aspalter (ed) *Discovering the welfare state in East Asia*, Westport: Greenwood Publishing.

Biffl, G. (1998) *Unemployment, underemployment and migration, a challenge for labor market policy in China*, WIFO Working Paper No 101, Vienna: Economic Research Institute, WIFO.

BLI (Bureau of Labor Insurance) ROC (1997) *Yearbook of labor insurance statistics Republic of China, 1996*, Taipei.

Chan, H.S.G. (1985) 'Taiwan', in J. Dixon (ed) *Social welfare in Asia*, Beckenham: Croom Helm.

Chan, H.S.G. (1998) Various lectures given at the Institute of Sociology, National Taiwan University.

Chan, R.K.H. (1996) *Welfare in newly-industrialised society*, Aldershot: Avebury.

Chan, R.K.H. and Tsui, M.S. (1997) 'Notions of the welfare state in China revisited', *International Social Work*, vol 40, pp 177-89.

Chen, S.Y. (1996) *Social policy of the economic state and community care in chinese culture, aging, family, urban change, and the socialist welfare pluralism*, Aldershot: Avebury.

Chen, Y.E. (1995) 'Lao Gong Yu Chuan Min Jian Kang Bao Xuan Xi Lie Tan', *Taiwan Laogong*, No 30.

Cheng, W.Y. (2001: forthcoming) 'Labor policies in transition in democratizing Taiwan', in C. Aspalter (ed) *Understanding modern Taiwan, essays in economic, politics and social policy*, Aldershot: Ashgate.

Chi, F.L. and Zhu, H.Y. (1998, 'China's anti-poverty strategy in the economic transition', in National Centre for Development Studies, The Australian National University (ed) *Social reform and development in the Asia Pacific*, Seoul: Korean Development Institute.

CHK (2000) *Annex II to the Constitution of the Hong Kong Special Administrative Region, PRC* (www.uni-wuerzburg.de/law).

CHKG, *Constitution of the Hong Kong Special Administrative Region, PRC* (www.uni-wuerzburg.de/law).

Chow, N.W.S. (1994) 'Welfare development in Hong Kong – an ideological appraisal', in B.K.P. Leung and T.Y.C. Wong (eds) *25 years of social and economic development in Hong Kong*, Hong Kong: University of Hong Kong.

Chow, N.W.S. (1995) 'Social security reform in China – an attempt to construct a socialist security system with Chinese characteristics', in L. Wong and S. MacPherson (eds) *Social change and social policy in contemporary China*, Aldershot: Avebury.

Chow, N.W.S. (1999) 'Ageing in China', *Journal of Sociology and Social Welfare*, vol 26, no 1, pp 25-49.

CIRD (China Institute for Reform and Development) and CASS (Chinese Academy of Social Sciences) (1998) 'A survey of China's social reform and development', in National Centre for Development Studies, The Australian National University (ed) *Social reform and development in the Asia Pacific*, Seoul: Korean Development Institute.

CLA (Council of Labor Affairs) ROC (1997) *Lao Gong Fa Gui Ji Yao*, Taipei: CLA.

CNT (2000) *China Today* (www.chinatoday.com/org/cpcelection/korea-south.htm).

CPRC (2000) *Constitution of the People's Republic of China* (www.uni-wuerzburg.de/law).

CROC, *Constitution of the Republic of China* (www.uni-wuerzburg.de/law).

Dickson, B.J. (1996) 'The Kuomintang before democratization: organizational change and the role of elections', in H.M. Tien (ed) *Taiwan's electoral politics and democratic transition: Riding the third wave*, New York, NY: M.E. Sharpe.

Dixon, J.E. (1981) *The Chinese welfare system, 1949-1979*, New York, NY: Praeger.

Domes, J. (1975) *China nach der Kulturrevolution, Politik zwischen zwei Parteitagen*, Munich: Wilhelm Fink Verlag.

Feldstein, M. (1998) *Social security pension reform in China*, National Bureau of Economic Research, Working Paper No 6794, Cambridge, MA.

Guo, N. (2000) 'Social security reform kept pace with economic changes', *China Daily*, 5 October, p 2.

Harding, H. (1990) *China's second revolution: Reform after Mao*, Washington DC: Brookings Institution Press.

HKE (2000) *Hong Kong election data* (www.elections.gov.hk/elections).

HKJD, *Joint Declaration of 1984* (www.info.gov.hk/info/jd-full2.htm).

HKCSS (Hong Kong Council of Social Service) (1987) 'Revamp on subvention system', *Welfare Digest*, April, No 155.

HKCSS (1996) 'Accountable NGOs in a new era', *Welfare Digest*, June, No 249.

HKGOV (Hong Kong Government) (1973) *The way ahead*, Hong Kong: Government Printer.

HKGOV (1984) *Hong Kong annual digest of statistics*, Hong Kong: Government Printer.

HKGOV (1994) *Hong Kong annual digest of statistics*, Hong Kong: Government Printer.

HKGOV (1996a) *Report on: review of CSSAS*, Hong Kong: Government Printer.

HKGOV (1996b) *Director of social welfare*, Hong Kong: Government Printer.

Hsiao, M.H.H. (1991) 'The changing state-society relation in the ROC; economic change, the transformation of the class structure, and the rise of social movements', in R.H. Myers (ed) *Two societies in opposition: The Republic of China and the People's Republic of China after forty years*, Stanford, CA: Hoover Institution Press.

Hsiao, M.H.H. (1992) 'The labor movement in Taiwan: a retrospective and prospective look', in D.F. Simon and M.Y.M. Kau (eds) *Taiwan: Beyond the economic miracle*, New York, NY: M.E. Sharpe.

Hsiao, M.H.H. (2001: forthcoming) 'Taiwan's social welfare movement in the 1980s', in C. Aspalter (ed) *Understanding modern Taiwan, essays in economics, politics and social policy*, Aldershot: Ashgate.

Hsu, I.C.Y. (1999) *The rise of modern China*, Oxford: Oxford University Press.

Hu, A.D. (1997) 'Reforming China's social security system', *International Social Security Review*, no 3, pp 45-65.

Huang, T.F. (1996) 'Elections and the evolution of the Kuomintang', in H.M.Tien (ed) *Taiwan's electoral politics and democratic transition: Riding the third wave*, New York, NY: M.E. Sharpe.

Hwang, Y.S. and Hill, M. (1997) 'The 1995 health reforms in Taiwan – an analysis of the policy process', *Hong Kong Public Administration*, vol 6, no 2, pp 79-95.

Jiang, P.L. and Wu W.C. (1992) 'The changing role of the KMT in Taiwan's political system', in T.C. Cheng and S. Haggard (eds) *Political change in Taiwan*, Boulder, CA: Lynne Rienner.

Kang, J. (2000) 'Smaller families, richer life', *China Daily*, 9 October, p 6.

Ku, Y.W. (1995) *Welfare capitalism in Taiwan: State, economy and social policy*, London: Macmillan.

Kuan, H.C. et al (eds) *The 1995 legislative council elections in Hong Kong*, Shatin: Chinese University of Hong Kong.

Lam, J.T.M and Lee, J.C.Y. (1993) *The dynamic political actors in Hong Kong's transition*, Hong Kong: Writers' and Publishers' Cooperative.

Lee, P.N.S. (1993) 'Reforming the social security system in China', in S.S. Nagel and M.K. Mills (eds) *Public policy in China*, Westport, CA: Greenwood Press.

Leung, B.K.P. (1990) 'Problems and changes in community politics', in B.K.P. Leung (ed) *Social issues in Hong Kong*, Hong Kong: Oxford University Press.

Leung, B.K.P. (1996) *Perspectives on Hong Kong society*, Oxford: Oxford University Press.

Leung, J.Y.H. (1998) 'Political parties: public perception and implications for Change', in I. Scott (ed) *Institutional change and political transition in Hong Kong*, New York, NY: St Martins Press.

Li, P.K. and Newman, D. (1997) 'Give and take: electoral politics in transitional Hong Kong', *Asian Perspective*, vol 21, no 1, pp 213-32.

Lin, T.M. and Zhang, B.H. (1998) 'Cross-cutting issues and the consolidation of democracy in Taiwan', in P. Burnell and P. Calvert (eds) *Democratization*, Ilford: Frank Cass.

Lin, W.I. (2000) 'Feeding the multitudes, not just a selected few', *Taipei Times*, 15 June.

Lo, S.H. and Yu, W.Y. (1996) 'The electoral system of Hong Kong's legislative council', in Low, S. (2000) 'Pension plan to start ahead of schedule', *Taipei Times*, 27 June.

Lu, H.L.A. (1997) *Zhong Shen Mei Li Dao*, Taipei: Taiwan Wen She Books.

Meisner, M. (1999) *Mao's China and after: A history of the people's republic*, New York, NY: Simon & Schuster.

Miners, N. (1998) 'Executive-legislative relations', in I. Scott (ed) *Hong Kong, politics and government*, New York, NY: St Martins Press.

Ngan, R.M.H. (1986) 'The overall governmental structure in Hong Kong', in A.Y.H. Kwan and D.K.K. Chan (eds) *Hong Kong society, a reader*, Hong Kong: Writers' and Publishers' Cooperative.

NHIB (2000) National health insurance bureau homepage (www.nhi.gov.tw).

Selden, M. and You, L.Y. (1997) 'The reform of social welfare in China', *World Development*, vol 25, no 10, pp 1657-68.

Shinn, R.S. and Worden, R.L. (2000) (www-chaos.umd.edu/history/toc.html).

Sung, C. (2000) 'Chen sets out pension plan', *Taipei Times*, 12 May.

TC, Constitution of the Republic of China (Taiwan) (www.uni-wuerzburg.de/law).

Tien, H.M. (1992) 'Taiwan's evolution toward democracy: a historical perspective', in D.F. Simon and M.Y.M. Kau (eds) *Taiwan: beyond the economic miracle*, New Yor, NY: M.E. Sharpe.

Tien, H.M. (1996) 'Elections and Taiwan's democratic development', in H.M. Tien (ed) *Taiwan's electoral politics and democratic transition: riding the third wave*, New York, NY: M.E. Sharpe.

Tien, H.M. and Chu, Y.H. (2000) *China under Jiang Zemin*, Boulder, CA: Lynne Rienner Publishers.

Walker, R.L. (1955) *China under communism, the first five years*, New Haven, CT: Yale University Press.

Wong, L. and Mok, K.H. (1995) 'The reform and the changing social context', in L. Wong and S. MacPherson (eds) *Social change and social policy in contemporary China*, Aldershot: Avebury.

Yee, S. (2000) (www-tech.mit.edu/V109/N60/china.60n.html).

Yeung, W.T. (1986) 'Occupational welfare in China: provisions and challenges', *The Hong Kong Journal of Social Work*, vol 20, no 1, pp 8-14.

Zhang, F. (2000) 'Rural areas need better clinics', *China Daily*, 3 October, p 5.

Zhao, S.S. (1996) *Power by design: Constitution-making in nationalist China*, Hawaii: University of Hawaii Press.

Zhu, B.X. (2000) '"Health for All" remains country's prime target, medical care reform pools funds from state, employees, employers', *China Daily*, 3 October, p 5.

NINE

The male part-time worker and the welfare state: minor problem or major challenge?

Zoë Irving

Introduction

Over the last two decades a substantial literature has developed around the theme of part-time employment and its links to various aspects of the welfare state. The vast majority of this body of theoretical and policy-related writing and empirical research has rightly focused upon women's part-time employment as both a contributing factor in the continuing economic inequality between women and men, and an outcome of the industrial transformation of pre-existing gendered divisions of labour. More recent comparative social policy literature has focused, sometimes implicitly, on the level and nature of women's part-time work as one of several indicators of the extent to which welfare regimes are gendered, or more precisely, how far the regimes diverge from the 'male model'. However, among the changes associated with the flexibilisation of labour, in most OECD countries rates of male part-time employment have been increasing over the last decade. This development raises interesting theoretical questions around the future use of the 'male model' as a standard by which the development of gender relations can be measured. At the level of material welfare, it is questionable whether male part-time workers share the disadvantages and inequalities experienced by women who work part-time. It is also possible that the male part-time worker is a yet more troublesome anomaly in welfare states founded on the 48:48:48 male model of employment: 48 hours a week, 48 weeks a year, for 48 years of a lifetime (Harker, 1996, p 5).

This discussion is a mapping exercise presented in three sections. First, there is a brief overview and comparison of the patterns of male and female part-time employment in selected countries. The incidence of male part-time employment is examined in relation to welfare regime types and other economic, social and political factors. Second, the chapter focuses on the extent to which the experience of part-time work and welfare is shared by women and men. The knowledge that women workers experience *diswelfare* because the structure of welfare states is based on male employment patterns is now well established, uncontentious and has led to limited national and European Union-devised modifications to the various systems. The chapter suggests that additional pressures for more far-reaching reform may become manifest where male workers are found to be excluded from a system based upon male work. Third, the chapter assesses the extent to which the increase in male part-time employment presents a challenge to the use of the 'male model' as an accurate representation of employment and welfare regimes. It does this with reference to gendered welfare regimes literature, and considers the implications for gender analysis.

Men's part-time work and welfare regimes

Although part-time employment represents the major source of job creation in Europe over the last two decades, as many analysts have pointed out it is its gendered nature which is by far its most striking characteristic (Rosenfeld and Birkelund, 1995; Fagan and Rubery, 1996; Hakim, 1996; Smith et al, 1998). Part-time employment is for the most part undertaken by women, whose employment accounted for 74.3% of the part-time total in the OECD countries in 1997 (OECD, 1998). The social and economic disadvantages which accrue to women from intermittent and partial labour market attachment have been well documented (and are discussed in more detail below) but despite this the trends away from full-time employment continue. Deindustrialisation, recession and the rise of the service sector in many countries have combined to create an increasingly insecure and diverse labour market experience (Meulders et al, 1994; De Grip et al, 1997). In response, a changing relationship to employment may be occurring, which is hinted at in Blossfeld and Hakim (1997) for example, and actively encouraged by more radical writers (Gorz, 1985; Forrester, 1999). Notwithstanding the prevalence of women part-time workers, men's patterns of employment have also been subject to change and restructuring, and given that welfare states have been designed around men's work these developments must be significant for the future of welfare generally and social protection in particular.

Before the significance (or insignificance) of men's part-time work can be established, some illustration of international variation in the evolving patterns is necessary. At its vaguest, the term 'part-time' employment describes work which is "for fewer contractual hours than are worked by a full-time employee in a given sector, enterprise or establishment" (Marullo, 1995, p 2). As a basis for international statistical comparison this definition and its derivatives are less than helpful, and can produce many anomalies including the situation where employees working the same hours are classified as full-time in one country and part-time in another (Marullo, 1995; OECD, 1997; Hakim, 1996, 1997).

It is argued that the differentiation which can be made between part-time workers is as important as that which can be made between part-time and full-time workers since employment and social security rights are based upon earnings, or hours worked or both (Meulders et al, 1994; Bruegel and Hegewisch 1994; Boje, 1996). Thus the experience of a 'part-time' worker whose hours of employment are nine tenths of full-time hours (the usual threshold for distinguishing between full and part-time hours (OECD, 1997)) is likely to be more akin to that of a full-time worker than a part-time worker whose employment is based upon short working hours (15 or less per week), and whose experience is argued to be the most precarious and disadvantaged (Sainsbury, 1996; Hakim, 1997). Data for 1985 and 1994 show an increase in proportions working less than 20 hours per week in every country listed except Spain (men) and in 10 out of the 20 countries listed (women) (OECD, 1998, pp 158-9, chart 5.2). This suggests that in the terms used by Hakim (1997), a trend may be developing from more secure 'reduced hours' or 'half-time' work towards 'marginal' part-time work.

Although categorisations relating to forms of employment are becoming harmonised in the European context, the OECD has identified three broad measures of part-time employment that are found in national and European data: self-classification; a 'cut-off' point at 30 or 35 hours per week based on usual hours worked; and, less commonly used, a cut-off based on actual hours worked in the reference week (OECD 1997, p 15). The differences in definition can have a significant effect on the comparability of figures produced: the OECD provide an example where the application of the 30 hours cut-off to Swedish data reduces the rate of part-time employment from 27% to 18% (OECD, 1997, p 6). In response to these problems in the comparison of part-time employment,

the OECD has undertaken to provide comparative tables that minimise
the limitations of national data through the use of national surveys based
on a usual hours cut-off of 30 hours. These data are summarised for
selected countries in Table 1 which outlines trends in the growth of part-
time work over the period 1983-98.

Some broad trends can be identified from Table 1 in relation to the
general rise or decline of part-time employment and the specific patterns
for women and men. As other authors have noted (Blossfeld and Hakim
1997a; O'Reilly and Fagan 1998) in countries where employment was
previously characterised by full-time patterns, a general expansion is
occurring in part-time employment. This is the case even in countries
with relatively low proportions of part-time workers: Finland, Greece,
Portugal and Spain. At the end of the 1980s a clear pattern could be
identified in relation to the countries with the highest rates of part-time
employment: the Nordic countries (Sweden, Denmark and Norway);
anglophone countries except the USA (Australia, Canada, New Zealand
and the UK); the Netherlands and Japan (OECD, 1999, p 37).

By 1998 some interesting changes had occurred. In Denmark, Norway
and Sweden a declining trend can be identified, in Sweden this decline is
apparent in both male and female rates, while in Denmark and Norway
male rates continue to rise. The only other country where part-time
employment is declining is the USA, which has been argued to represent
a unique case in relation to part-time employment (Rosenfeld and
Birkelund, 1995). Combined with the low status and poor employment
conditions attached to part-time jobs, the lack of both employer provided
health insurance and eligibility for publicly provided Medicaid are regarded
as factors explaining the USA's lower proportions engaged in this form
of employment (Drobnic and Wittig, 1997). With regard to the remaining
'anglophone' group, the Netherlands and Japan, the very high rate of
part-time employment continues to increase for men and overall, but in
Canada and the UK rates for women appear stable. The proportion of
male part-time workers appears to be expanding in all countries except
Austria, Sweden and the USA. Although a slight decrease is shown, in
the USA male rates remain high despite the disadvantages experienced
by part-time workers. The highest rates of male part-time employment
are to be found in Australia, Japan, the Netherlands, New Zealand and
Canada, closely followed by Denmark, the UK and USA, Norway,
Switzerland and Ireland.

Fagan and O'Reilly (1998, p 5) observe that "Differences in social
structures [therefore] have a central role in the production of satisfactory

Table 1: Trends in part-time employment in selected OECD countries (1983-98)[1]

	Part-time employment as a proportion of total employment		Part-time employment as a proportion of employment Women		Part-time employment as a proportion of employment Men	
	1983-98 % change	1998 %	1983-98 % change	1998 %	1983-98 % change	1998 %
Australia	Rising +6.9	Very High 25.9	Rising +5.2	Very High 40.7	Rising +5.2	Very High 14.4
Austria (1995-98)	Stable +0.4	Medium 11.5	Rising +1.2	Medium 22.8	Stable −0.4	Low 2.7
Belgium	Rising +6.5%	High 16.3%	Rising +9.8	High 32.2	Rising +1.7	Medium 4.9
Canada	Rising +1.9%	High 18.7%	Stable +0.5	Medium 28.6	Rising +1.8	Very High 10.5
Denmark	Decreasing −3.6%	High 17.0%	Decreasing −11.3	Medium 25.4	Rising +2.8	High 9.9
Finland	Rising +1.4%	Low 9.7%	Stable +0.5	Low 13.0	Rising +2.3	Medium 6.8
France	Rising +5.1%	Medium 14.8%	Rising +6.1	Medium 25.0	Rising +2.6	Medium 5.8
Germany	Rising +3.2%	Medium 16.6%	Rising +1.2	High 32.4	Rising +2.5	Medium 4.6
Greece	Rising +2.2%	Low 9.2%	Rising +3.2	Low 15.9	Rising +1.1	Medium 5.3
Ireland (1983-97)	Rising +7.5%	Medium 15.2%	Rising +9.8	Medium 27.2	Rising +3.8	High 7.0
Italy	Rising +4.0%	Medium 11.8%	Rising +6.2	Medium 22.2	Rising +1.8	Medium 5.5
Japan	Rising +7.5%	Very High 23.6%	Rising +9.5	High 39.0	Rising +5.7	Very High 12.9
Luxembourg	Rising +5.5%	Medium 12.8%	Rising +10.1	Medium 29.6	Rising +1.3	Low 2.6
Netherlands	Rising +11.2%	Very High 30%	Rising +10.1	Very High 54.8	Rising +6.8	Very High 12.4
New Zealand (1986-98)	Rising +6.3%	Very High 22.8%	Rising +5.9	High 37.6	Rising +4.9	Very High 10.6
Norway (1989-98)	Stable −0.1%	Very High 21.0%	Decreasing −4.0	High 35.9	Rising +1.9	High 8.1
Portugal (1986-98)	Rising +3.3%	Low 9.9%	Rising +3.6	Low 15.8	Rising +2.3	Medium 5.2
Spain (1987-98)	Rising +2.8%	Low 7.7%	Rising +4.5	Low 16.6	Rising +1.0	Low 2.9

continued

Table 1: Trends in part-time employment in selected OECD countries (1983-98) (continued)

	Part-time employment as a proportion of total employment		Part-time employment as a proportion of employment Women		Part-time employment as a proportion of employment Men	
	1983-98 % change	1998 %	1983-98 % change	1998 %	1983-98 % change	1998 %
Sweden (1987-98)	Decreasing −3.4%	Medium 13.5%	Decreasing −7.8	Medium 22.0	Decreasing +0.7	Medium 5.6
Switzerland (1991-98)	Rising +2.1%	Very High 24.2%	Rising +3.2	Very High 45.8	Stable +0.4	High 7.2
UK	Rising +4.6%	Very High 23.0%	Stable +1.1	Very High 41.2	Rising +4.9	High 8.2
USA	Decreasing −2.0%	Medium 13.4%	Decreasing −3.8	Low 19.1	Decreasing −0.9	High 8.2

Notes:

Total Employment: Very High = >20%; High = 16-20%; Medium = 10-15%; Low = <10%; Stable = change within 1% over period covered

Women: Very High = >40%; High = 30-39%; Medium = 20-29%; Low = <20%; Stable = change within 1% over period covered (except UK where year on year change is within 1.1% for all years)

Men: Very High = >10%; High = 7.0-9.9%; Medium = 4.0-6.9%; Low = <4%; Stable = change within 0.5% over period covered

Source: Adapted from OECD (1999, pp 36-9), Part-time employment as percentage of employment

accounts for international variations in part-time work among women", and in particular the role of social policies or welfare regimes. Presumably then, the type of welfare regime would be likely to have a similar impact on the patterns of part-time employment in which men engage. Following three of the various gendered typologies of welfare regimes (Lewis, 1992; Siaroff, 1994; Duncan, 1995, p 275, Figure 2) it is interesting that, although similar trends are found within clusters of countries, overall the variance in the patterns of part-time employment prevents any simplistic matching with these regime types. Although different approaches to analysis are taken by these three authors[2] and some countries do emerge in different groupings, differentiation can still broadly be summarised according to distinctions between Nordic countries, continental European countries, southern European or 'Latin rim' countries and the anglophone group. At a superficial level, these country distinctions are similar to those found in mainstream typologies of welfare regimes (Esping-Andersen, 1990, 1997a; Leibfried, 1993), and patterns of part-time employment also loosely fit into these clusters. In the 'Liberal' (for example, Australia, Canada, Japan, Switzerland) and 'Social democratic' (for example, Sweden, Norway) welfare states of Esping-Andersen's model it is clear that part-time work is more prevalent. In the 'Latin rim' countries identified by Licbfricd (Greece, Portugal, Spain) significant part-time employment is not a characteristic of employment regimes.

Thus, although the greater concentration of part-time employment can be narrowed to specific regime types, the patterns suggest that a more specific set of factors determine its nature and extent in each country. Both Blossfeld and Hakim (1997a) and O'Reilly and Fagan (1998) demonstrate that explanation of cross-national differences in the incidence of part-time employment requires exploration of a combination of economic, institutional and social factors. The welfare state typologies highlighted above do assist in providing a framework for this kind of exploration but are unable to account for all of the relevant explanatory factors. In his concluding discussion Blossfeld (1997, pp 318-23) provides an outline of the relative importance of a range of variables such as taxation systems, hours worked, demand for labour, pronatalism, entitlement to health insurance and secularisation, which link Denmark and Sweden, distinguish France from Germany and the Netherlands and separate Britain from the USA. In the case studies that form the basis of Blossfeld's analysis, the southern European countries remain united in following a full-time employment trajectory. Other factors identified in explanation of the divergence in patterns of part-time work include the deregulation (Dex and McCulloch, 1995) or regulation of the labour market and share of agriculture in the national economy (Meulders et al, 1994), the share of services and higher general rates of female participation (Bruegel and Hegewisch, 1994), employer demand (Fagan and Rubery, 1996), the rate of unemployment (De Grip et al, 1997) and the disincentive effect of tax and benefit systems (Doudeijns, 1998).

From their particularly revealing statistical comparison of nine OECD countries, Rosenfeld and Birkelund (1995) argue that part-time employment predominates in (mainly social democratic) countries where the historical strength of labour has facilitated the development of a large public sector. Within this sector a significant proportion of part-time jobs are provided in order to achieve both full employment and gender equality. These work or demand-side factors are combined with welfare supply-side factors such as financial and service support for working mothers and families, also provided in or through the public sector. Due to its very high rates of part-time employment but minimal public sector,

Japan is considered an 'outlier' in relation to many of the political-institutional variables considered by Rosenfeld and Birkelund (1995). The upward trend in Japan is attributed to employer strategies to reduce labour costs within the confines of a relatively rigid labour market (Houseman and Osawa, 1998). Employer strategies to increase workforce flexibility might be equally important in determining levels of part-time work in other deregulated 'Liberal' welfare states. In the long term, it may be that current production needs become increasingly based on previously 'feminised' working patterns, further promoting the importance of demand-side factors in the development of part-time work.

Characteristics of women's and men's part-time work

In terms of explaining the incidence of male part-time employment, a correlation is indentified between high female part-time rates and similar high rates for men (Delsen, 1998). But men's part-time employment is thus explained via the incidence of women's part-time employment rather than as a development with its own impetus and trajectory[3]. The data presented here suggest that trends in men's part-time work do not simply shadow those of women. For example, in Canada and the US where female rates are 'medium' and 'low', male rates are 'very high' and 'high', and in Belgium and Germany where female rates are high, male rates are relatively low. Where women are the focus, analysis of the gendered nature of part-time work is enhanced by greater attention not only to institutional factors but also to gender relations and the social and personal factors that contribute to its incidence. For example, the contributors to Blossfeld and Hakim (1997a) refer to a range of attitudinal and work orientation data while Sainsbury (1996, chapter 5), Pfau-Effinger (1998) and Daune-Richard (1998) consider, respectively, access to social protection, social practices and particularly the construction of childhood as a public or private concern and "the relationship between the public and private spheres and of individuality and citizenship" (Daune-Richard, 1998, p 227). Yet these approaches reflect the concerns foremost in the analysis of women's work patterns. There are difficulties in applying similar approaches to the analysis of men's part-time work since, although it may be a statistical corollary of that of women, it would be surprising to find, for example, that male part-time workers are attempting the reconciliation of family and employment rather than undertaking involuntary part-time work in a slack labour market, as is more often suggested (Rosenfeld and Birkelund, 1995; De Grip et al, 1997).

Before an attempt is made to analyse the male part–time worker evidence it makes sense to set out some of the characteristics attributed to men's part–time work and to compare them with those of women. Delsen (1998) provides a comprehensive account of current patterns of male part–time work in OECD countries which suggests that although in most over 80% of part–time jobs are found in the service sector, hours worked in manufacturing are beginning to show a shift away from the full–time model. The most obvious difference between the patterns of women and men is that while women part–timers tend to be found in the mid–working age groups, men are concentrated in the 15-24 years and over-55 age groups. Older male part–timers are more characteristic of central Europe and Japan while the younger age group is characteristic of the liberal anglophone countries, the Nordic countries and the Netherlands. Despite this pattern, Delsen notes that growth in men's part–time work is in the 'prime-age' group (25-49 years) where numbers increased in the EU by 50% between 1991-95 (1998, p 62). The main feature of the overall trends in part–time work is convergence: increases in rates across most countries, both between women's and men's rates and in the age groups involved (Delsen, 1998 and Table 1 above). Thus it appears that despite the negative perceptions of part–time work, there are economic pressures that are creating a discernible shift in men's employment towards patterns more associated with women's employment. The question, then, is whether this development poses problems or possibilities for the welfare state.

The 'problem' of the male part-time worker: mountain or molehill?

The 'problem' of part–time work is its construction as an inferior form of employment, predominantly based upon the needs of employers for numerical flexibility, although as Bruegel and Hegewisch (1994) argue, there are supply factors which sometimes oblige employers to offer employment in a format which suits women. Despite this proviso, and the recognised exceptions where full and part–time hours are indistinguishable, the status of part–time work is more often than not that of 'precarious' and 'marginal' employment where one would expect to find low rates of remuneration, inferior conditions of service, few opportunities for training and staff development, poor prospects for career progression and reduced rights to social protection. There are a variety of reasons why part-time work has failed to achieve equal status with full-time work:

1. The preponderance of women in part-time work which has led to it being considered as 'secondary' employment in terms of the income gained and the importance attributed to issues such as career development and training.
2. The sector and/or occupations in which part-time work is concentrated which are associated with an extension of low-skilled 'women's work' in the public rather than private sector, services such as cleaning, catering and caring, and any job with 'assistant' in the title.
3. Historically trade unions have been conspicuously unreceptive to the needs of (women) part-time workers in the belief that part-time employment represented an erosion of the conditions for effective (male) worker organisation and wage bargaining.
4. The 'fall-back' or 'bridge' status often attributed to part-time work in relation to full-time work and its construction as an 'involuntary' form of economic activity.

Essentially then, it is the gendered nature of part-time employment that forms the basis of its inferior status. As Delsen (1998) observes, men would be unlikely to want or choose part-time employment where it is characterised by 'junk jobs' that attract neither occupational status nor a 'family wage'. However, as an increase in the proportion of men engaging in this form of employment has been identified, it is necessary to explore first, the extent to which a negative experience of part-time work might be shared by men, and second, the possibility that men's involvement in part-time work may lead to a change in its status.

The gendered experience of part-time work

In the version of the human capital/work orientation thesis presented in Hakim (1996) and Blossfeld and Hakim (1997b), it is argued that part-time employment is a life-strategy for women that determines the choice to be a secondary earner and primary homemaker rather than adopting the male model and choosing a full-time career. This thesis is contested in the case of women (Fagan and Rubery, 1996), and from the literature available it appears that neither is it the case for men. Excluding reduced hours working in the manufacturing sector, in its 'short working hours' form, part-time work is presented as a stopgap for men. Fagan and

O'Reilly (1998) note that the supply of men for part-time work is an effect of the expansion in education in some countries. In the UK, for example, figures for the mid-1990s show that around 42% of male part-timers were students (Dex and McCulloch, 1995). Thus, when examined by age-group, the indication is that men tend to engage in part-time work to obtain income in addition to their main source of income, which is not the wage of a male breadwinner but some form of state transfer such as a student grant (or subsidised loan), a pension, or, in Australia, unemployment benefit (Burgess, 1997).

It has also been suggested that in the case of Denmark where men are engaged in part-time work these are generally employees whose part-time employment represents a second job (Boje, 1996). Within the EU, Eurostat data for 1997 show that the highest proportions of second job-holders (over 4% of the employed population) tend to be found in those countries with the highest rates of part-time employment (over 22% of total employment): Denmark, the Netherlands and the UK. However, Portugal, Austria and Finland also have high proportions of second-job holders combined with low rates of part-time employment (below 15% of total employment) (Eurostat, 1999, pp 136, 139). In the case of Australia, Burgess (1997) indicates that the male outflow from part-time to full-time employment is double that for women. Thus, part-time employment actually represents 'hidden unemployment' where, in their aspiration to work full-time, men attempt to retain at least some link to the labour market despite the disadvantages. This, combined with the evidence mentioned above, might suggest that the poor conditions and reduced entitlements to social protection may be of little consequence to male part-time workers. Unlike less qualified, 'prime-age', part-time women, as students they are building up or, as retirees, winding down strong links to the labour market rather than establishing a weak lifetime link. While it is possible to conclude that many male students and retirees are involved in part-time work for 'pin money' to supplement their main source of income, Delsen's (1998) suggestion that there is convergence between male and female part-time employment rates, and the incidence of second jobs, suggests there may also be a growing number of possibly low-paid or indebted male employees undertaking a part-time job (or jobs) to make ends meet. The presumption that for men part-time work is involuntary rather than a life-strategy may therefore be a little premature.

In relation to social protection and financial security, if part-time work constitutes only a minor proportion of a man's work history this may lessen.but not eliminate the impact of reduced entitlements to insurance-related benefits and pensions. In addition, the significance of supplementary income in preventing financial and associated crises should not be underestimated, and is recognised in studies of household expenditure. The loss of this extra income through for example, dismissal or redundancy, is unfortunate enough but this may then be compounded by a lack of compensation through entitlement to social security and related benefits. The consequences of men's employment choices are also of interest in relation to women's welfare; within the liberal and continental European welfare states there remains a substantial proportion of women whose benefit entitlements are based on their status as wives and they too may experience the 'diswelfare' which accompanies part-time work where their husbands engage in this form of economic activity. The 'gendered' comparisons of welfare states and part-time work mentioned earlier all confirm that the state privileges full-time paid work over unpaid work and part-time employment (Orloff, 1993). As Grimshaw and Rubery (1997) have argued, governments cannot reduce social division when combining flexibility and the male breadwinner model, because this model excludes those who are not employed continuously on a full-time basis. With increasing proportions of male part-time workers, it is likely that more not less exclusion from social and employment protection will result. Only those whose part-time work is characterised by high levels of remuneration would be in a position to compensate for the difficulties arising from the combination of contributory social insurance and intermittent employment or short working hours. Those for whom high earnings are not a feature of their part-time employment will experience disadvantage within all types of welfare state though the extent of this will differ. The greater importance of citizenship as a basis for entitlement in the Nordic countries has been eroded to some extent, but in Denmark, for example, unemployment insurance can be paid at a part-time rate, and a semi-retirement pension is available for those continuing to work part-time (Irving, 1998). Greater problems will be experienced where states adhere more strictly to a contribution and entitlement system based on the primacy of full-time work and a rigid distinction between being 'in work' or 'out of work'. Greater reliance on private and/or occupational provision will not favour part-time employees since, as Marullo (1995) indicates, exclusion from occupational pensions is a common disadvantage of part-time employment in Europe.

In terms of regulation relating to part-time work, it appears that at least in the 15 EU member states and Australia, equal rights are now offered to part-timers in regard to conditions of service, whether through collective agreement or statutory legislation. Differences are more significant when the permanence of employment is in question in Australia, the UK, Ireland and Sweden, where temporary contract workers do not attract the same protection as permanent workers (Marullo, 1995; Burgess, 1997). In Australia where two thirds of the part-time work force and 81% of male part-timers are 'casual', the cumulative disadvantages of partial employment may be felt much more widely than is imagined. If men are being pushed and pulled towards female patterns of employment then one outcome may be that the disadvantage associated with these will become a much more significant policy issue. In OECD countries, the part-time share of male employment was 6.6 % in 1997 (OECD, 1999, p 39) which in numbers represents around 34 million people.

A change in the status of part-time work?

If the feminised nature of part-time work is the key factor in its low status, then a process of masculinisation might lead to a raising of this status. As the country with highest rates of both female and male part-time employment, the Netherlands provides some indication of how this process might develop. Indeed Delsen (1998) posits the existence of a Dutch model in the evolution of part-time work. As a feature of employer's staff retention strategies, part-time work in the Netherlands continues to undergo a metamorphosis from "secondary jobs for married women to fully acceptable jobs for all women and increasing numbers of men" (Delsen, 1998, p 68). This has occurred because the formal status of part-time work in relation to the minimum wage, labour law and social protection has been placed on an equal footing with that of full-time work.

Using data for 1990, Fagan and Rubery (1996, p 240) find that "only 42% of female part-timers in the Netherlands work in occupations with 60 per cent or more women employed" compared to 85% for female part-timers in the UK. In 1990, at 13.4% the male part-time employment rate was at its peak in the Netherlands compared to a lower rate in the UK of 5.3% (OECD, 1999, p 39). The possibility that might be inferred from this is that a higher proportion of male part-timers could contribute to a reduction in levels of gender segregation and a concomitant improvement in the status of part-time jobs. If a move to part-time work is perceived as downward occupational mobility then, as several analysts suggest, the only way to make it acceptable (or attractive) to men is to ensure equal treatment between part-time and full-time workers (Delsen, 1998; Fagan and O'Reilly,

1998). The suggestion here is that with greater numbers of men already engaged in part-time work, the pressures for these improvements will become more compelling, particularly at the EU level where sympathy towards the needs of part-time workers has already been demonstrated in a recent directive[4], although the rationale for this was located in efforts to create jobs rather than improving gender equality.

The future of the 'male model' of employment

Terms such as 'atypical' work and 'non-standard' employment reflect the explicit assumption that the '48, 48, 48' male model is typical; that it represents some kind of gold standard against which a range of employment patterns can be measured. The use of these terms also reflects the implicit assumption that the male model of employment is superior, that it is the goal for all employees and that anything less signifies short-changing those concerned. In the most comprehensive recent comparative analysis of part-time work the editors conclude by suggesting that a key distinction to be made within the study of part-time work is between that which provides "an eventual stepping stone into full-time work" representing 'inclusion' and that related to "casualised employment and spells of unemployment" and 'marginalisation' (Fagan and O'Reilly, 1998, p 25). Thus, part-time employment continues to be presented as substandard in relation to the male model, despite the authors having pointed out that gender differences in all areas of life are "organised hierarchically, on the basis of the primacy or cultural prestige of the male norm" (1998, p 15). Put simply, the quality, and inherent desirability of all forms of employment are measured against the form that men have typically followed.

The arguments supporting this negative characterisation of part-time employment are convincing in the sense that for the majority of female part-time workers at present the work experience is one of low pay and expendability, and this is contrasted with the relative comfort and security experienced by the majority of male full-time workers. However, although the work of Blossfeld and Hakim (1997b) lacks sufficient recognition of the constraints on 'choice' produced by structural inequalities, they do explore the idea that a full-time, lifelong commitment to the world of paid work might not represent the pinnacle of individual achievement. This view is also shared by a range of radical and not so radical writers (Gorz, 1985; Bauman, 1998; Forrester, 1999, Gray, 1999). However, whereas Blossfeld and Hakim (1997b) focus on women's experience of part-time work, the focus of interest in this part of the discourse is men, and the extent to which a masculinisation of women's employment patterns may provide an opportunity for the transformation of the domestic division of labour.

The socialisation of care is regarded by many feminists as more emancipatory than the private market solutions available only to the better-off, the homemaker restrictions placed on the worse-off in the USA and UK, or the familism which characterises Germany and Belgium. The socialisation of care, however, reconstitutes women's work and is actually marketisation since care becomes a commodity even where it is funded by the state. More emancipatory still, then, would be the facilitation of men's choices to become genuinely involved in domestic work. Hakim (1993, p 106) argues that "part-time workers are unlikely to be major catalysts for change in the labour force", and that only women who follow the male model are challenging the sexual division of labour (Hakim, 1996). But what of men following the female model? First, it cannot be assumed that they are simply responding to rather than initiating changes in the labour market, particularly since it has not been established that male part-timers share the low status and relative powerlessness of their female counterparts. Second, changes in the labour market are mutually dependent on changes in the domestic division of labour. In Sweden, which has a moderate rate of male part-time employment, Daune-Richard (1994) observes that men have greater responsibility for childcare and devote more time to housework than men in either France or the UK. However, even assuming attempts to remove obstacles presented by welfare institutional arrangements and employment systems, as has occurred in Sweden, there is the more fundamental and unquantifiable issue of what Pfau-Effinger (1998) describes as 'gender culture', or more simply, domestic gender relations and attitudes to domestic and market work. What are these attitudinal obstacles to men's greater involvement in domestic work or even simply their reduced involvement in market work?

With regard to men's involvement in domestic work and childcare, the wide range of international studies summarised in Goodwin (1999, chapter 8) suggests that while it is the case that women are responsible for the vast majority of these tasks, one of the barriers to men's involvement is the time they spend in paid work. However, in Shelton's (1992) US study the opposite was indicated: that men's time spent on domestic work is not strongly linked to time in paid work. In Goodwin's (1999) own study a smaller proportion of non-standard workers (58.3%) than full-time workers (65.7%) thought that women and men should do the same jobs around the house, but in practice neither group actually did this. Overall, his analysis suggests that male non-standard workers are more likely to undertake domestic work. For men, higher levels of education are argued by some to correlate with greater levels of gender egalitarianism (Fagan and O'Reilly, 1998). However, Goodwin (1999) and Shelton (1992) found that in practice, higher levels of education for men correlated with participation in fewer household tasks. Shelton (1992) suggests that this outcome may be an effect of the higher occupational demands experienced by better-qualified men rather than opposition to gender equality. For some men then, changes in attitudes towards the work ethic combined with a taste of part-time work while engaged in further education may encourage a more amenable approach towards following the 'female model' in later life. These men might also be more likely to contribute to pressures for change in the status and rewards of part-time work.

In terms of the work ethic, there are serious issues surrounding the construction of part-time work as an indicator of a lack of commitment to or engagement with citizenship duties. At a personal level, the gendered nature of part-time work implies that men who follow this pattern may be regarded by their peers as 'feminine', although these gendered constructions do not seem to have afflicted men in higher status part-time occupations (consultants or company directors for example). Goodwin (1999) found that 'prime-age' male non-standard workers (who tended to be slightly better qualified than the three other groups identified) were the least likely to support traditional work ethic values and had the most positive attitudes to sex equality at work. Important factors in explaining these attitudes were found to be employment of the man's partner and having children. Nevertheless, in analysis of changes between 1981 and 1991 in their attitudes towards the importance of 'work', it appeared that as they aged, responses within this group of non-standard workers became increasingly traditional (Goodwin, 1999, p 132). In the case of women in the EU, Fagan and Rubery (1996) argue that contrary to Hakim's (1993) thesis, part-time employment is not an adequate indicator of work commitment. Similarly, then, assumptions should not be made regarding the part-time employment in which men engage.

Conclusion

The discussion above seems to have raised more questions than answers in terms of the effects of changes in part-time work on the construction of gender roles. Further research is therefore necessary to assess the extent to which part-time working will become a valued form of economic activity for men and women. What can be outlined though, are some implications for the use of the 'male model' within gender analysis. The only reasons for the continuing use of the male model as a valuable analytical tool are (a) that it continues to represent the experience of the better-off majority and/or (b) that it represents a model of aspiration. With regard to the first point, full-time permanent employment and its attached benefits does remain the model for most workers in OECD countries but despite polarisation between long and short working hours, overall, working hours are steadily declining (OECD, 1998). This points to the potential demise of the male model, which will be accompanied by a series of challenges to social insurance systems, principles of entitlement and the social relations of gender. These challenges should be regarded as the framework for a redistribution of paid and unpaid work. The second point is more suggestive of a reconceptualisation of paid and unpaid work which is not premised on the assumption that full-time paid employment is the only key to worth and identity.

The answer to the question of whether the male part-time worker represents a minor problem or a major challenge for the welfare state requires a more wide-ranging study of trends in part-time employment, the sectors of activity and occupations, the hours worked, the motivation and rewards and the age and general social profile of those involved, as well as the complementary roles undertaken when not engaged in paid work. However, from the discussion presented here the answer depends upon the view of the 'round hole' of the male model and the preferred response to the 'square pegs'. If it is accepted that the best way of organising employment is through the '48,48,48' model which should be preserved at all costs, then he is a minor problem. However, if it is accepted that post-Fordism is nigh, and a positive redistribution of work is desired, accompanied by an overhaul of outdated and 'perforated' systems of social protection, then he is a major challenge.

Notes

[1] The exclusion from the table of the Czech Republic, Hungary, Iceland, Korea, Mexico, Poland and Turkey is due to the fact that either (a) only very recent data exist for these countries, and/or (b) that their industrial and/or political development would require separate analysis in relation to part-time work. The

categories 'Very High' etc adopted are subjective and relate to the overall position of countries relative to one another.

[2] Lewis (1992) analyses the construction of women's roles as either mothers or workers and categorises her four countries according to the strength, modification or weakness of the breadwinner/homemaker model. According to this model, Sweden follows a dual/weak model and France a modified model, while the UK and Ireland represent strong breadwinner states. Siaroff (1994) explores the existence of a real work/welfare choice for women in 23 OECD countries, attaching a greater role to religion and women's political power in explanation of gender divisions. He identifies four regime types: the 'Protestant social democratic' Nordic countries where gender equality is most advanced; the 'Protestant liberal' anglophone countries where the work ethic combines with minimal welfare to create formal equality and informal inequality; the 'advanced Christian democratic' group of family-centred continental European countries organised around the principles of private patriarchy; and the 'late female mobilisation' countries which include the southern European countries, Japan, Switzerland and Ireland. This group is characterised by limited advances towards gender equality attributed to the relatively recent granting of women's suffrage. Duncan (1995, p 271) maps countries according to the form of the gender contract, that is, the "patriarchal compromise over gender divisions of labour and power". The southern European countries and Ireland are argued to be in a transitional phase from private patriarchy; Sweden and Denmark have equality contracts; Finland a dual role contract; the UK a mixture of a housewife/dual role contract; France a dual role contract; and housewife contracts are characteristic of Germany, the Netherlands, Belgium and Switzerland.

[3] That is, causation is assumed from correlation: where part-time jobs are characteristic of women's employment they become incorporated as a demand-side labour market strategy which men are then passively drawn into.

[4] Council Directive 97/81/EC of 15 December 1997 concerning the Framework Agreement on part-time work concluded by UNICE, CEEP and the ETUC – Annex: Framework agreement on part-time work. (OJ No L014, 20/01/1998 p.0009-0014)

References

Allan, G. (ed) (2000) *Social services parliamentary monitor*, 22 May, Issue No 045, London: Cadmus Newsletters.

Bauman, Z. (1998) *Work, consumerism and the new poor*, Buckingham: Open University Press.

Blossfeld, H.-P. (1997) 'Women's part-time employment and the family cycle: a cross-national comparison', in H-P. Blossfeld and C. Hakim (eds) *Between equalization and marginalization, women working part-time in Europe and the United States of America*, Oxford: Oxford University Press, pp 315-24.

Blossfeld, H.-P. and Hakim, C. (eds) (1997a) *Between equalization and marginalization, women working part-time in Europe and the United States of America*, Oxford: Oxford University Press.

Blossfeld, H.-P. and Hakim, C. (1997b) 'Introduction: a comparative perspective on part-time work', in H-P. Blossfeld and C. Hakim (eds) *Between equalization and marginalization, women working part-time in Europe and the United States of America*, Oxford: Oxford University Press, pp 1-21.

Boje, T. (1996) 'Gender, work time and flexible employment, the case of Denmark', *Time and Society*, vol 5, no 3, pp 341-61.

Burgess, J. (1997) 'Part-time employment in Australia: unusual features and social policy issues', *International Journal of Social Economics*, vol 24, no 7/8/9, pp 831-46.

Brown, P. and Compton, R. (eds) (1994) *A new Europe? Economic restructuring and social exclusion*, London: UCL Press Limited.

Bruegel, I. and Hegewisch, A. (1994) 'Flexibilisation and part-time work in Europe', in P. Brown and R. Compton (eds) *A New Europe? Economic Restructuring and Social Exclusion*, London: UCL Press Limited, pp 33-57.

Daune-Richard, A.M. (1994) 'A social policy perspective on work, employment and the family in France, the United Kingdom and Sweden', *Cross-National Research Papers*, vol 4, no 2, pp 68-79.

Daune-Richard, A.M. (1994) 'How does the 'societal effect' shape the use of part-time work in France, the UK and Sweden?', in J.O. Reilly and C. Fagan (eds) *Part-time prospects: An international comparison of part-time work in Europe, North America and the Pacific Rim*, London: Routledge, pp 214-31.

De Grip, A., Hoevenberg, J. and Willems, E. (1997) 'Atypical employment in the European Union', *International Labour Review*, vol 136, no 1, Spring, pp 49-71.

Delsen, L. (1998) 'When do men work part-time?', in J. O'Reilly and C. Fagan (eds) *Part-time prospects, an international comparison of part-time work in Europe, North America and the Pacific Rim*, London: Routledge, pp 57-76.

Dex, S. and McCulloch, A. (1995) *Flexible employment in Britain: A statistical analysis*, Discussion Series no 15, Manchester: Equal Opportunities Commission.

Doudeijns, M. (1998) 'Are benefits a disincentive to work part-time?', in J. O'Reilly and C. Fagan (eds) *Part-time prospects, an international comparison of part-time work in Europe, North America and the Pacific Rim*, London: Routledge, pp 116-36.

Drobnic, S. and Wittig, I. (1997) 'Part-time work in the United States of America', in H.-P. Blossfeld and C. Hakim (eds) *Between equalization and marginalization, women working part-time in Europe and the United States of America*, Oxford: Oxford University Press, pp 289-314.

Duncan, S. (1995) 'Theorizing European gender systems', *Journal of European Social Policy*, vol 5, no 4, pp 263-84.

Esping-Andersen, G. (1990) *The three worlds of welfare capitalism*, Cambridge: Polity Press.

Esping-Andersen, G. (ed) (1997a) *Welfare states in transition, national adaptations in global economies*, London: Sage Publications.

Esping-Andersen, G. (1997b) 'After the golden age? Welfare state dilemmas in a global economy', in G. Esping-Andersen (ed) *Welfare states in transition, national adaptations in global economies*, London: Sage Publications, pp 1-31.

Eurostat (1999) *Eurostat Yearbook, a statistical eye on Europe, Data 1987-1997*, Luxembourg: OOPEC.

Fagan, C. and Rubery, J. (1996) 'The salience of the part-time divide in the European Union', *European Sociological Review*, vol 12, no 3, pp 227-50.

Fagan, C. and O'Reilly, J. (1998) 'Conceptualising part-time work:the value of an intergrated comparative perspective' in J. O'Reilly and C. Fagan (eds) *Part-time prospects, an international comparison of part-time work in Europe, North America and the Pacific Rim*, London: Routledge, pp 1-31.

Forrester,V. (1999) *The economic horror,* Cambridge: Polity Press.

Goodwin, J. (1999) *Men's work and male lives, men and work in Britain*, Aldershot: Ashgate Publishing Limited.

Gorz,A. (1985) *Paths to paradise: On the liberation from work*, London: Pluto Press.

Gray,A. (1999) *Time off pays off. How reductions in working time can create jobs and promote lifelong learning*, Discussion Paper 46, London:The Fabian Society.

Grimshaw, D. and Rubery, J. (1997) 'Workforce heterogeneity and unemployment benefits: the need for policy reassessment in the European Union', *Journal of European Social Policy*, vol 7, no 4, pp 291-318.

Hakim, C. (1993) 'The myth of rising female employment', *Work, Employment and Society*, vol 7, no 1, pp 97-120.

Hakim, C. (1996) *Key issues in women's work, female heterogeneity and the polarisation of women's employment*, London: The Athlone Press.

Hakim, C. (1997) 'A sociological perspective on part-time work', in H-P. Blossfeld and C. Hakim (eds) *Between equalization and marginalization, women working part-time in Europe and the United States of America*, Oxford: Oxford University Press, pp 22-70.

Harker, L. (1996) *A secure future? Social security and the family in a changing world*, London: CPAG.

Houseman, S. and Osawa, M. (1998) 'What is the nature of part-time work in the United States and Japan?', in J. O'Reilly and C. Fagan (eds) *Part-time prospects, an international comparison of part-time work in Europe, North America and the Pacific Rim*, London: Routledge, pp 232-51.

Irving, Z. (1998) *Women's self-employment and the role of social policy: A comparison of Denmark, France and the UK*, Unpublished PhD thesis, Leeds Metropolitan University.

Jones, C. (ed) (1993) *New perspectives on the welfare state in Europe*, London: Routledge.

Leibfried, S. (1993) 'Towards a European welfare state?', in C. Jones, *New perspectives on the welfare state in Europe*, London: Routledge, pp 133-56.

Lewis, J. (1992) 'Gender and the development of welfare regimes', *Journal of European Social Policy*, vol 2, no 3, pp 159-73.

Marullo, S. (1995) *Comparison of regulations on part-time and temporary employment in Europe, a briefing paper*, Employment Department Research Series, no 52, Research Strategy Branch, Sheffield: Employment Department.

Meulders, D., Plasman, O. and Plasman, R. (1994) *Atypical employment in the EC*, Aldershot: Dartmouth Publishing Company.

OECD (1997) *The definition of part-time work for the purpose of international comparisons*, Labour Market and Social Policy Occasional Papers, no 22, Paris: OECD.

OECD (1998) *Employment outlook June 1998*, Paris: OECD.

OECD (1999) *Labour force statistics 1978-1998*, 1999 Edition, Paris: OECD.

O'Reilly, J. and Fagan, C. (eds) (1998) *Part-time prospects, an international comparison of part-time work in Europe, North America and the Pacific Rim*, London: Routledge.

Orloff, A.S. (1993) 'Gender and the social rights of citizenship: the comparative analysis of gender relations and welfare states', *American Sociological Review*, vol 58, June, pp 303-28.

Pfau-Effinger, B. (1998) 'Culture or structure as explanations of differences in part-time work in Germany, Finland and the Netherlands?', in J. O'Reilly and C. Fagan (eds) *Part-time prospects, an international comparison of part-time work in Europe, North America and the Pacific Rim*, London: Routledge, pp 177-98.

Rosenfeld, R. and Birkelund, G.E. (1995) 'Women's part-time work: A cross-national comparison', *European Sociological Review*, vol 11, no 2, pp 111-34.

Sainsbury, D. (1996) *Gender, equality and welfare states*, Cambridge: Cambridge University Press.

Shelton, B.-A. (1992) *Women, men and time, gender differences in paid work, housework and leisure*, New York, NY: Greenwood Press.

Siaroff, A. (1994) 'Work, welfare and gender equality: a new typology', in D. Sainsbury (ed) *Gendering welfare states*, London: Sage Publications, pp 82-100.

Smith, M., Fagan, C. and Rubery, J. (1998) 'Where and why is part-time work growing in Europe?', in J. O'Reilly and C. Fagan (eds) *Part-time prospects, an international comparison of part-time work in Europe, North America and the Pacific Rim*, London, Routledge, pp 35-56.

Part Three:
Historical and conceptual developments

The four chapters in this final section explore a range of issues that are broadly historical and/or theoretical in nature. In each case, the contributors either 'push the boundaries' of 'traditional' social policy in ways that encompass reinterpretations of historical events and issues, or examine the implications of newly emerging phenomena for our understanding of the role and nature of contemporary welfare.

Jean Carabine's chapter on sexuality and the New Poor Law (Chapter Thirteen) provides a Foucauldian reading of a landmark example of early social legislation which foregrounds sexuality as a central 'discourse'. As Carabine suggests, social policy conveys "messages about what is acceptable and appropriate (hetero)sexuality as well as what is inappropriate and unacceptable sexual practices and relationships", and she examines this 'normalisation process' in relation to bastardy, promiscuity and marriage. Importantly, of course, Carabine notes that traces of certain discourses, the origins of which can be traced to the NPL, have a resonance in 20th- and 21st-century social policy – the contemporary treatment of lone mothers being one example.

Bridging history and theory, Hewitt's chapter (Chapter Twelve) examines the role played by theories of human nature in the contemporary history of welfare reform. Identifying four ideal typical models upon which social democratic and neo-liberal accounts variously draw, Hewitt suggests that the (discrepant) elements of these models were held together – sutured – by the device of the National Minimum, the role of which was best exemplified in the 1942 Beveridge Report. The key argument, however, is that whereas both social democrats and neo-liberals "held coherent social policy discourses based on a range of different component models of human nature", New Labour's project as defined by the nebulous 'Third Way' lacks a coherent conception of human nature. Although Labour's social policy evokes elements of earlier models of human motivation, the party has evolved no suturing principle capable of holding together these potentially centrifugal components.

The two other chapters by Nixon and Keeble (Chapter Ten), and

Fitzpatrick (Chapter Eleven), move away from historical concerns to an examination of two concerns which hold important implications for contemporary social policy. Nixon and Keeble assess the impact of the new communication technologies and ask whether they are likely to influence the ways in which social policy is delivered, constructed and experienced. Taking 'active citizenship' as a central theme, the chapter suggests that the emergence of ICTs per se will not create any greater sense of equality until basic issues of access both to the new technologies and to online skills are properly tackled. New Labour, it is argued, is failing to address these matters with the result that existing inequalities in 'real' welfare services are being perpetuated in developments in online provision.

This concern with ICTs notwithstanding, Fitzpatrick is right to note that social policy has a stronger sense of the past than the future. His chapter attempts to correct this imbalance. Fitzpatrick deals with intergenerational justice and specifically with the various ways in which we tend to discount or 'devalue future costs and benefits against present benefits and costs', his aim being to discover a principled 'discount rate' to meet the demands of intergenerational justice. Following a theoretical discussion of possible approaches to this issue from the standpoint of environmental and social sustainability, Fitzpatrick moves to a consideration of contemporary biopolicy. He suggests that recent advances in biotechnology could undermine the basic principles of sustainable justice that he advances, arguing, for example, that continued biological diversity is more conducive to intergenerational justice than the prospect of future genetic homogeneity.

TEN

New communication technologies
– connected welfare: new media
and social policy[1]

Paul Nixon and Leigh Keeble

In a rapidly changing world in which the effects of the adoption of information and communications technologies (ICTs) are all pervasive, there is a growing recognition that the social diffusion of new media such as the Internet is likely to have a profound effect upon the future provision of welfare services (Loader, 1998; Burrows et al, 2000; Hardey, 1999). Recent policy directives foreground the importance to the UK government of new ICTs for the delivery of social welfare (Blair 2000; Cabinet Office, 2000; DoH, 2000). However, while politicians and policy makers in Britain and around the world are beginning to regard such ICTs as catalysts for modernising public service organisations and procedures, less has been written about the social shaping of the media or its potential impact on the social relations of welfare. In particular, we suggest that the enthusiastic adoption of ICTs for reforming welfare should be considered as an aspect of a contested policy formulation which regards the 'active citizen' as the central agent for resolving competing economic, social and political pressures (Williams, 1999). It is the interpretation or understanding of exactly what 'active citizenship' means and the values so suggested which affects how the social relations of welfare are changing. At the same time, such differences of interpretation and resulting, and sometimes, conflicting values are reflected in service provision.

This chapter identifies and considers areas where the increasing utilisation of ICTs could be important for influencing the restructuring of welfare provision. By briefly examining the conflicting meanings assigned to the idea of 'active citizenship' and the values implicit in the competing perspectives, it will demonstrate how the use of ICTs promote such ideas and the subsequent impacts on social policy. The paper will

207

examine how the use of ICTs could change the way we deliver, construct and experience social policy outcomes. The analysis will concentrate not just on service delivery but, by introducing examples from our own research, will also focus on the notions of democracy and social inclusion, examining the claims that the use of ICTs could bring greater equality and democratic input into policy and decision making.

It has been argued that the changing policy prescriptions of both the New Right and New Labour, together with the new forms of welfare politics developing within civil society, have resulted in challenges to the old welfare order and the construction of new visions of an 'active welfare subject' (see for example, Roche, 1992; Giddens, 1994; Dwyer, 1998). These processes have contributed to an expansion in our understanding of what Williams (1999, p 667) calls the 'moral repertoire' through which people engage with welfare.

However, the interpretation and understanding of 'active citizenship' (Lister, 1997) is not uncontested and the differing interpretations of the idea can produce different understandings of the social relations of welfare. At the same time, the different values implicit in these conflicting interpretations impact on the ways in which ICTs are adopted and used. It is not our intention to reproduce the analysis of the different values discussed by various authors such as Dean et al. (2000), Williams (1999) and Dwyer (1998), however, by drawing on the work of Fiona Williams (1999), we can examine the resulting impact on the delivery of welfare services via ICTs.

First, Williams (1999) argues that the period of New Right government in Britain was fundamentally important because it introduced the idea of a welfare citizen as being 'active'. Of particular significance was the fact that welfare subjects were reconstituted into two opposing categories during this time: the taxpayer/consumer and the welfare dependent. The key influence on the values of the active welfare citizen in the New Right vision was the assumption that the taxpayer/consumer could – and should – exercise choice in the welfare market.

Active citizenship and its impact on information society policies

This emphasis on active citizenship and choice impacted upon information society policies being developed in the UK during the period of the Thatcher/Major governments. These policies, which were motivated by market forces (Taylor, 1995), mirrored other similar policy developments around the world such as the Banngemann Report (in the European Union) and the National Information Infrastructure (in the United States). Even when the government announced the *IT for All* programme in 1996, with stated aims to improve the awareness of the benefits of ICTs to people in everyday life, Tang (1998) argued that government policy was still geared towards business and the one-way delivery of government services. It was 'active citizens' who had access to the new technologies to gain information and improve their choices.

The election of the Blair government in 1997 has led to a realignment of the meaning of 'active citizenship'. Williams (1999) notes that the new welfare programmes emerging from government put its 'customers' at the centre of service delivery. In this way, Williams (1999, p 671) argues that it "is *active* in its efficiency, its support, its transparency in tailoring its service to individual needs, in its use of information technology to coordinate the different sectors; it will also reclaim and reshape an ethos of public services".

The policies advocated by the New Labour government in relation to the adoption of ICTs reflect the belief in the potential of the new technologies to promote citizens' choices and make government services more accessible. However, also enshrined within New Labour's rhetoric of 'active citizenship' is the clear assertion of the 'responsibilities' of individual citizens (Dean et al, 2000). In the case of online service provision one can see how the developments of Web sites such as www.nhsdirect.nhs.uk could place responsibilities on individuals to access information provided by government, take account of that information and act on it accordingly.

Moving beyond taxpayer/consumers, other groups, which, according to Williams (1999), also promote the idea of 'active citizenship' but from a very different agenda and perspective to those already discussed, are the new social movements and self-help groups, which have grown in importance and influence since the 1970s. Although these groups are diverse both in their makeup and in their main aims and objectives, they share a common demand in relation to "the reconstitution of the welfare subject as an active citizen participating in the democratic organisation of welfare services" (Williams, 1999, p 673).

Such self-help groups, although focusing on specific needs, are seen by Williams as promoting and campaigning for welfare services to be delivered in ways that respect "identity and autonomy and treat people with equal worth" (1999, p 673). These values are reflected in the self-help, 'virtual' spaces that are currently developing on the Web.

There is no doubt that we are in a period of major social, economic and political change from which a new social welfare order is emerging. Chakravarti and Krishnan (1999) argue that governments need to move from forms of governance which are centralised and bureaucratic towards a model which is more fluid and devolved. Within the changes currently taking place we can also identify moves towards the characterisation of society as being increasingly 'information driven'. Governance is affected by such changes and governments are experiencing a "... paradigmatic shift in thinking, towards an interpretation of the State as being less concerned with provision and more with facilitation, enablement and partnerships in the management and delivery of public services ..." (Taylor, 1998, p 145). Welfare providers and regulators are being compelled to reassess their activities and to re-engineer their responses to social welfare related problems. These new forms of tasks and relationships require new answers which potentially involve changing the relationships both among and within government departments, agencies and other service providers – which implies a rethinking of organisational structures and operation processes. ICTs have been identified as contributing to this reorganisation process.

E-government strategy

In April 2000 the government published *E-government. A strategic framework for public services in the information age* (Cabinet Office, 2000). The strategy sets out to provide a common framework and 'direction for change across the public sector', and fulfils a commitment made in the *Modernising government* White Paper (1999) to publish a strategy for Information Age government. The underpinning component of the government's proposals is the stated aim for Britain to embrace the knowledge economy: "I strongly believe that the knowledge economy is our best route for success and prosperity" (Blair, 2000). To achieve this end, the government has three stated aims: to put all government services online by 2005; to ensure universal access to the Internet by 2005 (HM Treasury, 2000); and to ensure that all records are held in electronic form by 2004 (DoH, 2000).

The *E-government* strategy emerging is consistent with the reforming public sector service provision discussed in the *Modernising government* White Paper. The drive towards the use of ICTs in welfare, and in government in general, is premised upon both an ideological imperative to modernise government and a thematic urge to embrace modern technology, but also on aims of making services more efficient and effective.

The costs inherent in such a process are huge, both in terms of physical resources and the time needed to invest in operationalising, managing and maintaining such changes. This investment is acknowledged by the government which has announced a central funding stream to support *selected* priority services as plans are developed (HM Treasury, 2000).

The commitment from government is quite clear. Earlier this year Tony Blair reiterated his belief in the potential of the new media to increase the competitiveness of Britain and reduce social exclusion (Blair, 2000). The *E-government* paper (Cabinet Office, 2000) sets out the four guiding principles: building services around citizens' choices; making government and its services more accessible; social inclusion; and the better use of information. However, Day (2001) argues that the underlying priorities of the policy are economic efficiency and competitiveness. Day notes that even the language used to describe the developments – for example, 'information revolution' and 'knowledge economy' – highlights and reinforces the techno-economic determinism of government policy. Even so, we would also suggest that these developments help to demonstrate the interpretation of 'active citizenship' from the perspective of the New Labour government.

To date, the development of online government welfare services mainly centres on the provision of information, responsibility for its receipt, and any subsequent action, being left to individuals. For example, the DSS already has a comprehensive website which advises on, among other things, benefit entitlement (www.dss.gov.uk). Even at this relatively early stage of the development of online services, the site allows individuals to gather information about their eligibility for benefits. Such developments will continue and may lead to individuals being able to calculate their benefit entitlements online. This emerging scenario suggests that it would not be difficult to imagine the onus being placed on individual citizens to ensure that they claim their full entitlements. After all, government agencies could argue that, once the information is provided, it is the individual's responsibility to explore it fully in order to ascertain the nature and extent of their rights. In this way, the provision of information by central and local government on the Internet could lead to even greater responsibility being placed on individuals to act and behave in certain ways in, for example, protecting their own health (www.nhsdirect.nhs.uk).

Despite the concerns voiced by Day (2001), the sheer volume of consultation papers emerging from government indicates that there is clearly a growing emphasis on the potential use of ICTs as an aid in social welfare provision. Indeed, Burrows et al (2000) argue that the emergence and growth of Internet use in Britain has important implications for the analysis of social policy. Loader (1998) posits that the study of social policy must include the analysis of the restructuring of social relations and subjects that are mediated by the new ICTs.

New Labour's rhetoric in relation to the new technologies and welfare has been grounded within a perspective that ICTs are good per se. Loader (1998, p 227) suggests that the reason why government is keen to promote the development of online service provision can be directly related to what he identifies as the emergence of 'self service welfare', summarising its characteristics as follows:

- the welfare service commodity is transformed to enable it to be produced in the home or local community;
- the recipient is responsible for taking on almost all the labour costs for the service;
- the system may facilitate the transfer of capital costs to individuals, voluntary organisations or teleworkers;
- the system is built upon highly sophisticated informatics applications;
- the recipient may (at least in appearance) be empowered to contest the authority of professionals.

The benefits to government in delivering welfare services online seem apparent, not the least of which being that the costs of services can be dramatically reduced. At the same time, by encouraging the use of ICTs the government appears (at least at a rhetorical level) to be promoting the interactive abilities of the new technologies and so potentially allowing for meaningful consultation with citizens.

With the promotion of joint working in many local authority sections, a Web-based presence could be beneficial to individuals working in welfare services. The provision of detailed information can be effective in answering basic questions in relation to the structure of an organisation and its roles and responsibilities. At the same time, updating Web-based information has become relatively easy as software packages have developed. There is again a potential cost benefit to local authorities as the provision of information on a website might reduce their need to produce written information in the form of leaflets and so on, so reducing printing costs. However, the cost of maintaining the website should not be underestimated.

What, however, do these developments actually mean in relation to analysing social policy and the future implications for welfare delivery?

Burrows et al (2000) in their discussion of what they term 'virtual community care' argue that the emergence of self-help groups on the Internet could represent a potential challenge to the dominant post-war models of social policy. They note that in its current form, this phenomenon could represent:

> ... one element of a shift away from the conception of welfare based upon rationally administered state provision coupled with paternalistic professionally determined needs and bureaucratic organisational delivery systems towards one more characterised by fragmentation, diversity and a range of individualization processes. (Burrows et al, 2000, pp 104-5)

A double-edged sword?

If this is the case, the government could be faced with a double-edged sword. First, it may regard such developments as representing a successful shift in the burden of welfare provision. The development of 'self service' welfare results in the recipient of welfare taking on almost all of the labour costs for the service. Second, however, the interactive nature of the media could pose a threat to government. Individuals could become 'skilled up' to the extent that they can use the technology to gather support and challenge government decisions. Evidence of this can be seen in campaigns relating to issues as diverse as anti-globalisation, the environment and labour exploitation (see www.indymedia.org for examples of online activism).

The conflicting perspectives of 'active citizenship' already discussed are not the only perspectives influencing the provision of welfare services online. Individual local authority welfare organisations will ultimately be responsible for designing their own Web provision and these will be influenced by other cultural and organisational perspectives.

The literature on public services organisations clearly suggests that the design and delivery of public services has been shaped by values associated with professionalism (Hugman, 1991) and, in latter years, managerialism (see Clark et al, 1994; Clarke and Newman, 1997). As has been previously discussed (Hague and Keeble, 1999), such values are not necessarily conducive to the introduction and full exploitation of the potential of ICTs as a tool for empowerment. Professional groups, after all, place emphasis on autonomy and discretion and the maintenance of professional standards and protection of client interests through self-regulation and collegiate control. Such a value system is consistent with a view of ICTs as, on the one hand, a means of networking and information sharing with colleagues and associated professionals and, on the other, a means of providing information and possibly delivering services to clients. Goode (cited in Johnson, 1981) notes that professional monopoly is maintained by persuading society that not only can no one else do the job, but that it would be dangerous to let them try, the point being that the distinctive qualities of professional knowledge may be more attuned to the needs of professionals themselves than to those of clients and the wider community. Professional values, then, are not necessarily conducive to notions of empowering individuals and communities.

Managerialism and the market approach, by contrast, may encourage competition and efficiency drives but are not necessarily based on consumer benefit. The culture of managerialism that has colonised public services in recent years has established the achievement of economy, efficiency and effectiveness as a superordinate goal, with emphasis placed on 'economy' and the bottom line of cash savings. ICTs can be viewed as a tool to improve financial performance and accordingly, many public sector managers miss out on the significant potential of ICTs to enhance service delivery and relations with citizens (Milner, 1999). This perhaps is not surprising as the new managerialism places emphasis on financial performance above stimulating citizen demand.

Of course, there have always been tensions between these competing value systems, and both are now being challenged to some extent, at a rhetorical level at least, in a range of government documents (see, for example, Cabinet Office, 1999; DoH, 1998). These documents are littered with references to improving accountability and ensuring the participation of individuals and groups, who are variously referred to as 'citizens', 'customers', 'self-supporting persons', 'stakeholders', 'consumers', 'voters', and 'individuals with duties'.

It has been argued that the New Labour administration has continued with the agenda established by the previous Conservative government to change welfare citizens from passive beneficiaries to active subjects (Dwyer, 1998; Williams, 1999; Dean et al, 2000). Williams (1999) outlines a framework of principles that, she suggests, 'puts flesh' on the rhetoric of 'equal worth' in the Third Way debate. The 'good-enough' principles for welfare identified by Williams are: interdependence; care; intimacy; bodily integrity; identity; transnational welfare; and voice. For the purpose of this chapter, it is 'voice', identified by Williams as permeating each of the other principles she discusses, which the new technologies could potentially enhance.

Williams (1999, p 683) argues that what underpins the transition of welfare users as dependent subjects to active participants is a belief that "the experience of the users of welfare services and their own definition of their needs is central to the organisation and delivery of welfare". There are three competing definitions of active citizenship from the New Right, New Labour and new social movements, each invoking different meanings of 'active'. We will explore the implications of these different meanings in relation to ICTs and social policy.

Citizen empowerment

It was discussed earlier how there is the potential for the technology and new media to be developed in a much more interactive manner. Cyber visionaries have argued that ICTs offer opportunities for citizens to become empowered (Rheingold, 1993; Barlow, 1996). By starting from the premise that ICTs are shaped and developed through social relations, they offer the potential of being used as a tool by the disadvantaged and excluded 'to challenge entrenched positions and structures' (Loader et al, 2000). The Internet and the World Wide Web allow individuals access to global information and potentially provide a space for participation without preconceived socially constructed identities based on gender, age, sexuality, ethnicity, disability and so on constraining meaningful interaction.

Hague and Loader (1999) acknowledge the limitations of this cyber-libertarian approach while identifying the key features of the interactive media and the claims made about the benefits to individual citizens. Such benefits are perceived as including: interactivity, development of global networks, the potential for free speech, free association, and the breakdown of nation-state identity. This latter factor is important in a number of respects. There is, for example, the developing ability to form cross-national coalitions sharing information and expertise in order better to understand and compare differing approaches and policy solutions, as well as to provide the opportunity for more effective lobbying for social policy reform. The ability to share information across geographic boundaries is transformed as the Net shrinks the time-space continuum. As geographical and time obstacles to information sharing are reduced, the main barrier to information sharing, apart from that of access discussed elsewhere, becomes language. Although English remains the most commonly used language on the Internet and the World Wide Web, the potential for all to participate is limited.

These empowering, visionary perspectives are, however, not without their critics (see Hague and Loader, 1999). Even so, there have undoubtedly been some major developments in the UK. Such developments are reflected in the work of CIRA[2] whereby we have seen a growth in local community groups or local areas accessing the Internet (see, for example, www.trimdon.org.uk; www.tvco.org.uk; and www.hendon-hub.org.uk). In addition, communities of interest have been developed on the Web providing emotional support and advice to a whole range of different groups.

Burrows et al (2000) note the formation of new virtual spaces designed specifically to deal with the British context. These are often Usenet news groups. As such, the development of computer mediated social support (CMSS) provides individuals with knowledge and information that can allow them to challenge professionals from a position of power (Burrows et al, 2000). Evidence from our own research has demonstrated how empowered individuals can feel. For example, a woman used the Internet to find out more information about an illness, Attention Deficit Hyperactivity Disorder (ADHD), from which her child suffered. She reported that when she visited the specialist involved in looking after her child, the information gathered from the Internet gave her, for the first time, the confidence to ask questions of the specialist and challenge some of the decisions being made about her child's care. She reported feeling more in control of her child's treatment as a result of this information. This woman continues to use the Internet to gather information but also actively contributes to various support groups in which she is involved[3].

The Internet's potential to enhance decision making for individuals is also demonstrated by Hardey (2001) in his research into health information online. Hardey finds that the Internet can provide a great deal of health information, advice and treatment. As such, the Internet can act as a resource for the publication and consumption of health information and in addition, potentially challenges the doctor/patient relationship. As Hardey (2001) notes, the growth of CMSS on the Internet in relation to health could contribute to the end of the medical monopoly over medical information.

However, Pleace et al (2001) argue that rather than counteracting the undermining of social insurance and the welfare state resulting from successive governments' expenditure cuts, computer mediated social support could be an instance of the Internet acting as a catalyst towards greater social division and inequality. Potentially however, some of the social experiments discussed earlier have been empowering for the individuals involved as they have often created their own Web pages and used this facility to provide information about themselves, their areas and their concerns. How effective such activities have been in informing policy and decision making remains to be seen. In our work, though, we are aware of projects now being developed that involve channelling the available access to the new technologies into projects that are intended to inform decision making processes (such as Birmingham Youth Parliament, UK Youth Parliament, Evaluating Telematics Based Community Development project at the University of Sunderland, and the work of the Hansard Society).

As briefly mentioned earlier, Pleace et al (2001) argue that the Internet could actually exacerbate existing equalities. It is also acknowledged that the UK government has apparently attempted to counteract such an eventuality, as demonstrated in the establishment of the Social Exclusion Unit and the formation of the Policy Action Team 15 and their subsequent report (PAT 15, 2000). However, in relation to CMSS discussed by Pleace et al (2001), they note that it will "potentially reinforce the capacity of an increasingly self-sufficient and reflexive middle class to place themselves in an advantageous position". Hardey (2001) also discusses this issue in relation to health care. He notes how there are well-known social and economic inequalities arising from chronic illness and disability which may exclude patients from using the Internet. Yet, at the same time, the effective use of technologies by middle class patients to obtain information and advice, might lead to their placing disproportionate demands on health care resources at the expense of others. If this were to happen, the advantages already experienced by the middle classes in accessing health resources would be reinforced and perpetuated.

The issue for social policy remains, then, what happens to those who are not in the polarised group of middle-class Internet users who are developing their own form of social support and social welfare through the new technologies? We would propose that there remain two key areas – access and skills – which need to be considered to ensure effective use of the Internet for all is achieved.

With regard to access, while we acknowledge that levels of access to new technologies including the Internet and the World Wide Web has increased dramatically, evidence shows that the take-up among people living in deprived neighbourhoods is below national average (PAT 15, 2000). The PAT 15 report argues that there are gaps in provision and barriers that effectively prevent some people accessing ICTs. Limitations in physical access remain a concern in relation to online welfare service delivery. Unequal access indicates that those already excluded might potentially suffer a 'double whammy' by being further excluded from the information provided online.

At the same time, even with growing access, we would argue that access to 'what', still remains a pertinent question in relation to ICTs. Our earlier notion that government appears to regard ICTs as good per se is illustrated by the growth of government websites. Each central government department has its own site which generally provide a mass of information about that department's work, and there are central pages which provide an overview of government (see, for example, www.ukonline.gov.uk, www.dss.gov.uk and www.hm-treasury.gov.uk). At the same time, there has been a major expansion of local government websites, which provide a range of information about local services, leisure facilities, guides and so on. While we are not denying the importance of these sites or the value of the information they are providing, we question their lack of interactivity. If, as suggested here, one of the main potential benefits to individual citizens in this Information Society is the ability to use the Internet to inform the decision making process, then it is important to allow those previously without a voice an input into government. If government offices do not allow meaningful interactivity on their sites, their impact remains limited.

We would contest that the access issue remains extremely important and requires further consideration and research. We have noted that it is not just physical access that is essential but also the quality of the product being accessed. At the same time, such access is grounded on having the knowledge and skills to make meaningful use of the new technologies. This leads on to our next potential problem for individual citizens.

Negotiating the Web

While there has been a growth in the number of facilities providing access to the Internet and the World Wide Web and, indeed, an expansion in access at home, individuals must have the skills to negotiate what they access. As one participant in our recent research commented, "it's like an encyclopaedia without an index." Negotiating this 'encyclopaedia' is complicated and can be extremely frustrating.

There has been a range of government-backed initiatives aimed at improving skills, such as *IT for All* and *WebWise*. As part of the Lifelong Learning agenda, universities and other providers have developed community-based courses such as an introduction to the Internet and basic Web design which have proved an effective method of skilling individuals. However, our research indicates that such formal training programmes are not sufficient to reach all individuals or indeed to ensure continued use and development of ICTs. The problem of trying to engage disaffected people by formal education and qualifications has proved to be difficult in some areas of the community, in particular in relation to many young people. It is therefore important that we find other ways of engaging with people and attracting them to explore the technologies.

One method that has proved effective when first working with specific community groups is the running of awareness sessions. Individuals are encouraged and supported to explore the Internet by focusing on their own interests. Such an informal approach can then lead to them enrolling on more formal courses. A range of such projects in which CIRA has been involved include Trimdon Digital Village (www.trimdon.org.uk), the Terminus Project at Saltburn[4] and the Ayresome Community Enterprise[5] At South Bank Women's Centre, 73 women enrolled on formal university courses with 30 completing and passing an introductory Internet/Web authoring course in 1999/2000.

In addition, the running of awareness sessions has proved extremely positive in a relatively new project, Tees Valley Communities On-Line[6]. The project manager and technician have worked informally with the communities involved, leading to the development of a website (www.tvco.org.uk) to which individual communities contribute. This site has been used to campaign against specific local issues and has also been used to positively promote the image of the local communities involved. Participants are learning technical skills but are also participating in the steering committee; perhaps as importantly, the project is extremely effective in breaking down some of the barriers which existed between these communities despite their geographic close proximity.

Another method, cascade training, has been developed by a local project, Hendon Hub (www.Hendon-Hub.org.uk) in Sunderland. This method has led to the appointment and training of an access worker in five community projects. The worker then supports other members of the group with the skills they have. Ultimately, it is intended that the access worker will pass on skills to other members of the projects so they can then go on to support other community members and so on. This approach has proved popular and effective at Hendon Hub, with some community members going on to more formal training courses and the development of other more informal training sessions in specific projects. For example, the Sunderland Catholic Youth Centre (www.hendon-hub.org.uk/scyc.htm) has established informal training for parents of young people who access the centre. Both the access workers and the young people support this training. In addition, the access worker in the Hendon Community Care Project (www.hendon-hub.org.uk/hccc.htm) has established a training suite that provides informal training to both its workers and the general public.

The key finding for us in relation to making full use of the new technologies in specific community projects relates to having a person working in the project capable of using the technology and engaging with others to develop their skills. The dilemma here, of course, is that many voluntary and community organisations have scarce resources and identifying the need for such a worker and securing funding can be problematic.

The potential problem for individuals, therefore, is gaining the skills necessary to make really effective use of the interactive aspects of new technologies. It is necessary to demonstrate to individuals not only how the new technologies are relevant to their lives and circumstances but also how they can use them to give themselves a voice. The key here, we would suggest, is that the training in using new technologies should not just be about training for work. While that is important, it is not the only benefit that can be derived.

Perhaps it is relevant to indicate the paradox here in relation to these two issues, access and skills, and government rhetoric. Perhaps the emphasis by government on formal training assists in limiting knowledge and ensures that individual citizens do not explore and develop their skills fully in relation to the new technologies. While government sites (and many others) remain providers of information only, there seems little need to encourage skill development beyond basic Web surfing. The challenge, therefore, is to find effective means of providing the skills necessary to make full use of the new technologies. In particular, providing these skills to those most disaffected and excluded is important when formal education might be something they want little or nothing to do with.

Conclusions

We are experiencing a major period of social, political and economic transformation from which a new welfare order is emerging. Within the context of this changing welfare order we can identify a clear move by government to introduce ICTs both to transform welfare and to deliver aspects of welfare. The key questions, however, are, first, what values are likely to inform the new welfare order and, second, how will these values impact on the adoption and the use of ICTs? We have put forward different interpretations of 'active citizenship' and argued that these are reflected in the way that the perspectives discussed have embraced the interactive capabilities and potential of the new technologies. However, the dominant influence on both the values of the new welfare order and, indeed, the use of new technologies to promote these values, are those of the New Labour government, the new social movements and self-help groups. We would argue that New Labour's assumption that ICTs are good per se, together with the growth of the use of the technology by the emerging self-help groups, mask the inequalities that continue to persist in relation to access and skills. Both of these perspectives in relation to social policy and ICTs have an idea of 'active citizenship' which are clearly different: nevertheless, to be 'active' in both cases assumes not just physical connectivity but also a desire to connect.

The impact of ICTs on welfare is, we note, complex and contradictory. Although the government might be trying to get as many people as possible online to reduce divisions in access based purely on wealth, how and whether people will participate remains unclear. To be an 'active citizen' in cyberspace requires the skills and confidence to engage with the technology – assets already identifiable with the middle-class participants of CMSS.

The discussion and debate we have highlighted here suggests the emergence of a multi-tiered 'wired welfare' community (Burrows et al, 2000). However, the question for social policy in many ways remains the traditional one of how we address existing inequalities in 'real' welfare services – but now in a period when inequalities seem set to be perpetuated by the developments of provision and delivery of services online. This raises a further issue, which cannot be fully considered here: while government proceeds with its agenda to wire people up and provide information and services online, there is still a whole range of welfare services which cannot be delivered by computer. The need for a home help, for example, is based on a very human – and in many ways 'physical' – need.

The final point, therefore, is that despite the potential of ICTs to encourage 'active citizenship', there is a danger that the provision of those more traditional, human welfare services will not be addressed. It may also be the case that the continued impact of the cultures of professionalism and managerialism within agencies and individual local authority departments could colonise ICT-mediated social policy service delivery and undermine many of the potential benefits that could accrue to online active citizens. As ever, the focus of contention concerns the utilisation of the means of production, with the new bourgeoisie of the 21st century apparently being unwilling to allow wider 'ownership' to develop. Are we doomed to repeat the errors of the past and will this Internet revolution prove to be yet another false dawn?

Notes

[1] The authors would like to express their thanks to Brian Loader for his comments on earlier drafts of this article.

[2] The Community Informatics Research & Applications Unit (CIRA) was established by the University of Teesside to investigate and critically analyse the social and economic factors shaping the development and application of new information and communication technologies (ICTs), such as the Internet, and their consequences for community development, economic restructuring and social exclusion. It is a multidisciplinary unit where social scientists, computer scientists, software engineers, project managers and designers are encouraged to combine their respective talents on particular research projects.

[3] The evidence referred to here relates to an ongoing evaluation of the impact of the introduction of Internet access to South Bank Women's Centre, part of an ERDF funded project.

[4] Terminus, in the centre of Saltburn, is a community facility which provides space for small businesses and houses an IT training suite. Set up in 1998, it is now a very successful venue for the University of Teesside's Local Learning Scheme. CIRA has equipped Terminus with 15 PCs all with Internet access and has organised a number of awareness events. For more information contact Terminus on tel 01287 624843, or e-mail: admin@terminus.org.uk.

[5] Ayresome Community Enterprise (ACE) is a volunteer-run community venture in central Middlesbrough. CIRA has facilitated a number of awareness and training events with ACE. In 1999 we were able to establish a suite of 10 computers linked to the Internet. ACE is a successful venue for delivery of University of Teesside Local Learning courses such as an introduction to IT, and Internet and Web authoring. For more information contact Ayresome Community Enterprise on Middlesbrough (01642) 649100, or e-mail: ace@tvcol.org.uk

⁶Tees Valley Communities On-Line (TVCO) is a project designed to use Internet technology to link six communities (Grangetown, Dormanstown, St. Hildas, South Bank, North Ormesby and Owton/Rossmere) as means to foster community development and economic regeneration. The project is funded by ERDF Resider funding.

References

Barlow, J.P. (1996) 'Declaration of the independence of cyberspace', *Cyber-Rights Electronic List*, 8 February.

Blair, T. (2000) Speech by the UK Prime Minister to the Knowledge 2000 Conference, 7 March, reproduced at www.guardianlimited.co.uk/ Archive/Article/0,4273,3971304.000

Burrows, R., Nettleton, S., Pleace, N., Loader, B. and Muncer, C. (2000) 'Virtual community care? Social policy and the emergence of computer mediated social support', *Information Communication & Society*, vol 3, no 1, pp 95-121.

Cabinet Office (1999) *Modernising government*, London: The Stationery Office.

Cabinet Office (2000) 'E-government – a strategic framework for public services in the information age', www.iagechampions.gov.uk/ strategy.htm

Chakravati, A.K. and Krishnan, A.S.A. (1999) 'Electronic government and the international scenario', Seminar on Electronic Governance, 27 January, Jaipur, Rajcomp.

Clarke, J., Cochrane, A. and McLaughlin, E. (eds) (1994) *Managing social policy*, London: Sage Publications.

Clarke, J. and Newman, J. (1997) *The managerial state: Power, politics and ideology in the remaking of social welfare*, London: Sage Publications.

Day, P. (2001) 'Participating in the information society: community development and social inclusion', in B.D. Loader and L. Keeble (eds) *Community informatics: Community development through the use of ICTs*, London: Taylor Francis/Routledge.

Dean, J., Goodlad, R. and Rosengard, A. (2000) 'Citizenship in the new welfare market: the purposes of housing advice services', *Journal of Social Policy*, vol 29, no 2, pp 229-45.

DoH (Department of Health) (1998) *Modernising social services*, London: The Stationery Office.

DoH (2000) *Information for social care. A framework for improving quality in social care through better use of information and information technology*, Consultation draft, www.doh.gov.uk/scg/information.htm

Dwyer, P. (1998) 'Conditional citizens? Welfare rights and responsibilities in the late 1990s', *Critical Social Policy*, vol 57, pp 493-517.

Giddens, A. (1994) *Beyond Left and Right: The future of radical politics*, Cambridge: Polity Press.

Hague, B. and Keeble, L. (1999) 'Good technology? Information and communication technologies and cultural change in the voluntary and community sector', Conference paper presented to the 5th NCVO, Researching the Voluntary Sector Conference, City University, London, 7-8 September.

Hague, B.N. and Loader, B.D. (eds) (1999) *Digital democracy*, London: Routledge.

Hardey, M. (1999) '"The story of my illness": personal accounts of illness on the internet', *Sociology of Health and Illness*, vol 21, no 6, pp 820-35.

Hardey, M. (2001: forthcoming) '"E-health": the internet and transformation patients into consumers producers of health knowledge', *Information Community and Society*.

HM Treasury (2000) *Spending review 2000: Cross-departmental review of the knowledge economy*, www.hm-treasury.gov.uk/sr2000/associated/knowledge/index.html

Hugman, R. (1991) *Power in the caring professions*, Basingstoke: Macmillan.

Johnson, N. (1981) *Voluntary social services*, Oxford: Basil Blackwell & Martin Robertson.

Lister, R. (1997) *Citizenship: Feminist perspectives*, Basingstoke: Macmillan.

Loader, B.D. (1998) 'Welfare direct: informatics and the emergence of self-service welfare?', in J. Carter (ed) *Postmodernity and the fragmentation of welfare*, London: Routledge.

Loader, B.D., Hague, B. and Eagle, D. (2000) 'Embedding the net: community empowerment in the age of information', in M. Gurstein (ed) *Community informatics*, Canada: IPG.

Loader, B.D. and Keeble, L. (eds) (2001) *Community informatics: Shaping computer-mediated social relations*, London: Taylor Francis/Routledge.

Milner, E. (1999) 'The "problem" of electronic government', in B.N. Hague and B.D. Loader, *Digitial democracy*, London: Routledge.

PAT 15 (2000) *Closing the digital divide: Information and community technologies in deprived areas*, Report by Policy Action Team 15, London: DTI.

Pleace, N., Burrows, R., Loader, B., Nettleton, S. and Muncer, S. (2001) 'The safety net? Some reflections on the emergence of virtual social support', in L. Keeble and B. Loader (eds) *Community informatics: Computer mediated social networks*, London: Taylor Francis/Routledge.

Rheingold, H. (1993) *The virtual community*, Reading, MA: Addison-Wesley.

Roche, M. (1992) *Rethinking citizenship: Welfare, ideology and change in modern society*, Cambridge: Polity Press.

Tang, P. (1998) 'Managing the cyberspace divide: government investment in electronic information services', in B.D. Loader (ed) *Cyberspace divide: Equality, agency and policy in the information society*, London: Routledge.

Taylor, I. (1995) 'Developing superhighways in the United Kingdom', *International Technology and Public Policy*, vol 13, no 3, pp 194-5.

Taylor, J.A. (1998) 'Governance and electronic innovation: whither the information polity?', *Information Communication & Society*, vol 1, no 2, pp 144-62.

Williams, F. (1999) 'Good-enough principles for welfare', *Journal of Social Policy*, vol 28, no 4, pp 667-87.

ELEVEN

Dis/counting the future

Tony Fitzpatrick

Introduction

Social policy has always had a stronger sense of the past than of the future. Systems of social insurance were meant to pool collective risks across time, with contributions appending the present to the past as a shelter against the uncertainties of the future. So even though the insurance principle is an actuarial fiction it established a de facto intergenerational contract. Even at its best, however, this contract extends across no more than two generations – a time horizon of about 50 years, too short for the challenges that we now face – and the rising inequalities of the last 20 years have placed social insurance under strain (Thomson, 1992). Why have *social* insurance systems when people are less willing to pay contributions to help insignificant others? Surely the affluent can pay for themselves and the poorest helped with various forms of means-tested provision! This is not to claim that social insurance is dying but neither can it be claimed that social insurance has been central to the socio-economic reforms of the last 20 years.

What this means is that an orientation to the known past is replaced by an orientation to a future that appears inherently unknowable. Therefore, the present takes on a vertiginous quality and the future seems always to fall away from us even as we tumble towards it with ever-greater velocity. And as time becomes a source of psychosis, a temporal anomie, so politicians and policy-makers reach for the pragmatic, the safe, the predictable. The new social democracy is merely that which demands that we streamline our descent for the sake of efficiency. Yet the more we apply a post-ideological managerialism to social reform, subjecting the present to a perpetual audit, the faster the rabbit-hole seals behind us.

So if social insurance systems lack a proper sense of the future, and if contemporary policy reforms treat the past as a sacrificial resource, can we devise a new temporal narrative (Kim and Dator, 1999)? Are we still capable of mirroring the shadows of the many possible futures that are cast upon the present through acts of collective imagination, or has this political imagination been lost forever? This chapter attempts to answer this question with reference to two of the greatest challenges we now face. Fitzpatrick (2001a) addresses environmental issues; here, we cover the main theoretical ground in greater depth and conclude by examining the new genetics.

The theoretical ground referred to is that of the debate concerning intergenerational justice. There is no space to cover anything but the margins of that debate (Sikora and Barry, 1978; Feinberg, 1980, pp 180–3), but we can extract from it what we need to construct a new narrative for policy making. To this end, we shall now discuss utilitarian, contractarian and communitarian approaches to the issue of intergenerational justice[1].

Parfit and the repugnant conclusion

Parfit (1984, p 377) begins with the Non-Identity Problem (N-IP):

> If a choice between two social policies will affect the standard of living or the quality of life for about a century, it will affect the details of all the lives that, in our community, are later lived. As a result, some of those who later live will owe their existence to our choice of one of these two policies. After one or two centuries, this will be true of everyone in our community.

What this means is that we cannot harm future generations. Imagine two policy options: policy R will give rise to Red people while policy B will give rise to Blue people. If we choice policy R will we be hurting anybody? According to the N-IP we will not. We cannot harm any Blue people, since they will now never exist, and we cannot harm our Red descendents because their existence is axiomatically preferable to the non-existence that would have resulted had we chosen policy B. Now think of a parallel scenario. Policy D leads to the depletion of natural resources and so to future generations whose lives are barely worth living; policy C leads to the conservation of resources and so to future generations whose well-being is comparable to our own. If the N-IP is correct then we may as well choose policy D (because C requires undesirable short-term sacrifices) without worrying about the consequences. In other words, the N-IP allows us to do whatever the hell we want without having to worry about future generations.

Parfit suspects that the N-IP can be overcome with reference to some objective standard of assessment: Theory X. However, in searching for Theory X Parfit (1984, p 388) encounters the Repugnant Conclusion: "For any possible population of at least ten billion people, all with a very high quality of life, there must be some much larger imaginable population whose existence, if other things are equal, would be better, even though its members have lives that are barely worth living."

Imagine two societies. In society A, 10 billion people each possess 100 utility units each (= 1,000 billion units); in society Z, 2,000 billion people each possess 1 utility unit each (= 2,000 billion units). On strictly utilitarian grounds we ought to prefer society Z, because 2,000 billion units is larger than 1,000 billion units, even though its inhabitants live lives of unimaginable suffering. Therefore, utilitarianism seems to demand the indefinite growth of future populations so long as total utility increases also. Few would regard this as desirable and yet Parfit insists that attempts to avoid the Repugnant Conclusion are inadequate (for example, Boonin-Vail, 1996).

Let us consider two such attempts. First, perhaps, we should apply a principle of *average* rather than total utility. This would imply that we should only permit the human population to increase to the point where mean utility begins to peak, that is, a point significantly less populated than society Z. Yet Parfit dismisses this escape route as it would prevent us from adding to the population those individuals who, although they would have lives worth living, would reduce the overall average. Second, perhaps, we should place a ceiling on the population's expansion on the grounds that, beyond a certain point, the value of additional utility diminishes at an ever-accelerating rate. Yet Parfit closes off this escape route also by observing that if we devalue additional utility then we are logically compelled to devalue additional *disutility*, that is, the equivalent of being increasingly untroubled at a society where there was more and more pain and suffering. We find it far easier to appeal to diminishing marginal utility than diminishing marginal disutility.

Ultimately, though, Parfit draws us back to the Repugnant Conclusion because of the Mere Addition Paradox (MAP)[2]. Imagine three possibilities:

A Ten billion people (Ax) who possess 100 utility units each;
B Twenty billion people who possess 75 utility units each;

$A+$ Ten billion people (Ax) who possess 100 utility units each plus, on another planet, an additional 10 billion people (Ay) who possess 25 units each.

Intuitively, most of us would claim that A is preferable to B and B is preferable to $A+$. Yet, according to Parfit, $A+$ is no worse than A because $A+$ has all of the attractions of A as well as an additional 10 billion people who live reasonably desirable lives. But if B is preferable to $A+$ and if $A+$ is no worse than A then we should, when all is said and done, prefer B overall, that is, more people with less utility per person. If the MAP is then applied consistently we eventually arrive back at the Repugnant Conclusion where we ought to create enormously large future populations even if their lives are barely worth living.

Attempts have been made to avoid the MAP and so the Repugnant Conclusion (Temkin, 1993, pp 218-27; Adams, 1997). For instance, if $A+$ *is* worse than A, on the grounds of it being more unequal, then our original intuition stands firm. Parfit resists this suggestion, though. Because $A+$ has everything that A has, in addition to the group Ay whose lives are worth living and who do not affect Ax, then the appeal to in/equality is the same as claiming that Ay should not exist. However, a counter to this argument might attack Parfit's requirement that Ax and Ay do not affect each other. If they do not affect each other (by being on different planets) then they cannot be considered as part of the same moral community and so $A+$ does not exist; but if they *are* part of the same moral community then the principle of equality is surely as important as the principle of utility.

Yet what this kind of philosophising does is to ignore the problem of transition. If A, B and $A+$ are compared in abstract isolation then the MAP may or may not follow, but in the real world of policy making we also have to consider the complex disutilities of transforming one kind of society into another:

> ... there may be no way of separating the question of whether one outcome is better than another from the question of whether one outcome *together with its history* is better than another outcome together with its history.... This would be contextualism with a vengeance, and to the extent that such worries have force, they must surely make us wonder whether consequentialist reasoning – which depends on our being able to arrive at a meaningful ranking of outcomes – must ultimately be jettisoned altogether. (Temkin, 1997, p 334; cf Hare, 1993, p 76)

Such suspicions are multiplied when we remember that our contexts also consist of (both present and future generations of) animals and the entire eco-system. Can a better approach to future generations be taken, therefore?

Rawls and just savings

Social policy has taken much less notice of the 'just savings principle' than it has of the 'difference principle'. Rawls (1972, pp 284-93; 1999, pp 145-7; Barry, 1989, pp 197-201; Hooft, 1999; Langhelle, 2000) introduces into the original position an ignorance as to where the participants are in history, meaning that they have to determine a savings rate that every actual generation would find to be just. In effect, all future generations are represented in the original position and all can expect to gain through the just savings principle, with the exception of the first generation who shoulder the initial burden but receive nothing in return. However, because each generation is assumed to care for its immediate descendants the first generation, too, can be expected to accept the just savings principle. This means that the synchronic and diachronic dimensions of Rawlsian justice are equally dependent upon one another: the task of each generation is to realise the demands of liberal justice while contributing to an intergenerational process of accumulation that enables closer and closer approximations to the just society which is contracted to in the original position.

The notion of 'immediate descent' is crucial in actually determining the appropriate rate. Those in the original position must ask themselves how much it is reasonable to save for the next generation based upon what they feel entitled to claim from the preceding generation. This parent/child model not only enables a fair rate of saving to be determined but ensures that no generation can envy the stock of resources possessed by either its ancestors or its descendants. Consequently, although the members of the original position do not know where they are in time, they do know that they are contemporaries who have sentimental ties to successive generations. Basically, then, a contractualist theory of justice must take into account the least advantaged of every generation:

> Whereas the first principle of justice and the principle of fair opportunity limit the application of the difference principle within generations, the savings principle limits its scope between them.... Saving is achieved by accepting as a political judgement those policies designed to improve

the standard of life of later generations of the least advantaged, thereby abstaining from the immediate gains which are available. (Rawls, 1972, pp 292-3)

It means that duties are inter- as well as intra-generational and that we harm future generations if we bequeath to them conditions that we, ourselves, would not consent to in an original position – arguably sidestepping the N-IP (but see below).

There are two main problems with Rawls's account. First, it is arguably too ambitious in its stipulation that the participants in the original position may be located *anywhere* in time. Although a *theory* of justice can afford to be this impartial, if we are to establish institutional systems of justice-enhancement then we must acknowledge the intuition that we should care more for our immediate predecessors than for those who will live many centuries and millennia after us (a discount rate). To exclude totally the particulars of our temporal situations from considerations of justice would seem too abstract and formal an approach. Of course, Rawls then reinserts a discount rate but one which is far *too* stringent, extending across no more than two future generations. So the second problem is that the just savings principle is not ambitious enough, having the quality of a personal inheritance made through ties of sentiment rather than a true cross-generational scheme of accumulation. Therefore, Rawls' theory of intergenerational justice is both too abstract *and* too sentimental.

Can we resolve this difficulty by (a) including all generations within the original position, and (b) eliminating the sentimental motivation? The problem with (a) is that it runs up against a version of the N-IP. Do we include everyone who *will* ever live? Yet this presupposes an advanced knowledge of the policies and principles that we are to adopt when it is precisely those policies and principles that we are trying to formulate. But perhaps we can include in the original position everyone who *could* ever live. Yet how would it be meaningful to include all potential people when such numbers would be infinite? Therefore, critics have demanded that we fall back on (b). Barry (1989) argues that Rawls' Humean influences must be discarded as justice cannot be founded upon the sentimental ties that we have for our successors and Rawls (1993, p 274) himself came to accept this. For Barry, then, Rawls is formulating not a theory of *inter*generational justice, as justice implies the kind of reciprocity and mutual advantage that cannot obtain between generations due to the unidirectionality of time; instead, Rawls is formulating principles to which all generations should rationally agree, what we might call a theory of 'meta-generational justice'.

However, this still leaves the objection that Rawls is being too ambitious. Although it might be the case that justice cannot be founded upon sentiment this does not mean passion and sentiment are irrelevant to considerations of justice. In short, we have yet to consider communitarian or solidaristic critiques of intergenerational justice.

A transgenerational community?

There are few communitarian critiques of the intergenerational debate (Renzong, 1998). Avner de-Shalit (1995) is one of the few to have attempted a communitarian account, one that essentially depends on hypothesising the existence of a transgenerational community. If communities are spatial entities then it seems absurd to deny that they are also temporal entities; and if communities are the most important source of identity and obligation then the future must be an important source of identity and so a referent to which I bear obligations. As Dobson (1998, p 105) points out, de-Shalit is here echoing O'Neill's (1993, pp 28-38) depiction of the transgenerational self. For although I, the being now in existence, cannot be harmed 50 years after my death, my reputation and my legacy *can* be damaged. Similarly, then, not only can the present generation harm future ones but *future generations can harm us and we can harm long-dead generations*! Therefore, there may well be a loose reciprocity between generations that grounds the notion of intergenerational justice after all.

The problem here, though, is that the present generation has to care that its legacy may be harmed. What if it does not? What if I don't give a damn what people think about me after my death? This implies that my reputation cannot be posthumously harmed precisely because my reputation is of somebody who didn't care about his reputation in the first place! Therefore, the communitarian account falls back upon the requirement that the present generation hold ties of sentiment to the future, that is, cares about its legacy; but if it does not care then mere appeals to sentiment are circular and so carry no weight. Therefore, we are referred back to a meta-generational theory of justice.

Take Goodin's (1985, pp 177-78; Agius, 1998) attempt to derive intergenerational obligations from the unilateral power that we hold over our descendants. Any capacity that they will possess to harm us is far outweighed by our capacity to harm them. In short, it is the vulnerability of others (humans, animals and future generations) that operates as the source of our duties: those duties may decline in intensity, with nearer generations counting for more than farther ones, but if we recognise as part of our moral community those over whom we have power then the discount rate will be far less myopic than that which we currently apply.

Unlike de-Shalit, however, Goodin allows sentimental ties to supplement rather than replace the contractarian approach. Once we remember that, for Rawls (1972, p 50; 1993, pp 3-46), the original position is a site of 'reflective equilibrium', and political rather than metaphysical, then our concern for the vulnerable is permitted to creep beneath the veil of ignorance. So we find a middle way between the over- and under-ambitious sides of Rawls' just savings principle: the original position is not locatable anywhere in time but nor are its inhabitants concerned only with their offspring.

According to what I would call 'Affective Meta-Generational Theory' (AMGT) the moral community extends beyond the human and beyond the present without the pretence that we can legislate for all beings at all times. It also allows us to factor problems of transition into our notion of well-being, for example, although on utilitarian grounds society P may be preferable to society Q, the affective elements of AMGT may disallow a transition to society Q if we, as members of society P, were being called upon to make unbearable sacrifices. In short, AMGT balances partiality and impartiality with reference to the particular (the established and imagined needs of the present and future, respectively) and the universal (the just savings principle). It is a contractualist theory tempered by elements of communitarianism[3]. In order to see how and why this theory translates into the debate concerning biopolicy we must first determine a desirable rate of discount.

Discount rates

We discount the needs and interests of our future selves for a variety of reasons: short-termism, uncertainty and a consciousness of our mortality. Technically, discounting refers to the means by which we gradually devalue future costs and benefits against, respectively, present benefits and costs (Lind, 1982; Portney and Weyant, 1999). At one extreme, we can imagine a refusal to discount at all, so that the interests of people a million years from now would mean as much to us as our interests – we will call this a discount rate of 0%; at the other, we have a refusal to value the interests of any generation but our own – we will call this a discount rate of 10%[4].

How are we to determine a discount rate which, lying between these extremes, is both practical and desirable? By and large, two answers have been given to this question.

First, there are those who favour a market discount rate. A benefit-cost analysis focuses upon the real rate of return on investment over a particular time horizon. What this implies is the use of real interest rates in calculating the discount rate and a 'private time preference' in which the time horizon is relatively short. The problem with this method is that the medium- to long-term future is discounted fairly heavily (Amsberg, 1995). For instance, let us imagine that an asteroid is passing close by which, during its next orbit in 200 years time, will hit Florida (Nordhaus, 1999, p 148). If the damage is estimated at $2 trillion at today's prices, and if we apply a 7% per year discount rate (a rate sanctioned by the US government) then it is not worth us currently spending anything more than $3 million in trying to save Florida 200 years from now!

Therefore, a second method defines a social discount rate where equity and fairness are as important as efficiency. This 'social time preference' looks farther than the lifespan of individuals and so favours a lower discount rate. For example, public sector projects tend to apply a social rate because governments can borrow at lower interest rates than those offered to private sector investors and because the risks attached to the investment are lower. (So the UK's Private Finance Initiative represents the intrusion of market discount rates into public sector projects.) The problem with this method is that the calculation of the actual rate becomes more a matter of prescriptive guesswork regarding the desirable distribution of costs and benefits across different generations (Cowen and Parfit, 1992).

The debate over discounting returned with the growth of environmental economics in the 1990s. If we set a discount rate that is too high (profligacy) then we might not be able to create and maintain a sustainable eco-system; if we set a rate that is too low (asceticism) then the present generation may be called upon to make sacrifices that are politically and culturally unrealistic. Is there an alternative? A complication in finding one involves what we might call the 'savings paradox'. Since material well-being has improved throughout recorded history it seems reasonable to assume that the future will be materially better-off than the present. Therefore, saving for the future by reducing present expenditure will only increase the gross wealth of the future, at a cost to the present, and so undermines the rationale for saving; however, if we do not save for future sustainability by reducing present consumption, then although the future may be materially better-off it will have to spend a far higher proportion of its wealth on environmental protection, thus increasing the rationale for saving. Is there a way around the savings paradox that allows us to determine an appropriate discount rate that ties into AMGT (cf Kula, 1997)?

Sustainable justice

The real problem with the paradox may be too narrow a conception of savings, investment and consumption. If these are conceived in terms of resource depletion then, because resources are ultimately finite, we are certainly left with a conflictual model of intergenerational relations: more burdens today means more benefits tomorrow, and vice versa (Schelling, 1995). Even if we assume a positive sum game, where the wealth of both the present and future can be simultaneously enhanced, any economy based upon resource depletion must make trade-offs between present and future needs: technological fixes and the like can postpone the trade-offs but cannot avoid the conflictual model itself. In short, resource depletion gives rise to intergenerational conflict. But what if we turn things on their head and imagine that our environmental economics derives from a cogent theory of meta-generational justice? Since this theory will demand concordance rather than conflict then our economic ethic will be based less upon depletion and more upon resource *preservation*. If what we consume are finite resources then higher savings may well imply lower consumption, and vice versa; but if what we consume (that is, enjoy as essential to our well-being) is the preservation of resources and the flourishing of the non-human then higher *savings* might well be a condition of higher *consumption*. So, the savings paradox is avoided by replacing a material with non-material conception of well-being (Tacconi and Bennett, 1995, p 218).

Let us recap before moving on. Contractualism is the best approach to the intergenerational justice debate. However, it is necessary to revise Rawls to avoid the problem of his original position being too impartial *and* too partial. This revision necessitates the introduction of some affective (communitarian) elements, yielding an AMGT where what is important is not so much what generations owe to one another, but their adherence to principles of social justice that, while not being ahistorical, span a greater time horizon than those we currently apply. How wide is this horizon, that is, what is the appropriate rate of discount? To decide this we need to overcome the savings paradox by adopting a non-conflictual model of non-material well-being. My argument now will be that AMGT translates into principles of sustainable justice. To see why, let us return to our ascetics and profligates.

Ascetics favour a high-low approach, that is, high savings plus a low discount rate; profligates favour a low-high approach, that is, low savings plus a high discount rate (cf Dahle, 1998; Neumayer, 1999). Since asceticism seems to be far closer to the non-material ideal should we choose a high-low approach as our principle of sustainable justice? If we could instantly transport ourselves into an economy based upon resource preservation that answer might well be yes. But two objections should give us pause. First, since we used the problem of transition against Parfit it would be inconsistent to ignore the hows and whys of transition from one type of economy to another. Second, since we also drew a distinction between theories of justice and systems of justice, vis-à-vis Rawls, then we have to allow for a shortfall between the one and the other during the transitional period. To put it simply, pragmatics and political expediency might require a more moderate principle of sustainable justice (there is also a more ethical reason, see below).

So an alternative is a low-low approach where the discount rate is low but so, in the short-term at least, is the savings rate[5]. The rationale here is to apply a low discount rate in order to effect the cultural revaluation which, in the course of time, would alter collective notions of savings and consumption (along the lines suggested above) and permit the economic transition which is crucial; in the interim, we have to work within an economy of resource depletion which may well mean not asking people to make burdensome sacrifices. If social and environmental sustainability become associated with grim austerity (as the Right wing hope they will) then the case for social and environmental (or sustainable) justice will be defeated. If, however, sustainable justice can be established as meaning not less investment, consumption and spending but different ways of investing, consuming and spending then the Green argument can become a new orthodoxy. This means that we have to both count the future (low discount rate) and discount it (low savings rate) at the same time. (Before misunderstanding sets in, an important qualification should be added. Although a low savings rate is being advocated, this rate would still be higher than the one that currently prevails. So although it is wrong to assume that the road to sustainability is paved with the ruins of a consumer society it *is* the case that Green consumption implies less overall consumption than current levels.)

Does a low-low approach satisfy the contractualist theory defended above (putting aside the caveat of endnote 3)? Rawls was criticised because he (a) locates the original position anywhere in history, and (b) specifies that participants all belong to a single generation. By contrast, AMGT allows the participants to know approximately where they are in history while including within the original position all representatives from within that time horizon. Let us assume a horizon of 200 years stretching from 2000 to 2200[6]. The participants know this, and are therefore aware of what is at stake environmentally, though none of the individuals know where they themselves belong. Individuals are unlikely to advocate profligacy in case they should find themselves in an environmental wasteland of later generations; though nor is asceticism likely to be popular as this imposes draconian sacrifices on earlier generations. So, a low-low approach seems like a reasonable compromise in that all generations are valued (low discount rate) but earlier generations are permitted to use and transform the world's resources so long as, in doing so, they improve both the condition of the eco-system and humans' ability to appreciate non-monetary values.

If these assumptions are correct then we are left with a principle of sustainable justice that includes:

1. Intragenerational equity (difference principle).
2. Intergenerational equity (just savings).
3. The question of transition.
4. Cultural revaluation (a revision of our economic ethics).

So although (1) and (2) do not necessarily lead to a conflictual model, (3) suggests that some conflict cannot be avoided though it can be smoothed out over time with reference to (4). If welfare means GDP growth then, given finite resources, there are trade-off decisions to be made regarding the distribution of sacrifices, that is, between (1) and (2). But if welfare were to imply a revaluation of wealth so that it embodies the non-material – point (4) – then trade-offs become less urgent, for example, the future's enjoyment of the natural environment is not reduced by our enjoyment of the same, and vice versa. We make all generations wealthy by revaluing what we mean by wealth. In addition to reasons of political expediency, though, there is an additional consideration: what about the poor? How do we make the difficult distributional decisions now?

We could argue that inequality is damaging to sustainability for two main reasons (Stymne and Jackson, 2000). First, because those at the bottom over-consume resources as a means of trying to catch the affluent and perform environmentally damaging practices as a side-effect of coping with their deprivation. Second, those at the top over-consume resources as a means of maintaining their relative position and so pollute in greater proportions also. Consequently, reducing inequality leads to sustainability. However, others disagree. If equality contradicts our acquisitive instincts, our desire for positional goods, then it will itself be unsustainable and load additional pressures upon the environment as people attempt to recreate a stratified society.

As an egalitarian, this author would acknowledge the force of this argument at a lower level of economic development, that is, an equality of scarcity is likely to be unsustainable. But does the argument carry the same force against an equality of affluence (Perrings and Ansuategi, 2000)? Where both basic needs and acquisitive desires can be satisfied then any society which does not reconfigure its economic values resembles a collection of adults who still imagine that they are children by refusing to release the toys that they used to depend upon. Therefore, an equality of affluence has a prima facie desirability. But what kind of temporal trade-off does equal affluence require? Here, we are faced with another paradox: if we prefer present redistribution then we reduce the resources that are available for future redistribution; however, if present redistribution is effective then there may be no need for future redistribution! Therefore, an equality of affluence has to imply redistribution that is more efficacious and long term than that of the welfare state. Can we square the circle of assisting both the present and future poor? This challenge is taken up in Fitzpatrick (2001a).

Biopolicy

Sustainable justice therefore seems to require a low-low approach where we allow for the problem of transition and the urgent interests of the poor. We are ready to say something about the new genetics, for the new genetics has the power to upset the principle of sustainable justice if biotechnology is misapplied. To put it simply, a progressive biopolicy is that which either facilitates or does not contravene sustainable justice. Therefore, any application of biotechnology that undermines the difference and the just savings principles should be avoided. This means adapting the directive noted earlier: we should not require the future to inherit genetic characteristics that we, ourselves, would not consent to in an original position. As Harris (1998, p 214) points out, this can require genetic intervention (to remove harmful dangers) *and* non-intervention (so that we do not cause harm), although with a presumption in favour of the latter. For Buchanan et al (2000, p 342) this presumption on the side of caution is because the well-being of the future is guaranteed by preserving the ability of future people to make their own autonomous decisions, that is, by not narrowing their options through reckless engineering. For Fitzpatrick (2001b) this translates into a defence of the precautionary principle and of an ethic of 'differential egalitarianism' in order that the conditions of autonomy can be protected.

Fitzpatrick (2001b) argues that we must avoid over-prescriptive views of what a meaningful human life involves in order to avoid assumptions regarding normality that invoke homogenous notions of what it means to be human. A progressive biopolicy therefore requires an application of biotechnology that avoids reductionism by allowing difference-respecting discourses and practices to circulate within socially egalitarian environments. This implies that in addition to the usual values upon which social policy is based – welfare, equality and liberty – a respect for difference demands the addition of a fourth: precaution. Fitzpatrick (2001b) then illustrates what an egalitarian biopolicy might mean in practice through an investigation of the following.

First, there are the issues that genetic screening raise for health and life insurance. One danger is that of a 'laissez faire eugenics' where, in a purely free market, those who are both poor and genetically disadvantaged may experience a double discrimination. In the case of health insurance the obvious solution is to strengthen socialised forms of insurance in order to ensure that the costs of genetic conditions are absorbed into the collective pooling of risks. Where social insurance is less feasible, as in the case of life insurance, and a private market is permissible, then the private market could reasonably be required to pay a sumptuary tax in return for being allowed to profit in what is essentially a public good. Therefore, rather than accepting the insurance industry's line that adverse selection demands the compulsory disclosure of genetic information we should be redefining the costs of adverse selection as such a tax.

Second, there are issues relating to gene therapy (Engelhardt, 1998). At present there is a broad consensus in favour of distinguishing: (a) treatment versus enhancement, and (b) somatic cell therapy versus germ cell therapy. If this is the case then somatic cell therapy designed to aid the medical treatments of the present generation seems relatively unproblematic. However, some have questioned whether these distinctions can be maintained forever. For instance, if I am free to influence and even determine my descendants' future by providing them with a private education and other social advantages, then why should I not be able to influence/determine their future through germ-line intervention as well? One way of answering this question is to point out that enhancement and germ cell therapy are not desirable because they contravene the just savings principle (fair equality of opportunity between generations) by allowing today's affluent to maintain their advantages through each and every tomorrow (Kahn, 2000).

Genetically modified foods also raise questions relevant to intergenerational issues. The advocates of GM foods (Ridley, 1999) argue that they are more resistant to pesticides and produce the yields necessary to feed the world's already underfed populations. The critics (Rifkin, 1998) argue that the opposite is true because GM foods reduce genetic diversity, make Third World agriculture dependent upon First World agribusiness, could *increase* the use of pesticides by creating 'superweeds' through cross-pollination, and may introduce unanticipated effects into plant and animal (and human) species.

In the absence of conclusive evidence for or against GM foods vis-à-vis sustainable justice, the precautionary principle suggests that nations impose a moratorium upon the use of GM foods, one that might need to be indefinite should experiments upon GM foods be impossible without generating the kind of risks that moratoria and experiments are meant to reduce in the first place. Essentially, the argument is that, without compelling reasons to the contrary, we should regard biological diversity as more conducive to intergenerational justice than genetic homogeneity (Tacconi and Bennett, 1995). Similar arguments apply to the commodification of the genome, where biotech companies who devise methods of screening and engineering patent the genes disclosed by such techniques (Agius, 1998). This has implications for public sector research and treatment should royalties be payable to those biotech companies who are successfully privatising the biological commons. The principle of sustainable injustice warns against this dual process of genetic homogeneity and commercial monopolisation (Juengst, 1998).

Finally, Fitzpatrick (2001b) deals with the emerging conflicts between reproductive freedoms and social diversity. Biotechnological control can involve the filtering out of undesirable qualities (certain diseases and syndromes) and the 'filtering in' of qualities that are regarded as socially desirable (height, attractiveness, intelligence). These are issues that have exercised and worried the disability rights movement. If we can prevent suffering by eliminating syndromes that offer their bearers only a low quality of life then why hesitate? The problem is, who is to decide what constitutes a 'low quality of life'? If we allow physical and mental disabilities to be wiped from the human genome then is this vastly different from the 'designer babies' that so many find distasteful? Fitzpatrick (2001b) defends a regulated approach to these issues, where we attempt to both reduce suffering and respect the diversity of human experience.

So, the intergenerational debate impacts on the new genetics directly. If we start to genetically engineer on a frequent basis then we may be engaging in a high-risk strategy where future generations inherit characteristics that were either unintended or that they regard as undesirable. Then again, a strategy of non-intervention may produce similar effects. Surely they will not thank us for failing to eliminate certain debilitating syndromes and conditions that have a direct genetic causation. Therefore, the term 'regulated eugenics' is meant to convey the notion that although erring on the side of non-intervention may be the right thing to do, we should not imagine that this absolves us from making complex decisions about the genetic characteristics of future generations, nor from responsibility if the decisions we make turn out to be incorrect.

Obviously, this is not intended to be the last word on the matter. Many more questions have occurred during the writing of this chapter than there has been time to address. However, given social policy's general neglect of such questions, the hope is that the discussion here has stirred something. Do you disagree with the arguments advanced above? Good – now explain why.

Notes

[1] I am going to ignore libertarian approaches (Epstein, 1992; cf Braybrooke, 1992) as too simplistic.

[2] What follows is a simplified and adapted version of the first MAP (there are three in all).

[3] However, we are still left with the N-IP and the impossibility of populating the original position with all those who either will or might exist. An alternative is to imagine, say, 12 possible policy regimes, leaving us with an original position that is large but not infinite in size. The problem with this is that individuals could be expected to vote for a high-population regime (regardless of the implications for justice) on the grounds that they might be voting themselves into non-existence otherwise! A solution is either to exclude population policy from the original position or, if this is unrealistic, to acknowledge the limits of

any anthropocentric philosophy, since population size must take into account present and future generations of animals and the entire eco-system. In short, we avoid the N-IP by subsuming contractualism within an ecocentric ethic and arguing that we *can* harm future generations (whoever they may be) by bequeathing to them an unsustainable environment (cf Page, 1999).

[4] For simplicity's sake I am using a 0-10 scale and I am assuming no overlap between generations. Nor am I going to discuss whether the discount rate is constant or non-constant.

[5] A high-high approach is self-contradictory.

[6] The precise length of the time horizon will vary; for example, biopolicy makers might have an horizon of two centuries (8-10 generations) whereas policy concerning nuclear energy must have a time horizon of several millennia.

References

Adams, R. (1997) 'Should ethics be more impersonal?', in J. Dancy (ed) *Reading Parfit*, Oxford: Blackwell.

Agius, E. (1998) 'Patenting life', in E. Agius and S. Busuttil (eds) *Germ-Line intervention and our responsibilities to future generations*, Dordrecht: Kluwer Academic Publishers.

Amsberg, J. (1995) 'Excessive environmental risks: an intergenerational market failure', *European Economic Review*, vol 39, pp 1447-64.

Barry, B. (1989) *Theories of justice*, Hemel Hempstead: Harvester Wheatsheaf.

Boonin-Vail, D. (1996) 'Don't stop thinking about tomorrow: two paradoxes about duties to future generations', *Philosophy & Public Affairs*, vol 25, no 4, pp 267-307.

Braybrooke, D. (1992) 'The social contract and property rights', in P. Laslett and J. Fishkin (eds) *Justice between age groups and generations*, New Haven and London: Yale University Press.

Buchanan, A., Brock, D., Daniels, N. and Wikler, D. (2000) *From chance to choice*, Cambridge: Cambridge University Press.

Cowen, T. and Parfit, D. (1992) 'Against the social discount rate', in P. Laslett and J. Fishkin (eds) *Justice between age groups and generations*, New Haven and London: Yale University Press.

Dahle, K. (1998) 'Toward governance for future generations', *Futures*, vol 30, no 4, pp 277-92.

de-Shalit, A. (1995) *Why posterity matters*, London: Routledge.

Dobson, A. (1998) *Justice and the environment*, Oxford: Oxford University Press.

Engelhardt, H.T. (1998) 'Human nature genetically re-engineered: moral responsibilities to future generations', in E. Agius and S. Busuttil (eds) *Germ-line intervention and our responsibilities to future generations*, Dordrecht: Kluwer Academic Publishers.

Epstein, R. (1992) 'Justice across the generations', in P. Laslett and J. Fishkin (eds) *Justice between age groups and generations*, New Haven and London: Yale University Press.

Feinberg, J. (1980) *Rights, justice and the bounds of liberty*, Princeton, NJ: Princeton University Press.

Fitzpatrick, T. (2001a) 'Making welfare for future generations', in M. Cahill and T. Fitzpatrick (eds) *Social Policy & Administration*, special edition.

Fitzpatrick, T. (2001b: forthcoming) 'Before the cradle', *Journal of Social Policy*.

Goodin, R. (1985) *Protecting the vulnerable*, Chicago, IL: University of Chicago Press.

Hare, R.M. (1993) *Essays on bioethics*, Oxford: Clarendon Press.

Harris, J. (1998) *Clones, genes and immortality*, Oxford, Oxford University Press.

Hooft, H. (1999) *Justice to future generations and the environment*, Dordrecht: Kluwer Acadmic Publishers.

Juengst, E. (1998) 'A global human resource?', in E. Agius and S. Busuttil (eds) *Germ-line intervention and our responsibilities to future generations*, Dordrecht: Kluwer Academic Publishers.

Kahn, J. (2000) 'Genetic fixes and future generations', *Journal of Andrology*, vol 21, no 3, p 356.

Kim, T.-C. and Dator, J. (eds) (1999) *Co-creating a public philosophy for future generations*, Westport, CN: Praeger.

Kula, E. (1997) *Time discounting and future generations*, Westport, CA: Quorum Books.

Langhelle, O. (2000) 'Sustainable development and social justice: expanding the Rawlsian framework of global justice', *Environmental Values*, vol 9, pp 295-323.

Lind, R. (ed) (1982) *Discounting for time and risk in energy policy*, Baltimore, MD: John Hopkins University Press.

Neumayer, E. (1999) 'Global warming: discounting is not the issue but substitutability is', *Energy Policy*, vol 27, pp 33-43.

Nordhaus, W. (1999) 'Discounting and public policies that affect the distant future', in P. Portney and J. Weyant (eds) *Discounting and intergenerational equity*, Washington, DC: Resources for the Future.

O'Neill, J. (1993) *Ecology, policy and politics*, London: Routledge.

Page, E. (1999) 'Intergenerational justice and climate change', *Political Studies*, vol 47, pp 53-66.

Parfit, D. (1984) *Reasons and persons*, Oxford: Oxford University Press.

Perrings, C. and Ansuategi, A. (2000) 'Sustainability, growth and development', *Journal of Economic Studies*, vol 27, no 1/2, pp 19-37.

Portney, P. and Weyant, J. (eds) (1999) *Discounting and intergenerational equity*, Washington, DC: Resources for the Future.

Rawls, J. (1972) *A theory of justice*, Oxford: Oxford University Press.

Rawls, J. (1993) *Political liberalism*, New York, NY: Columbia University Press.

Rawls, J. (1999) *Collected papers*, edited by Samuel Freeman, Cambridge, MA: Harvard University Press.

Renzong, Q. (1998) 'The eugenics of the future', in E. Agius and S. Busuttil (eds) *Germ-line intervention and our responsibilities to future generations*, Dordrecht: Kluwer Academic Publishers.

Ridley, M. (1999) *Genome*, London: Fourth Estate.

Rifkin, J. (1998) *The biotech century*, London: Orion Books.

Schelling, T. (1995) 'Intergenerational discounting', *Energy Policy*, vol 23, no 4/5, pp 395-401.

Sikora, R. and Barry, B. (eds) (1978) *Obligations to future generations*, Philadelphia, PA: Temple University Press.

Stymme, S. and Jackson, T. (2000) 'Intra-generational equality and sustainable welfare: a time series analysis for the UK and Sweden', *Ecological Economics*, vol 33, pp 219-36.

Tacconi, L. and Bennett, J. (1995) 'Economic implications of intergenerational equity for biodiversity conservation', *Ecological Economics*, vol 12, pp 209-23.

Temkin, L. (1993) *Inequality*, Oxford: Oxford University Press.

Temkin, L. (1997) 'Rethinking the good, moral ideals and the nature of practical reasoning', in J. Dancy (ed) *Reading Parfit*, Oxford: Blackwell.

Thomson, D. (1992) 'Generations, justice, and the future of collective action', in P. Laslett and J. Fishkin (eds) *Justice between age groups and generations*, New Haven and London: Yale University Press.

TWELVE

New Labour, human nature and welfare reform

Martin Hewitt

In recent years the notion of human nature has returned to centre stage of social policy and politics. According to Alan Deacon "the debate about the future of welfare has entered a crucial and extraordinarily interesting phase" characterised by "the prominence accorded ... to questions of character, behaviour and morality" (1997, p 131; see Hewitt, 2000). Politicians and academics have shown renewed interest in the importance of theories of human nature and character in public policy. Margaret Thatcher claimed that the success of her policies was based on "clear, firmly held principles which were themselves based on a right understanding of politics, economics and above all human nature" (quoted in Shrimsley, 1996). Critical of this view, Tony Blair (1995) has argued that his politics "draws on a broader and therefore more accurate notion of human nature than one formulated on insular self-interest." Yet the debate about the importance of self-interest in defining human nature is no longer one between the Right and the Left, but is found at the hub of centre-left politics. Politicians such as Frank Field now argue that self-interest is the most important among the different human motivations that welfare reform should address (1997, p 165). Today, leading politicians use theories of human nature as one of the principal means of justifying policy.

One reason for the renewed interest in human nature is the realisation that the justification for different political values derives from differing and often competing views of human nature. During the postwar decades, the Right saw human nature as driven by the dominant motivation of self-interest, while the Left saw more collective sentiments as dominant. For a free-market thinker like Sir Keith Joseph (1976, pp 59-60), the principal human "motive is not goodwill.... [I]t is enlightened self-interest", whereby through the market "the self interest of the businessman is harnessed to the interest of his customer by competition". For a socialist like Titmuss (1970, p 225), a "deep human motive" of altruism resides in human nature such that "the ways in which society organises and structures its social institutions – and particularly its health and welfare systems – can encourage or discourage the altruistic in man".

Although there has been a major reconfiguration of the politics of Left and Right since the 1970s, human nature remains an important issue defining politics. Jordan's recent analysis (1998, p 38) of, among other things, the "characteristic view of human individuality" underpinning the Blair–Clinton orthodoxy sees human nature in terms of sentiments of obligation and self-interest – sentiments we will examine in more detail later. Obligations are fulfilled in the 'moral economy' of households, voluntary associations and communities, and self-interest in the market economy of work, based on relations of equivalent exchange rather than mutual obligation. However, national prosperity in the changed world of international competition requires individuals to extend their obligations from the moral economy to the market economy of work, which is now invested with a new work ethic and is no longer a matter solely of freedom of choice (as it was for neo-liberals). The duty to work and contribute to greater national prosperity is as important as the duty to be good parents, neighbours and citizens. To this end governments now promote greater skills flexibility, productivity and competitively priced goods, higher rewards for work including welfare supplements to low wages and childcare, and improving standards of living (Jordan, 1998, pp 38-43).

Notwithstanding the interest in human nature, the appeal to motivational assumptions as justifications for social policy has its critics. Welfare policy has emphasised one propensity to the detriment of others –altruism rather than self-interest (for example, Bell et al, 1994); has failed to give a balanced account that reflects the complexity of human motivation, "where altruism is more equally weighted with self-interest" (Field 1996, p iii; also Green 1993, p 1); and has failed to address the fundamental changes in post-traditional societies that impact on the nature of selfhood (Giddens, 1994).

Troubled by the uncertainty over exactly what constitutes human nature, Julian Le Grand (1997) argues that policy makers should design policies that do not require accounts of human nature for their justification – accounts of motivation he caricatures as altruistic *knights*, self-interested *knaves*, and compliant *pawns*. He proposes (Le Grand, 1997, p 165) that we should "accept our ignorance about what actually motivates people and ... try and design what might be termed *robust* strategies: strategies or institutions that are robust to whatever assumption is made about human motivation". This robustness treats assumptions about human nature as ideologies that can dominate and even mislead public policy.

However, this suggests that arguments in social policy based on human nature tend to focus on one dominant motivation or principal reason for human conduct to the exclusion of others. In fact, human nature is made up of complex motivations and reasons for action.

In examining human nature reasoning in social policy this chapter seeks to show that theories of human motivation are more complex than is often supposed, and that they are constructed around conflicting ideas (for a development of this approach see Hewitt, 2000; for a broader perspective see Cowen, 1994). It will further show that this complexity has until recently been held together by a – not always explicit – suturing device conjoining different principles about how welfare institutions should distribute resources to those in need. However, the profound social and economic changes shaping welfare, the emergence of greater cultural diversity in society, and the demands for new forms of welfare more sensitive to this diversity, all mean that traditional unifying principles – such as the national minimum – are no longer tenable for a transformed welfare state. This poses a serious challenge to New Labour in its desire to modernise welfare in keeping with traditional albeit broader ideas about human nature, and to marshal welfare provisions for the task of developing human potential in an age characterised by cultural diversity and international competition.

Models of human nature

Discourses on human nature in 20th century social policy, whether social democratic or neo-liberal, consist in complex accounts that draw on four distinct ideal typical models – presently termed *atomistic, organic, basic needs* and *mutualist* – derived from single axiomatic principles of human motivation. These different models have been combined into different accounts that have each played a role in the formation of social policy during the last century, as seen in particular in the roles played by social democratic and neo-liberal accounts of human nature.

First, the *atomistic model* held by neo-liberals proposes that human nature consists of individuals motivated by self-interest. In this individualist theory of motivation, individuals rely primarily on the market for their needs (Hayek, 1943, p 27), are bound by the rule of law (Hayek, 1943, p 54), and conform to moral rules (Hayek, 1960, p 62).

A supplement to this model – important for social policy – argues that individuals who are unable to participate in the labour market because of age, disability or sickness should have their needs met by residual state welfare and charity. In this way the atomistic model of human nature supports a *residual needs* model of human needs, found in 19th century Poor Law and 20th century means-tested provisions. This residual model complements the atomistic model by assuming that, because the non-active residuum of dependants can be differentiated from the economically active, they will have a minimum effect on the free circulation of labour and commodities in the market.

Second, the *organic model* represents an enduring conception of human nature in the social democratic tradition, and in some strands of rightist thought – specifically Conservative and Christian Democratic – about the sentiments of identity binding the family, community and nation. It asserts that individuals have a natural tendency to live in social groups in order to fulfil their physical, emotional and spiritual needs and that individual fulfilment is contingent on the welfare of society at large. The common good depends on the welfare of each individual; and the individual's welfare on the maintenance of the common good. This model became more interventionist with the emergence of the British Idealists and New Liberals in their response to the social upheavals of 19th century industrialisation and urbanisation. It has a long pedigree that extends from the Charity Organisation Society (Vincent and Plant, 1984) to the recent communitarian movement in America and Britain (for example, Etzioni, 1995). The organic model is now central to Tony Blair's vision of the Third Way in welfare reform (Blair, 1998; Blair and Schroeder, 1999).

Third, the *basic needs model* is found in the proposals of the Webbs and of Beveridge for a national minimum. It argues that individuals have common basic needs that must be met before their individually different needs are met. This division between two orders of needs provides the grounds for different political and economic arrangements for meeting need: basic needs should be met collectively and individually different needs privately in the market (Beveridge, 1942, pp 6-7). In democratic societies all individuals have a universal right to sufficient resources to meet their basic needs. It therefore implies a moral as well as an empirical demarcation of individuals. Individuals are divided into those who, on the one hand, once their basic needs are met, have the physical and mental capacities to live independently and to help their less fortunate neighbours, and those who, on the other hand, have a claim on collective welfare because they are insufficiently endowed with these capacities, or because these capacities remain unrealised because of misfortune or deprivation. The model of common basic needs assumes a level of need-satisfaction that is universal to all, unlike the residual model that acknowledges a narrower range and lower level of needs, with provisions targeted selectively at the poorest.

Finally, social policy employs a fourth model based on the principle of *mutualism*. Like the organic model, it is premised on the assumption that human beings meet their needs by working cooperatively with others. Human fulfilment and well-being are founded on relationships of reciprocity and cooperation among individuals engaged in the work of producing goods and services for each other. Thereby individuals come to recognise their common human nature in each other. Reciprocity creates the conditions for realising universality and solidarity among humankind within a framework that includes a large element of voluntary obligation. This model was present in the British Idealists whose ideas appealed to New Liberals and the Charity Organisation Society. The model resurfaces in Tawney (1964), Beveridge (1948) and Titmuss (1970), and in the recent debates on mutuality (for example, Holman, 1993; Blair, 1995; Field, 1996) and stakeholding (Hutton, 1996a, chapter 12, 1996b, chapter 12).

Social democracy and human nature

The social democratic philosophy of welfare influenced social policy from the early part of the 20th century to the Labour governments of the 1970s, and embraced the ideas of reformers as politically distinct as Fabians, such as the Webbs, and liberals such as Keynes and Beveridge. This section examines the social democratic tradition as a standard by which to compare and contrast New Labour's position on human nature in the following section.

The social democratic conception of welfare is based on a complex account of human nature that draws on all of the four simple or axiomatic models described above. The *organic model* had a formative influence at a time when late 19th century liberalism was developing a more collectivist approach to government in response to the problems of industrial society. In the 20th century the *basic needs* model influenced thinking about the government's role in managing the problems of social deprivation, especially in developing universal policies guaranteeing national minimum protection for all. The *mutualist model* appealed to voluntary forms of collective welfare begun in the late 19th century by Friendly Societies, mutual aid, and cooperatives, which survived well into the 20th century but became more marginal after 1945.

For key writers who identified with or were close to the social democratic tradition, such as the Webbs and Beveridge, state welfare was concerned to meet universal basic needs and organised in terms of a range of national minima. Beyond the minimum, an 'extension ladder' of voluntary provision (Webb and Webb, 1911, p 252) was provided by charities, supported by voluntary donations and dispensed by volunteers or paid professionals, by 'voluntary insurance' based on occupational or private insurance, and by the 'mutual aid' of community organisations and cooperatives (see Brenton, 1985, p 17; Williams and Williams, 1987, pp 20-1; Hewitt, 1992, p 27). While market provision, giving choice and command over resources to the better off, was throughout given a place in social democratic welfare, it was supplementary to basic needs provision. In this way the *atomistic model* of human nature also informed social democratic welfare, though given a subsidiary role to state welfare. Social democrats could claim with some justification that the provision of universal services for common needs helped to prevent the dangers of rampant individualism, inequality and social fragmentation which an unregulated market could have unleashed (Crosland, 1956, pp 141, 145; Marshall, 1963, p 107 and passim; Titmuss, 1968, p 135 and passim; Townsend, 1979, p 64). In the postwar decades, social democrats who supported the mixed economy of private and public provision implicitly or explicitly adhered to this complex account of human nature based on the component notions of basic needs, mutualism and delimited self-interest (Crosland, 1956, pp 105-12; Marshall, 1963, p 87; Robson, 1976, p 82).

The British welfare state was predicated on each of these four notions of human nature, with the notion of the state's obligation to meet need providing the dominant theme. The National Minimum formed a particular institutional and discursive device or 'suture' (see Laclau and Mouffe, 1985) joining universal, individual and mutual needs constituting the complexity of human nature (see Hewitt, 1998). This suture or 'line' represented a discursive figure that signified several kinds of division, unification and classification, which can be seen most clearly in the Beveridge Report (1942). First, the National Minimum articulated an institutional principle unifying the different sectors of state and non-state provision in 'cooperation'. Thereby, in establishing a national minimum, the state would "leave room and encouragement for voluntary action by each individual to provide more than that minimum for himself and his family" (Beveridge, 1942, p 7). Second, it signified a principle of classification demarcating common needs from individually different needs. Throughout, the Report distinguished between the "normal needs" (Beveridge, 1942, p 15) or "essential universal needs" (Beveridge, 1942, p 273) that all individuals possess, and "other needs" which are less "uniform and less universal" (Beveridge, 1942, p 273). This in turn gave rise to a fundamental, distinction between what the state and the individual should provide for, namely 'social' and 'voluntary' insurance. Social insurance organised by the state is designed to guarantee "a basic income for subsistence" (Beveridge, 1942, p 121). Voluntary insurance meant that "making provision for these higher standards is primarily the function of the individual" (Beveridge, 1942, p 121). Third, the national minimum implied a classification between contributors and recipients, between individuals who in contributing were contributing to the common good and who, at a different stage in their life, would also benefit from the common good. In social insurance "organised by the community ... each individual should stand in on the same term" (Beveridge, 1942, p 13) so that each can receive benefits in return for contributions. Fourth, it provided a juridical principle demarcating two related spheres of rights and duties. On the one hand, the state had a duty towards all individuals of providing a universal national minimum, and toward the poorest of providing residual means-tested assistance. On the other, in the market individuals had responsibilities – if not exactly duties – to provide for their own and their families' needs without state support (Beveridge, 1942, p 7). Fifth, it provided an incentive principle (in effect the principle of 'less eligibility') that differentiated individuals on subsistence national insurance from individuals on more adequate 'voluntary' insurance by ensuring that the level of national insurance would "leave room and encouragement" for voluntary insurance (Beveridge, 1942, p 121); and, further, it demarcated between individuals on national insurance and those on slightly lower national assistance, by making assistance "something less desirable than insurance benefit" (Beveridge, 1942, p 141). Finally, it furnished conceptual principles for defining different kinds of needs: common basic needs, residual needs and individually different needs. Each of these divisions, unifications and demarcations defined different sectors of the welfare state that were sutured together into a complex discourse of social democratic solidarity.

In the 20th century, leading neo-liberals as well as social democrats held complex positions on human nature. They recognised that an 'unbounded' mix of different motivations (for example, Hayek 1960, p 86) governs individuals. For this reason both the social democratic Left and the free-market Right have recognised that policies must be based on principles that appear to run counter to the different institutional designs that these two political movements would logically pursue. Social democrats accept the existence of market institutions as long as they are underpinned by welfare institutions meeting basic needs; the Right accepts residual welfare institutions as long as they do not undermine the efficiency of market institutions. The compromises made in both cases have less to do with intellectual slippage from principle to expedience and more with recognising the complex reality of human motivation that must operate in the practical context of everyday policy making and delivery.

Social democrats and neo-liberals traditionally held coherent social policy discourses based on a range of different component models of human nature. Currently New Labour is more explicitly following a project of welfare reform that embraces different models. However, it does so without the underlying principles – or sutures – that were available to earlier political projects.

New Labour and human nature: redefining principles, 1994-97

In the mid-1990s, the Labour Party and organisations close to it entered into discussion about the theoretical principles guiding social policy. This theoretical discourse retained broadly the same configuration of the four components of human nature that has defined the social democratic tradition in the 20th century, with basic needs remaining a founding principle. The focus of this tradition in the mid-1990s was the issue of social justice and its definition (see, for example, Borrie, 1994; Cohen, 1994; Townsend, 1995; Page, 1996). Yet this debate reveals a new tendency to question the principle of meeting basic needs as of right and to recast social justice in terms of social obligations.

The presence of these four models in Labour's thinking is seen in the following strands of policy discussion. First, of prime importance has been the right of citizens to have their *basic needs* met. An influential example of this is found in the Report of the Commission on Social Justice (CSJ) (Borrie, 1994; see also the Rowntree Commission's *Inquiry into Income and Wealth*, Barclay, 1995). The Commission outlines four principles of social justice which continue to draw on social democratic notions of human nature. The overriding value of social justice is the "equal worth of all citizens" achieved by means of civil, political and legal rights. This principle echoes the tradition of social democratic thought from Tawney's 'equality of consideration' (1964) and Marshall's citizenship (1963). For the CSJ this principle requires three foundations: (a) "every one is entitled, as a right of citizenship, to be able to meet their *basic needs* for income, shelter and other necessities"; (b) "opportunities and life-chances" should be provided to enhance self-respect and equal citizenship; (c) in social justice "unjust inequalities should be reduced and where possible eliminated" (Borrie, 1994, p 18, stress added). The notion of social justice rested securely on the premise that government should maintain the individual's status as a citizen with equal rights to welfare as part of a wider portfolio of rights. However, this notion need not lead inevitably to redistributive policies committed to achieving substantial material equality "primarily through tax and benefit systems" (Borrie, 1994, p 4), which was dismissed by Borrie as the "levellers' approach" (1994, p 96; but see Townsend, 1995; Page, 1996). The introduction of arguments for economic efficiency alongside arguments for basic needs signalled the beginning of an important shift in the social democratic discourse on human nature (see Levitas, 1998, pp 33-4).

Second, New Labour has revived the *social organic* model of human nature in drawing on its ethical socialist roots. Blair, for example, stresses the "view that individuals are socially interdependent human beings – that individuals cannot be divorced from the society to which they belong" (1994, p 4). Thus the individual's interests are advanced through "the collective powers of all used for the individual good of each" (Blair, 1994, p 7). In this vision of a 'united society', the voices of T. H. Green, Hobhouse and the British Idealists (Vincent and Plant, 1984) are clearly audible.

This organic view is seen clearly in New Labour's appeal to communitarianism as part of the 'Third Way'. Communitarianism appeals to the individual's sense of duty which "is at the heart of creating a strong community or society" (Blair, 1995, p 4). At the same time, duty "draws on a broader and therefore more accurate notion of human nature than one formulated on insular self-interest" (Blair, 1995, p7). The idea that fulfilling certain duties should be a condition for receiving welfare, thereby balancing rights and duties, is central to Labour's social policy (Dwyer, 1998).

A further development of the organic view is seen in Labour's stakeholder pension (DSS, 1998c, p 12). However, unlike Field's proposals for stakeholding (1996), the government's proposal does not prescribe a *mutualist* framework giving members shared ownership of the assets –

although some scheme in the traditional mutual sector will already be based on this principle. Rather the stakeholder pension is a device providing cost-efficient pensions by limiting the amount of deductions insurance providers can take in marketing and administration costs and profits. Indeed, mutualism is largely absent from New Labour's philosophy of human motivation. Rather the aim is the organic one of enhancing the collective good for all, in which there is sufficient space for each individual to enjoy his or her own stake in this good. In sum, the collective good of an inclusive society demands duties of each individual, and at the same time provides opportunities for each to enjoy the fruits of their own efforts.

Third, as we have seen, the renewed interest in *mutual human nature* with its view of individuals with different needs and abilities meeting their needs through socially organised acts of cooperation, is central to New Labour's communitarian ethic and its governance by partnership. However, in practice mutualism plays a minor and at best rhetorical role in New Labour's policies.

On the fourth – *atomistic* – component of human nature, Labour has clearly departed from the social democratic tradition by seeking to find new ways in which markets rather than governments can provide basic provisions such as health and education. In this respect it is retaining elements of market-based allocation and delivery of social provisions, by continuing the Tories' Private Finance Initiatives, by establishing local action zones and regeneration partnerships which draw partly on private provision, by extending the notion of competitive tendering in its Best Value assessments of local government (see Geddes and Martin, 2000), by redesigning the Tories' quasi-market arrangements between purchasers and providers into larger Primary Care Groups and Trusts, and by extending contractual 'service agreements' in health care from one to three years (DoH, 1997).

However, since coming to government Labour now claims that these arrangements do not signify the continuation of the atomistic model of market welfare (in which the majority would be left to fend for themselves and the poorest to rely on means-tested welfare), as long as social policy achieves a stronger organic unity between the individual and society that redraws the balance between rights and duties and between state dependence and individual independence. The organic unity of society embracing state *and* market, rather than the market and state basic minimum as mutually exclusive approaches, becomes the precondition for fair distribution. For, as Blair (1998, p 3) has argued recently, society is strong if there is "a thriving civil society, comprising strong families and civic institutions buttressed by intelligent government. When society is weak, power and rewards go to the few and not the many". For Blair (1998, pp 14-15), this means that, rather than "champion indiscriminate and often ineffective public spending", Labour should offer more "adequate services and not just cash benefits", with "greater emphasis to partnerships between public and private provision".

These four models were advanced by different left-of-centre groups within social democracy at the turn of the new century. However, they do not represent a coherent political project. It can be argued that as presently conceived New Labour's project lacks a coherent conception of human nature as the philosophical foundation for its welfare reform strategy.

New Labour and human nature: from principles to practice – redefining welfare subjects

In putting principles into practice, New Labour has significantly reconfigured the four models of human nature. Broadly conceived, Labour has relegated the basic needs model, as the first principle of traditional social-democratic social policy, in favour of a renewed organic model, in which individuals are expected to fulfil their role as good citizens, workers and parents and contribute to the common good of all as a condition for exercising their rights as citizens of the new welfare state. Underlying the appeal to organic human nature are repeated references to motivations of self-interest which Tory reforms did much to instil and New Labour has so far done little to dispel.

We can follow more closely the implications of Labour's unsteady mix of organicism and self-interest in its welfare to work and social security policies. For the Labour government – and the Tories – the task of redefining human motivation in social policy has involved two related tasks: reconstructing social security minima as part of a wider project of redefining the subjects of welfare and investing them with a new and expanded range of motivations. The two processes of redefinition are linked in that redefining the appropriate level of welfare provision assumes a redefinition of the kind of individuals, with their specific needs and abilities, who are subject to welfare. We will expand on these two areas of redefinition.

But first a brief word about the way welfare subjects have been constructed from the time of the classic welfare state to the present. The provision of a national minimum, based on universal national insurance, NHS and education, meant that in principle all individuals were universal subjects of the welfare state, prone at one time or another to be subjects of education, health, pensions and unemployment benefits. The ideal of the universal welfare state produced a single subject with rights to a range of welfare provisions. With national insurance and full employment, most individuals could switch between work and welfare with relative ease, subject only to the strictures of a straightforward incentive structure based on the principle of less eligibility. The welfare state provided for some degree of overlap between worker and welfare subjects. At the same time, in reality, fractions of some social groups, such as married women and lone mothers, were treated as less than universal subjects and given a more limited range of rights – the married woman, for example, on the grounds that, compared to the single woman, "she has other duties" (Beveridge, 1942, p 51). Nonetheless, the notion of the universal citizen subject represented an ideal for different groups to demand as of right.

During the last 50 years successive governments have restructured welfare minima and in so doing redefined welfare subjects. During the postwar period of full employment, the national minimum was available to individuals leaving the labour market for short periods to compensate for interrupted earnings. In the 1970s, the Labour government raised the subsistence level of long-term benefits by indexing them to earnings, so contributing towards a more adequate national minimum (but also splitting the minimum into long- and short-term benefits). However, in the 1980s the Tory government replaced the national minimum with a series of means-tested residual minima which no longer indexed long-term benefits to wages and extended the use of means-testing. These developments replaced the notions of universal basic needs and the universal citizen subject by an atomistic notion of the welfare subject driven by personal self-interest and the fear of unrelieved poverty as state benefits were lowered in relation to earnings and new incentives provided to buy into private pensions. The notion of a unified welfare subject defined by the national minimum gave way to the consumer subject and welfare subject. In turn welfare subjects were grouped into those deemed deserving of benefits because they were unable to work (the retired, older workers who retired early, the sick and disabled and lone parents) and the unemployed who were subject to increasingly stricter benefit regimes from the 1980s onwards (Finn, 1998). This dual treatment signified a division that was further opened up by New Labour.

These reforms used compulsion and incentives to encourage the unemployed to participate in the labour market, especially in the low-paid sector, and gave financial incentives to the employed to invest greater portions of earnings in private and occupational benefits, including government subsidised private pension plans. The assumption was that individuals motivated by self-interest and self-preservation seek remunerated work and private welfare when alternative sources of state support are less attractive – in short the motivation underlying the poor law principle of 'less eligibility'. However, on balance the reforms provided little in the way of respite for the elderly and disabled, apart from those with severe disabilities.

Today under New Labour, there is a further move to redefine welfare subjects into three groups. The first two groups comprise the objects of Labour's twofold strategy of "work for those who can, and security for those who can't" (DSS 1998a, p iii). The first group of welfare subjects is defined by its participation in the low–paid labour market and the New Deal. In becoming *in-work welfare subjects* they take the first step to becoming independent worker subjects, the ultimate aim of welfare rebuilt around work. The second group are defined by their inability to work because of age and/or severe disability, namely *out-of-work welfare subjects*. The third group, and the one Labour is least explicit about, comprises a residual group of individuals who fall into neither of the first two groups. This third group consists of those whom the government believes could work but who for various reasons persist in not working, so resisting the blandishments of the government's two–fold strategy. The lack of reference to this group in the welfare Green Papers (1998a,b,c) lends a mantle of invisibility to its identity. As *invisible welfare subjects*, their motivations are described in negative terms, as the lack of required motivation. Only by joining the first group of welfare subjects, will its members benefit from measures that remotivate and 'incentivise' them into becoming good workers, parents and citizens. The government's assertion that for school leavers and the long-term unemployed "there will be no fifth option of remaining on benefit" (1998a, p 25) – after refusing the four New Deal options of employment, education, voluntary work and environmental task forces – further compounds this invisibility.

The broadly three-way classification of welfare subjects maps onto a restructured system of welfare minima, forging a new account of human nature. Since 1997 Labour has modified Tory welfare minima in two ways which reflect its own twofold construction of the aims of welfare, rebuilding it around work for those who can and security for those who cannot.

For the first group of workers in low-paid work and moving from the New Deal gateway into its work options, namely *in-work welfare subjects*, the minimum is redefined in terms of in-work benefits such as tax credits for working families and the disabled and 'benefit plus' enhancements to the Job Seeker's Allowance. This provides a higher level of remuneration than out-of-work means-tested benefits. Though also based on means-tested minima, the new in-work benefits are meant to appeal to the worker's sense of self-interest within the labour market and self-worth within an inclusive society. This suggests a motivational strategy for in-work welfare subjects of reinforcing the link between the organic motivation to belong and the individualist motivation to secure self-interest. New Labour appeals to self-interest in the way it continues to employ a core set of assumptions advanced during the 1980s and 1990s about the relationship between wages and welfare benefits based on the belief that differentials must be sufficiently wide to encourage individuals to abandon welfare dependency for work (see McLaughlan et al, 1989, pp 12-14). Whereas the Tory strategy was to lower benefit levels in relation to low wages, Labour has raised low wages above the level of out-of-work and mainly mean-tested benefits by supplementing wages with new in-work tax credits (Oppenheim, 1997).

The definition of this group is being extended to cover individuals who were traditionally not encouraged to work such as lone parents, the disabled, older workers and partners of the unemployed (mainly housewives). Symptomatic of the thrust towards the 'active society' of economically active individuals now being adopted by governments in many advanced industrial societies, these traditionally *out-of-work welfare subjects* are now being redefined as *in-work subjects* and encouraged back into the labour market (Walters, 1997). In principle, the extension of 'can-work' welfare subjects to cover both low-paid employees and individuals traditionally unavailable for work implies New Labour's desire that the in-work minimum should in time become a new more widely established minimum. (Presumably, this aspiration further assumes that the means-tested, out-of-work minimum will recede back to the residual status Beveridge accorded it in 1942.) The welfare of this group is pivotal to achieving Labour's goal of an inclusive society based on the organic links forged through work between each individual and the social whole. Under the New Deal each group is subject to policies and stricter benefit regimes that augment notions of 'ability' and 'employability' and diminish notions of 'disability' and 'unavailability' for work. These groups are not unambiguous independent workers, but a mix of traditionally deserving and less deserving welfare subjects. However, the success of this project to endow these welfare subjects with a new active and visible status in the labour market has yet to be demonstrated (cf Millar, 2000).

Further measures to support in-work welfare subjects are the national minimum wage, which raises earnings above out-of-work benefit rates, and New Deal job search and training programmes (with different degrees of compulsion) for lone parents, the disabled, the young unemployed and the long-term unemployed and their partners. Lund has speculated that the gap between in- and out-of-work income may be further widened by using the tapered child tax credit for working families to replace the universal child benefit, leaving the latter as a residual benefit with parental obligations attached for unemployed families (Lund, 1999, p 454). Certainly, the proposed employment tax credit is intended, among other things, to widen the net of in-work benefits to include households without children (Howard, 2000). Further, the thrust of recent area programmes, such as Sure Start, New Deal for Communities, Employment Zones and Health Action Zones, deliberately focuses additional health, education and early years provisions on family and their children to enable parents to enter and to sustain employment. Though not exclusively for the employed these programmes are of greater value to the employed than the unemployed (for an extensive list of incentives to the working poor, see Millar, 2000, pp 8-9).

For the second group of *out-of-work welfare subjects* – pensioners and the disabled – the government's 'guaranteed minimum income' is conditional on receiving Income Support. Their subject status is defined in relation to a new enhanced residual minimum that, though so far uprated in line with earnings, is calculated to have a minimum impact on economic prosperity, which is in keeping with the principle of residual minima. On the one hand, the income guarantee raises the income level of the poorest to a minimum tied to annual increases in earnings, a gesture towards meeting basic needs. However, on the other hand, this linkage is selectively tied to means-tested Income Support, and so cannot meet the basic needs of those who cannot work. Indeed the deliberate separation of welfare minima for the basic needs of those who work and for those who cannot fundamentally undermines the principle of universal basic needs.

For the third, less visible, group of individuals refusing New Deal options, the government is retaining the residual mean-tested minimum and extending the Tories' stricter regime of benefit reductions in the hope of compelling individuals into the labour force (Finn, 1998).

Conclusion

In sum, each of the three minima for specific welfare subjects – namely a guaranteed minimum for the most vulnerable, an enhanced low-earnings minimum for New Deal workers, and the residual minimum for non-workers – provides a structure for work and welfare by which New Labour is seeking to create a new construction of human motivation entailing self-interest, organic reciprocity and residual needs. However, unlike earlier constructions of human nature, Labour has yet to invent a suturing principle that holds together these discrepant notions of human nature. It no longer has a national minimum tying together different types of benefit and supporting a complex though coherent notion of human motivation. Its embrace of the residual minimum and the principle of means testing, central to neo-liberal reforms, has been equivocal and at variance with its opposition to means testing when in opposition (see Blair, 1996, pp 144-5, 147, 300; Field, 1996, p 11).

As an alternative interpretation, Labour's Third Way suggests that welfare reform should abandon the doctrinaire choices of the Old Left and the New Right (DSS, 1998a, pp 2,19) and design policies justified on pragmatic grounds alone (Blair and Schroeder 1999, p 4). However, Labour's extension of the means-tested residual minimum to cover Tax Credits and the national insurance Incapacity Benefit claimed by occupational and private pension beneficiaries would signify that it is instead, at least in this respect, advancing the Tories' agenda based on an appeal to a sense of fear in means-tested claimants and self-interest in independent workers. In a similar way, Labour is beginning to break down the traditional conceptual and institutional divisions between work and welfare and to reconstruct the poor law and neo-liberal distinctions between the identities of individuals in work and on welfare. The result has been the creation of hidden subjects in need of welfare whose identities are defined neither by work nor welfare.

The lack of unifying notions of human nature, work, welfare and need places Labour's social policy in a different world from earlier social policy, one which lacks a dominant theory of motivation and an associated normative viewpoint which can provide guiding objectives for social policy. At best, the idea of founding policy on diversely different motivations leads to a pragmatic, rather than principled, stance. Human nature in particular is no longer the basis for axiomatic statements about social policy. Consequently, there is no clear way of employing notions of human nature to distinguish New Labour from Tory policy, unless a revived notion of work as the source of social inclusion, fulfilment and welfare entitlement for all including those who cannot work – that is, 'rebuilding welfare around work' – is possible. However, this remains a doubtful prospect even in times of apparent economic growth and stability (Jordan, 1998; cf Lund, 2000).

References

Barclay, P. (1995) *Inquiry into income and wealth*, Volume I, York: Joseph Rowntree Foundation.

Barclay, Sir P. (chair) (1995) *Inequalities in income and wealth*, York: Joseph Rowntree Foundation.

Beveridge, W.H. (1942) *Social insurance and allied services*, Cmd 6404, London: HMSO.

Beveridge, W.H. (1948) *Voluntary action*, London: George Allen and Unwin.

Bell, I., Butler, E., Marsland, D. and Pirie, M. (1994) *The end of the welfare state*, London: Adam Smith Institute.

Blair, T. (1994) *Socialism*, Fabian Pamphlet 565, London: Fabian Society.

Blair, T. (1995) 'End the give and take away society', *The Guardian* 23 March, p 24.

Blair, T. (1996) *New Britain: my vision of a new Britain*, London: Fourth Estate.

Blair, T. (1998) *The Third Way*, Pamphlet 588, London: Fabian Society.

Blair, T. and Schroeder, G. (1999) *Europe: The Third Way/Die Neue Mitte*, London: Labour Party.

Borrie, G. (chair) (1994) *Social justice: Strategies for national renewal* (The Report of the Commission on Social Justice), London: Vintage.

Brenton, M. (1985) *The voluntary sector in British social services*, Harlow: Longman.

Cohen, G.A. (1994) 'Back to socialist basics', *New Left Review*, vol 207, pp 3-16.

Cowen, H. (1994) *The human nature debate*, London: Pluto.

Crosland, C.A.R. (1956) *The future of socialism*, London: Jonathan Cape.

Cutler, T., Williams, K. and Williams, J. (1986) *Keynes, Beveridge and beyond*, London: Routledge and Kegan Paul.

Deacon, A (1997) 'Self interest and collective welfare', in A.R. Morton (ed) *The future of welfare*, Edinburgh: Centre for Theology and Public Issues, University of Edinburgh.

DoH (Department of Health) (1997) *The new NHS: Modern, dependable*, Cm 3807, London: The Stationery Office.

DSS (Department of Social Security) (1998a) *A new contract for welfare: New ambitions for our country*, Cm 3805, London: The Stationery Office.

DSS (1998b) *A new contract for welfare: Principles into practice*, Cm 4101, London: The Stationery Office.

DSS (1998c) *A new contract for welfare: Partnership in pensions*, Cm 4179, London: The Stationery Office.

Dwyer, P. (1998) 'Conditional citizens? Welfare rights and responsibilities in the late 1990s', *Critical Social Policy*, vol 18, pp 493-517.

Etzioni, A. (1995) *The spirit of community: Rights, responsibilities and the communitarian agenda*, London: Fontana.

Field, F. (1996) *How to pay for the future: Building a stakeholders' welfare*, London: Institute of Community Studies.

Field, F. (1997) 'The welfare debate: managing self-interest, self-improvement and altruism', in P. Askonas and S.F. Frowen (eds) *Welfare and values: Challenging the culture of unconcern*, Basingstoke: Macmillan.

Finn, D. (1998) 'Labour's 'New Deal' for the unemployed and the stricter benefit regime', in E. Brunsdon, H. Dean and R. Woods (eds) *Social Policy Review 10*, London: Social Policy Association.

Geddes, M. and Martin, S. (2000) 'The policy and politics of Best Value', *Policy & Politics*, vol 28, no 3, pp 379-95.

Giddens, A. (1994) *Beyond Left and Right: The future of radical politics*, Cambridge: Polity Press.

Green, D.G. (1993) *Reinventing civil society: The rediscovery of welfare without politics*, London: Institute of Economic Affairs.

Hayek, F.A. (1943) *The road to serfdom*, London: Routledge.

Hayek, F.A. (1960) *The constitution of liberty*, London: Routledge and Kegan Paul.

Hewitt, M. (1992) *Welfare, ideology and needs: Developing perspectives on the welfare state*, Hemel Hempstead: Harvester Wheatsheaf.

Hewitt, M. (1998) 'Social policy and human need', in N. Ellison and C. Pierson (eds) *Developments in British social policy*, Basingstoke: Macmillan.

Hewitt, M. (2000) *Welfare and human nature*, Basingstoke: Macmillan.

Holman, B (1993) *A new deal for social welfare*, Oxford: Lion Press.

Howard, M. (2000) 'Designing the employment tax credit', *Poverty*, vol 107, pp 6-10.

Hutton, W. (1996a) *The state we're in*, London: Vintage.

Hutton, W. (1996b) 'The stakeholder society', in D. Marquand and A. Seldon (eds) *The ideas that shaped post-war Britain*, London: Fontana Press.

Jordan, B. (1998) *The new politics of welfare*, London: Sage Publications.

Joseph, K. (1976) *Stranded in the middle ground: Reflections on circumstances and politics*, London: Centre for Policy Studies.

Laclau, E. and Mouffe, C. (1985) *Hegemony and socialist strategy: Towards a radical democratic politics*, London: Verso.

Levitas, R. (1998) *The inclusive society? Social inclusion and New Labour*, Basingstoke: Macmillan.

Le Grand, J. (1997) 'Knights, knaves and pawns: human behaviour and social policy', *Journal of Social Policy*, vol 26, no 2, pp 149-69.

Lund, B. (1999) '"Ask not what your community can do for you": obligations, New Labour and welfare reform', *Critical Social Policy*, vol 19, no 4, pp 447-62.

Lund, B. (2000) 'Work and need', in H. Dean, R. Sykes and R. Woods (eds) *Social Policy Review 12*, Newcastle: Social Policy Association.

Marshall, T.H. (1963) 'Citizenship and social class', in T.H. Marshall, *Sociology at the crossroads and other essays*, London: Heinemann.

McLaughlan, E., Millar, J. and Cooke, K. (1989) *Work and welfare benefits*, Aldershot: Avebury.

Millar, J. (2000) *Keeping track of welfare reform: the New Deal programmes*, York: Joseph Rowntree Foundation.

Oppenheim, C. (1997) 'Welfare to work', *Renewal*, vol 5, pp 50-62.

Page, R. (1996) *Altruism and the British welfare state*, Aldershot: Avebury.

Robson, W.A. (1976) *Welfare state and welfare society: Illusion or reality*, London: Allen and Unwin.

Shrimsley, R. (1996) 'Thatcher savages Blair', *Electronic Telegraph*, Issue 549, 23 November.

Tawney, R.H. (1964) *Equality*, London: Allen and Unwin.

Titmuss, R.M. (1968) *Commitment to welfare*, London: Allen and Unwin.

Titmuss R.M. (1970) *The gift relationship*, London: Allen and Unwin.

Townsend, P. (1979) *Poverty in the United Kingdom: A survey of household resources and standards of living*, Harmondsworth: Penguin Books.

Townsend, P. (1995) 'Persuasion and conformity: an assessment of the Borrie Report on social justice', *New Left Review*, vol 213, pp 137-50.

Vincent, A. and Plant, R. (1984) *Philosophy, politics and citizenship: The life and thought of the British Idealists*, Oxford: Blackwell.

Walters (1997) 'The "active society": new designs for social policy', *Policy & Politics*, vol 25, no 3, pp 221-34.

Webb, S. and Webb, B. (1911) *The prevention of destitution*, London: Longman Green.

Williams, K. and Williams, J. (eds) (1987) *A Beveridge reader*, London: Allen and Unwin.

THIRTEEN

Through a lens darkly: sexuality and the 1834 New Poor Law

Jean Carabine

This paper will examine a key piece of social policy – the 1834 New Poor Law Amendment Act and related Royal Commissioners' Reports[1] – through the lens of sexuality[2] to see if this can add anything new to our understandings, not only of the 1834 Act, but also about social policy more broadly.

The term 'sexuality' is used here to refer to (and to encompass) sexual identity, practices, acts, intimate relations and relationships of individuals, groups, and even populations. It is taken to refer to a category of person (heterosexual, homosexual, lesbian, queer, bisexual and so on), the focus of their desire (same-sex, opposite sex, and so on) as well as embracing all sexual practices, acts and relationships (marriage, cohabitation, reproduction, parenting, partnering or otherwise) and the meanings attached to those acts and practices. It also refers to a system of knowledge encompassing what we know as sexuality, what dominates as the 'truth' of sexuality at any moment in time, and the power effects and relations (generally those of heterosexuality) which result.

Accounts of the history of the development of social policy in Britain rarely deal either explicitly or implicitly with the role played by sexuality in that development. This is surprising, as sexuality is often the explicit focus of policies whether as in the Contagious Diseases Acts of the 1860s, or as with sex and relationship education or teenage pregnancy in the 21st century. However, social policy does not have to be specifically concerned with sexuality for it to 'speak' of sexuality and for it to regulate sexual relations and behaviour, as we shall see. Social policies about, for example, housing, health, income support, or parenting can also contain assumptions and convey messages about appropriate, acceptable and normal sexual relations and practices. The *Supporting Families* Green Paper (Home Office, 2001) acknowledges that successful parenting can be found in a diversity of family arrangements while continuing to assert that the heterosexual married couple is the best arrangement for parenting, thereby conveying messages about what is the preferred and acceptable sexual relationship for parenting.

Ideas about what sexuality is, and about what is acceptable sexuality, are conveyed through sexuality discourses that also in part inform social policy. In this way, sexuality can be said to have a constitutive role in relation to social policy. That is, ideas about what sexuality is at any given time, in part, constitute academic social policy and welfare practice (see Carabine, 1996a, b). Relatedly, social welfare can itself be understood as a discourse,

> ... a 'discourse of social welfare' comprises an organisation or matrix of knowledges – a culturally constructed and politically sanctioned framework for defining experience and for realising definitions in practice. A discourse of social welfare gives definition to the world in both conceptual and material senses of this term. (O'Brien and Penna, 1998, p 8)

Knowledges or ideas about sexuality are one such part of the 'matrix of knowledge' to which O'Brien and Penna refer. Social policy/welfare discourses are themselves comprised of a range of discourses specifically about welfare but also about family, mothering, and, of course, sexuality. Discourses are variable ways of 'speaking' about an issue which cohere to produce the object of which they speak, for example, sexuality or welfare, a category of person, such as a welfare subject (the unemployed, teenagers or lone mothers). Discourses are also fluid and often opportunistic, at one and the same time, drawing upon existing discourses about an issue while utilising and interacting with, and being mediated by, other dominant discourses (about, for example, family, poverty, welfare, morality, gender, race, ethnicity, sexuality, disability, and class) to produce potent and new ways of conceptualising the issue or topic. In so doing, discourses 'hook' into normative ideas and common-sense notions about, say, sexuality (that for example, heterosexuality is natural and normal, that homosexuality is something to be tolerated), or poverty, morality or motherhood, to produce shortcut paths into ideas which convey messages about, for example, 'good' and 'bad' (mothering, sexualities, and so on), morality and immorality (behaviours and relationships), deserving and undeserving (benefits and welfare recipients), and acceptable and unacceptable practices. Discourses are historically variable ways of speaking, writing and talking about an issue, as well as practices around it, which have specific outcomes and identifiable effects specifying what is morally, socially, legally and culturally un/acceptable at any given moment.

All of us – heterosexual or not – are affected by the assumptions about sexuality and sexual relations and practices that are contained in social policies. The argument here is that social policies convey messages about what is acceptable and appropriate (hetero)sexuality as well as what is inappropriate and unacceptable sexual practices and relationships. In this way, social policy can be said to perform a normalising role in relation to sexuality. Foucault (1990, 1991) has shown that through 'normalisation' individuals are compared and differentiated according to a desired norm. Normalisation establishes the measure by which all are judged and deemed to conform or not. This normalisation process produces homogeneity through processes of comparison and differentiation. Normalising judgement is not simply about comparing individuals in a binary way – as in good/bad, mad/sane or healthy/ill. It is also a 'norm' towards which all individuals are expected to aim and seek to achieve, and against which all are measured – 'good' *and* 'bad', sick *and* healthy, 'mad' *and* 'sane', heterosexual *and* homosexual. For Foucault, normalisation is one way that power is deployed. In his notion of 'norm' Foucault did not conceive power as being imposed by one section, class or group of society on another. Rather, he saw it as circulating and operating at all levels of society. The relationship between normalisation and discourse is that discourse conveys messages about what is the norm and what is not. In effect, discourses establish the norm. Normalising sexuality discourses specify not only what sexuality is at particular moments in time but also what is natural and normal sexuality while establishing the boundaries of acceptable and appropriate sexualities. Normalisation is consequently a means through which power is deployed. It is a dynamic of knowledge, practised and learnt, dispersed around various centres of practice and expertise. Both social policy and sexuality can be understood as such centres of expertise and practice.

Foucault's notion of normalisation has been adapted and applied to the social policy context where, it is suggested, it operates in three main ways. First, it 'constitutes' appropriate and acceptable sexuality. Second it produces differentiating effects and fragmented impacts which may be variously regulatory, penalising or affirmative in respect to different groups of, for example, women (for a full discussion of this and examples see Carabine, 1996a). Third, the normalisation process operates in a regulatory capacity through which heterosexuality is not only established and secured, but also, bodies and sexualities are disciplined and controlled. This final function is important. It operates, *explicitly*, through legislation and statutes, and *implicitly* both through normative assumptions about (hetero)sexuality as 'normal' and natural underpinning and informing social policy, and through the linking of notions of eligibility for welfare to ideas about appropriate and acceptable sexuality. The adaptation of Foucault employed in this chapter, however, stresses that the effect of normalisation is never overwhelming or totalising. Normalising strategies can be contested and may not necessarily lead to successful and complete regulation or outcomes. Although discourses may have regulatory intentions, this does not mean that they ultimately result in regulatory outcomes.

We can use this concept of normalisation to illustrate how in the 1834 New Poor Law reports, social policy is in part constituted by sexuality discourses, and second, that through social welfare practice and policy sexuality is itself constituted. This shows that not only are discourses of sexuality 'played' through social policy as an effect of normalisation, but also that sexuality discourses interact with and traverse other discourses central to welfare and social policy, and, in so doing, are mediated by those discourses. Thus it is argued that 19th century ideas about the sexuality of the labouring classes, especially female sexuality, marriage and population are interwoven with the poverty discourse that is central to the New Poor Law reports.

The 1834 New Poor Law through the lens of sexuality

Briefly, the 1834 New Poor Amendment Law was an attempt to reduce the increasing costs of poor relief through the introduction of a centralised, more efficient, but less generous system of relief. Central to achieving these aims were the principles of less eligibility, the workhouse and the work ethic. A primary concern of the NPL was undeniably to achieve the "objective of convert[ing] paupers into independent labourers" (Dean, 1991, p 14) The NPL is in the main directed almost entirely at the able-bodied male labourer with the family dependent upon him: women were generally ignored except when being treated as men's dependants (Webb and Webb, 1910, p 6; Thane, 1978, p 31; Ginsburg, 1979, pp 79-87; Daly, 1994). However, reading the 1834 Poor Law reports through the lens of sexuality shows that the 19th century Poor Law Commissioners were concerned with much more than merely the administration, organisation and relief of poverty. It reveals that the poverty discourse of 1834 is 'shot through' with sexuality discourses. With the lens of sexuality it is possible to see that the commissioners were also concerned with imposing emergent middle-class values about morality, acceptable and appropriate sexualities, family, marriage and domesticity on the labouring classes, and upon women in particular, and, in so doing, regulating working-class behaviour and relationships. Reading the Poor Law through sexuality therefore can tell us not just about sexuality or about poverty but can also inform wider understandings of the role and function of social policy in conveying ideas and values about appropriate behaviour and practices.

To illustrate this contention, the first section of the paper will set out the context of the commissioners' concerns about female sexuality and explore how these were constituted and formulated through a 'discourse of bastardy'. In the next section, the commissioners' concerns about marriage, appropriate sexuality and population will be examined. It will be suggested that these aspects are illustrative of two key processes in the relationship between sexuality and social policy – namely, 'normalisation' and 'constituting'. The final section considers to what extent these 19th century Poor Law discourses resonate in late 20th and early 21st century discourses about lone mothers. Finally, it is suggested that an analysis of the 1834 New Poor Law illustrates that the relationship between sexuality and social policy can be mutually constitutive.

Female sexuality and the discourse of bastardy

The commissioners' concern with female sexuality is to be found primarily and most significantly in their focus on illegitimacy in the sections of the reports and the Act dealing with the relationship between poor relief and bastardy. Indeed, these sections dealing with illegitimacy represent those parts of the NPL[3] which are more explicitly infused with sexuality. All of the assistant commissioners' reports contain commentaries on bastardy and the commissioners themselves include a separate section – known as the Bastardy Clauses – in the main part of their report and recommendations. The Bastardy Clauses arose out of concerns that illegitimacy was increasing and with it the costs of poor relief. The commissioners believed that the easy availability of poor relief for unmarried mothers and the existing bastardy legislation which allowed women to swear a man as the father of her child, thereby making him financially liable, 'caused' illegitimacy. In the Bastardy Clauses their three chief concerns are identified as the support of illegitimate children, the amount of relief paid to unmarried mothers by the parish and, finally, attempts to obtain repayment for maintenance from fathers. However, these became reconstituted as a concern about women's sexual immorality and power.

This concern with female sexuality is expressed through what is referred to here as the discourse of bastardy. This played a significant part in constituting single pregnant women and unmarried mothers as undeserving welfare subjects. Such women were presented as morally corrupt welfare recipients through a negative discourse of female sexuality that deployed three discursive strategies. The first of these constructed women as immoral welfare subjects through a process of negative depiction and by associating them with immorality. The second constructed women as predatory while positioning men as victims of female sexuality. The third constructed unmarried mothers as undeserving recipients of poor relief. This is mapped out briefly below.[4]

In their treatment of the bastardy issues the commissioners paint a picture of single pregnant women and unmarried mothers as immoral, predatory and lying, and as seducers of men deliberately getting pregnant so as to secure a husband and/or poor relief. The tone and language used in the Bastardy Clauses is judgmental, damning and moralistic, and conveys to the reader that such women are sexually immoral and should be punished for having a child outside of marriage whom they cannot support. For example,

> ... the female in the very many cases becomes the corruptor; ... the women, ... feel no disgrace, either in their own eyes, or in the eyes of others, at becoming mothers of bastards have still less reluctance in allowing the claims of a husband to anticipate the marriage ceremony, in fact they are almost always with child when they come to the church. (Mr Richardson, quoted in Main Report, 1834 [1971 edn], vol 8, p 96)

and

> The consequence is, that a woman of dissolute character may pitch upon any unfortunate young man whom she has inveigled into her net, and swear that child to him: and the effect of the law, as it now stands, will be to oblige the man to marry her. (Mr Walcott quoted in Main Report, 1834 [1971 edn], vol 8, p 98)

By contrast, in the sections dealing with bastardy, fathers are neither sexualised nor subjected to a judgmental or damning discourse for their failure to support either their illegitimate child or its mother. Nor are they condemned as immoral for having sex or for fathering children outside of marriage. They are not presented as seducers, promiscuous, licentious or as irresponsible. Instead, men are portrayed as victims of women's sexuality and as innocents seduced by scheming women. In a debate on the New Poor Law the Bishop of Exeter pointed out to the House of Lords how "fathers of bastard children were uniformly spoken of as 'unfortunate persons' while whenever the mother was mentioned allusion was made to 'vice'... the language of the report was that 'The female is most to blame'" (House of Lords [*Hansard*], 3rd series, xxv 586–94, 28 July 1834).

The less eligible device, a hallmark of the NPL, was also applied to unmarried mothers who compared against other recipients of relief, such as widows and the elderly, were considered less deserving. Widows and the elderly had, in the eyes of the commissioners, an unquestioned and right to relief. Unmarried mothers, on the other hand, were described as "defrauding of the relief of the impotent and aged, *true poor of the same parish*," (vol 8, p 92). Not only did unmarried mothers receive benefits for which they had not earned rights (through marriage), but these were earned through illicit intercourse. Widows are presented as possessing an unquestionable right to relief by virtue of being married – "this was one of the many premiums on marriage" (vol 8, p 196). After all, the "unmarried mother had voluntarily put herself into the situation of the widow: she has voluntarily become a mother, without procuring for herself and her child the assistance of a husband and father" (18th Recommendation, Main Report, 1834, p 198; George Taylor's Report vol 8, p 128).

This device of comparing unmarried mothers against others, judging them less eligible and as undeserving of poor relief for immoral behaviour and the lack of a husband was employed to stigmatise them as a group. Their eligibility for relief was in this way determined on the basis of their sexuality. This is significant, because it shows how ideas about appropriate and acceptable sexuality can be seen to inform and influence access and eligibility to welfare[5].

Through identifying unmarried mothers as predatory, undeserving and immoral and by associating this with unacceptable and inappropriate sexual practice a 'norm' of what of acceptable and appropriate sexual/moral practice was also being asserted. This process can be read as an attempt to impose a different, middle-class norm of female sexuality on labouring women.

Why present women as immoral, deceitful and lying? There are a number of explanations. First, in the decades prior to the 1832/34 Reports and the NPL, unmarried motherhood was widely tolerated both within most working-class communities and to a lesser extent among the middle, and even upper-classes as a fact of life. It was common practice, especially in rural areas, for conceptions to occur prior to marriage. Illegitimacy and common-law marriage were part of an "alternative plebeian morality" and for many of the labouring classes "premarital sex after the promise of marriage [w]as acceptable" (Clark, 1995, p 43; Laslett, 1977, p 128). Indeed, premarital pregnancy was seen as an important economic consideration in determining a woman's fertility (Weeks, 1981, p 60; Perkins, 1989, pp 182-3; Rendall, 1985, p 194). Under the old Poor Law an informal but strict moral code concerning premarital pregnancy and illegitimacy existed which was variously enforced and involved various forms of public shaming (Weeks, 1981, p 22). However, as a result of increasing industrialisation, urbanisation and economic insecurity marriage did not always follow.

In assessing attitudes prior to the introduction of the NPL it seems that bastardy was generally tolerated particularly by local labouring communities, with people tending to sympathise with the mother's situation. In part, this was in recognition of the widespread acceptance of the tradition of prenuptial pregnancy. This tolerance is also reflected in the stance adopted by many magistrates, who were generally presented as being reluctant to imprison unmarried mothers. One could also surmise that the incidence of illegitimacy reflected, to some extent, its widespread acceptability, although clearly, many women became pregnant in the expectation that marriage would follow. There is little doubt that the commissioners were also of the view that the incidence of illegitimacy reflected its widespread acceptance as well as being indicative of a lack of female virtue and morality.

To pre-Victorian middle-class society, women's 'immorality' was symbolic of a greater social ill and it became emblematic of the breakdown of national morality and through this the social order of society as a whole. Concerns about national morality and the possible collapse of society were fuelled by fears about the deterioration of society as a result of believed increasing immorality on the part of the labouring classes and as witnessed in profligate families, fears about population growth (the Malthusian effect) and of course, increasing illegitimacy – all expressed in the Poor Law Reports. As a result, illegitimacy, in common with venereal disease at the beginning of the next century (see Bland, 1983), became both a metaphor and signifier of national immorality with pauper unmarried mothers as its personification. Central to the development of new found middle-class morality were women as the torchbearers of men's and the nation's sexual morality. To pre Victorian Poor Law reformers unmarried mothers were the negative embodiment of the emergent Victorian ideal of female sexuality, perceived as sexually active, immoral and deceitful.

That national morality was so tied to women's morality also meant that to ensure the former the latter had to be maintained. Thus, we see reference, especially in the parliamentary debates on the Bastardy Clauses, to their importance in protecting female virtue[6]. Only by maintaining female virtue could the nation's virtue be secured. For example, "[t]he present laws.... Deteriorate the morality, and ... blunt the feelings of the lower orders of this country – the most numerous part of our population – the foundations of our prosperity – the sinews of our strength" (Bishop of London, *Hansard*, Lords, 3rd series, vol XXV, 1834, p 602). Again, "though want of chastity was a crime, a sin in man, it was still greater in a woman, whose error corrupted society at its very root" (Lord Althorp, the Lord Chancellor, *Hansard*, Lords, 3rd series, 1834, vol XXV, p 607) and "if female chastity was once at a discount, not merely would the bonds of society be loosened, but actually burst asunder" (Lord Althorp, *Hansard*, Lords, 3rd series, 1834, vol XXV, p 609).

It was necessary, therefore, to bring about a shift in public opinion (the widespread acceptance of unmarried motherhood) and practice (of prenuptial pregnancy). This required that the commissioners utilise some device whereby all sympathy for unmarried mothers would be negated and their situation no longer tolerated. Their plight had again to become despised and stigmatised. The commissioners sought to achieve this objective through the representation of unmarried mothers as liars, immoral, and undeserving[7]. Additionally, they were eager to make bastardy onerous for unmarried mothers and recommended that the full financial responsibility for illegitimate children be placed onto mothers[8]. In the section outlining their proposed Remedial Measures for dealing with bastardy the commissioners state:

> The shame of the offence will not be destroyed by its being the means of income and marriage, and we trust that as soon as it has become burthensome and disgraceful, it will become as rare as it is among those classes in this country who are above parish relief. (Main Report, 1834, p 197)

The invoking of sexualised images through the representations of unmarried mothers as fallen women and temptresses was further used to establish as the norm the idea of women as virtuous and moral. It did this by castigating alternative forms of sexuality – as in the established tradition of premarital sex and pregnancy "carried on from time immemorial" among the lower classes (Walcott's Report, 1834, Appendix A, p 180) – as unacceptable, inappropriate and as immoral. That is, by 'othering' unmarried mothers. So, the discourse of bastardy can be interpreted as a means of conveying to women that only virtuous and modest women are entitled to husbands and the security that entails. Enshrined in this is the notion of women's dependency on men, as other writers have noted (Thane, 1978; Ginsburg, 1979, pp 79-87) along with a privileging of marriage. The discourse of bastardy therefore conveys that the ideal norm is marriage and reproduction within it. Thus, the discourse functions to impose morality and moral responsibility upon women and leaves them little option but to marry men if they are to achieve economic security.

Of course, discourses may be influential and powerful but they do not necessarily determine practice – and there is often a dislocation between discourse and practice. Although the stigmatising of unmarried mothers was to some extent successful it did not immediately achieve this end. It was not until 1868 that the whole country came under the 1834 Act, resulting in widespread variation (see Webb and Webb, 1910, p 42). This variation was due to local resistance to the clauses – many people believed the practice of punishing the mothers and leaving the men to get off 'scot-free' was unjust – and, in part, due to the widespread existence of premarital pregnancy, irregular marriage, and a continued reluctance or inability on the part of many of the working classes to marry.

Family, marriage and population

A second means by which sexuality was invoked in the pages of the Poor Law Reports is through a focus on family, marriage and population; the numerous volumes of the reports are full of contributors' views and fears. These echo Malthusian anxieties about population growth, especially among the labouring classes, outstripping the means of subsistence[9]. Indeed, a repeated theme is that both the allowance system and poor relief lead to an increase in population. At the heart of these concerns was a belief that the labouring classes should not have children for whom they could not provide. It was in such circumstances that Thomas Malthus counselled moral restraint until couples, that is men, were financially secure. Those influenced by Malthus' work argued that poor relief combined with the allowance system encouraged the poor to marry early and to have large families that they could not, or would not, support. These views about population, particularly when combined with a general condemnation of working class 'marriages', can also be seen as part of a process of constituting appropriate working-class sexuality or to use the language of the time – appropriate working-class moralities.

The focus of this discourse is upon the labouring poor and especially those dependent on parochial relief rather than exclusively women as in the bastardy discourse. As a consequence it can be said to be a class rather than a gendered discourse. The discourse comprises various components and is at times contradictory and even muddled. This is partly because a range of different ideas is expressed, especially with reference to marriage. Although discourses are often inconsistent and uneven they can still manage to establish a powerful representation of an issue. This is true of the marriage/population/family discourse which, despite its unevenness, is able nonetheless to establish a normative notion of marriage. That a marriage/population/ family discourse can be traced in the reports is also significant because it illustrates that dominant and popular ideas about marriage/population/family informed and intersected the poverty discourse of the 1834 New Poor Law.

Mapping the family/marriage/population discourse

The poor are criticised for marrying early. They are presented to us as reckless and irresponsible. They marry before securing adequate means of support to sustain marriage and/or a family and as a result have unhappy and improvident marriages, which multiply the population with a disorderly and profligate progeny who go on to become surplus labour. In the eyes of the commissioners such marriages are clearly ill advised. Numerous references are made in the reports to the improvidence, wastefulness and irresponsibility of the poor in marrying. Without a doubt, labourers are "reckless and dissolute beyond belief. They were said to be living almost promiscuously, and that large families, legitimate or not, were considered by them as an advantage" (Villiers' Report, 1834, Appendix A, 1971 edn, vol 9, p 34). The discourse for the most part is aimed at those labourers on poor relief.

A number of devices are used to construct a negative image of the labouring classes. First, they are condemned for marrying without having adequate means to support a wife and family. Next, they are characterised almost as 'deliberately' marrying so as to obtain parochial benefits. For example, "it is quite a common thing for mere lads to get married in order to get families and by this means get the benefit of parish allowance" (Villiers' Report, 1834, Appendix A, 1971 edn, vol 9, p 91a) and "Ah, but sir, I married yesterday and I expect the parish to find a place for me to live in" (Villers' Report, 1834, Appendix A, 1971 edn, vol 9, p 29a). The suggestion throughout much of the reports, as these extracts show, is that most of the poor marry so as to obtain welfare benefits. Consequently, "[I]n those parishes which seem over-peopled, improvident marriages are most usual; the labourers enter into that state with utter recklessness, feeling secure that they and their families will be well paid according to the scale of relief" (Majende's Report, 1834, 1971 edn, vol 8, p 457).

In this way, the poor are constituted as self-seeking, wanting something for nothing, taking advantage of the relief system, and as lacking in self-restraint – being unprepared to wait until they can afford to marry.

The old Poor Law and allowance systems are also constituted as having immoral outcomes – encouraging early and improvident marriage, overpopulation and dependency in the labouring classes. Throughout the reports the poor are criticised for thinking parochial support was theirs as a 'right' and the old poor law condemned for discouraging individuals (men) from making future provision for themselves and their families in times of birth, sickness, unemployment and old age. The old Poor Law was criticised for encouraging dependency and blamed for sapping men's incentive to work:

> By making their marriages and the numbers of their children the great conditions of relief, by encouraging the opinion that having a family was a service to the state, by fostering among them the notion that their disasters were natural, and not to be provided for by themselves ... the poor have been taught to believe that they are released from many of the consequences which should properly attach to improvidence and bad character. (Mr Villiers, 1834, Appendix A, 1971 edn, vol 9, p 14)

The idea that the provision of poor relief produced unwanted immoral outcomes was influenced in part by Malthus's work on population. In men, poor relief eroded their incentive to work while in women it encouraged unwanted sexual behaviour. Taylor-Gooby (1994, p 82) refers to this as a process whereby those "who wish to see welfare activity constrained have argued powerfully for the restriction of state provision on the grounds of 'moral hazard' – the argument that benefits put people at risk of undesirable behaviour because they provide incentives to seek, for example, to evade work". The idea that poor relief weakens men's initiative and individual responsibility to work and to provide for their wife and children along with destroying the work ethic was central to the main part of the NPL. By contrast, the moral hazard produced in women encouraged inappropriate and unacceptable sexual behaviour, resulted in illegitimacy and undermined the nation's morality by threatening the formation of the family and the institution of marriage.

Second, pauper men are vilified as callous, greedy, dishonest, and idle. To demonstrate this, accounts are provided of men's dishonesty in claiming poor relief in one parish while working in another. One such man it was alleged also "had two grown-up daughters living in his house, notoriously prostitutes", whose gains from that source were said to be considerable. Another man it was testified, "regretted publicly the loss of his children on account of his pay from the parish being withdrawn, saying he should have been well off if they had lived" (Villiers' Report, 1834, Appendix A, 1971 edn, vol 9, p 16).

As with the examples of unmarried mothers used in the reports the evidence cited is used to condemn the labouring classes and is also often extreme and one-sided. Not only are the men condemned but so too is the whole family. "The wives of the paupers are dirty, and nasty and indolent; and the children generally neglected, and dirty, and vagrants and immoral" (Chadwick's Report, 1834, Appendix A, 1971 edn, vol 9, p 2a). Again, as was the case with unmarried mothers, a comparative device is employed and the poor are judged as lacking in comparison with their working neighbour. "How are the cottages of the independent labourers', as compared to them? – The wife is a very different person; she and her children are clean, and her cottage tidy ... the difference is striking to me ..." (Chadwick's Report, 1834, 1971 edn, vol 9, p 2a).

Indeed, so irresponsible and self-seeking are the labouring classes that they will even marry in order to obtain employment. In many parishes especially where the allowance system has ceased, "a superior claim in the married man over the single is recognised" so that "... where steady employment is to be given, the man with children is preferred ... thus in fact a bounty upon early marriage is presented to the labourer as having advantages independent of its natural object" (Mr Villiers' Report, 1834, Appendix A, 1971 edn, vol 9, p 13).

The implication is that giving work to married men with families encourages the poor to marry and to have kids, suggesting that it is not

enough that they should exercise restraint and wait until they have work
and the finances to support marriage. It is that they should not marry at
all. One assistant commissioner, George Taylor, went as far as to suggest
that legislation be introduced to prohibit anyone in receipt of poor relief
from marrying at any age. Realising that there might be some objections
to his proposal, Taylor suggested instead that "there could at least be no
injustice, and probably no offence to public feeling, in an enactment
depriving all benefit from the Poor Laws the issue of such marriages ..."
(Taylor, 1834, Appendix C, 1971 edn, vol 17, p 132).

In different places the commissioners have different things to say about
marriage. In the context of unmarried motherhood, as we have already
seen, women are condemned for having children outside of marriage
and criticised for having children without a husband and father to support
them and their children. "The unmarried mother has voluntarily put
herself into the situation of a widow: she has voluntarily become a mother
without procuring to herself and her child the assistance of a husband
and a father. There can be no reason for giving to vice privileges which
we deny misfortune" (18th Recommendation, Main Report, 1971 edn,
vol 8, p 198).

Marriage after pregnancy is similarly condemned, regardless of, or rather
because of, it being a commonplace practice of the labouring classes.
The picture painted by the commissioners is as with other examples of
plebeian marriages that they are unhappy, improvident. They believed
many of these post-pregnancy marriages to be 'forced' by parish officials
keen to keep parish rates and expenditure low: "improvident marriages
[were] not only promoted but compelled in order to save the parish
money" (Main Report, 1834, 1971 edn, vol 8, p 98).

In his report Edwin Chadwick argues that the law that allows a woman
to swear a man to be the father of her child, "has many injurious effects.
One of the most obvious is that thereby innumerable marriages in all
parts of England are brought about ... it has become the general rule, not
the exception for the parties not to marry until sexual intercourse has
produced pregnancy" (Chadwick's Report, 1834, Appendix A, 1971 edn,
vol 9, p 216).

In other reports the case against allowing marriage between minors is
made, a practice it is claimed that is 'notorious' in the manufacturing
districts where "the high wages occasionally obtained by boys and girls
... produces early actual emancipation or independence on the parents,
and instead of the young people forming a fund for supply in hard times
of less prosperity, they rush into marriage, depending on the Poor Laws

for supply of future want" (Taylor's Report, 1834, Appendix C, 1971 edn, vol 17, p 132).

While it would be misleading to suggest that the commissioners 'speak with one voice' their remarks do provide us with an insight into the attitudes of influential middle-class individuals (doctors, magistrates, JPs, overseers, clerics) towards the labouring classes. While their collective comments may not present a coherent approach or view on marriage, population and the labouring classes, what they do reveal is an overwhelming, if sometimes contradictory, discourse which constituted the marriages of the labouring classes as improvident, and labouring classes as immoral and profligate: on the one hand, as never having the foresight to think about the financial responsibilities of marriage and family and, on the other, as deliberately marrying for material advantage (to obtain work, poor relief, allowances, bread, accommodation, and clothes, and so on.).

Moral reformers of the early 19th century were outraged by the sexual behaviour and practice of the labouring classes, and regarded them with disgust and fear. By the 1830s the line between sexual respectability and 'irregular' behaviour began to harden (Taylor, 1983, p 201). The middle-class ideal of the family – the father and husband out at work and the mother and wife engaged in domestic duties within the home – had become firmly embedded in dominant English culture as acceptable intimacy and domesticity. Evangelism, which "denounced sexual indulgence as sin" (Clarke, 1995, p 188), heightened middle-class awareness to working-class 'immorality' (Taylor, 1983, p 335) and sought to put "the houses of the poor in order" (Hall, 1992, p 79). Marriage, home and family were key to middle-class morality. This has been identified as an ideology of domesticity (see Weeks, 1981, and Hall, 1992) which encapsulated ideas about appropriate morality, sexuality, social and sexual roles and responsibilities, marriage and family. This was the ideal, the 'norm' that everyone was expected to aim for and against which all would be judged and compared.

The middle classes were convinced that the labouring classes were immoral and that morality was at a premium. Mort (1987, p 37) has shown how, during this period, sexual reform was central to moral reform and a key component of disciplining the labouring classes. Mort (1987) maps out how, during the 1830s, health and morality become negatively conflated and this was reflected in the way that sexuality was constituted in and through medico-moral writings of the time. In Mort's work we can see how welfare reform and remoralisation went hand in hand in the early part of the 19th century. An examination of the NPL reveals how remoralisation was also constituted through discourses that centred *on poverty and welfare*. Whereas in medico-moral discourses it is the unhealthy and immoral behaviour of the poor that is pivotal in a negative construction of sexuality, in the NPL it is poverty and immorality (female sexuality, working class family and marriage, and poverty) that are the key axes in negative constructions of the working class poor.

Virtually absent from the discourse is any reference to the middle classes but this does not mean that they were not also part of the discourse. In focusing on what constituted inappropriate or 'bad' marriages and by associating this with the labouring classes the inference is that 'proper', acceptable marriage is well-advised, provident, happy, financially secure and self-sufficient, independent of poor relief and not financially motivated. The negative emphasis on improvident, early, and ill-advised marriages of the labouring classes therefore operates to normalise 'proper' marriage. Indeed, the middle-class idea of marriage, family and home is the silent presence in the discourse.

Taken together the two discourses of bastardy and marriage are not just about illegitimacy or marriage, or even poverty or simply a negative discourse about the labouring classes. They can be understood as part of a process wherein what we know as sexuality, or at least acceptable and appropriate sexuality, was discursively produced; they are both part of a process of normalisation and constitution in relation to sexuality.

Albeit differently discursively constituted – through gender and class – a picture of the labouring classes as immoral and of their sexuality – marriage, reproduction and family – as inappropriate and unacceptable is constructed. By presenting them and their practices as 'other', a 'norm' of acceptable and appropriate moral and sexual behaviour was asserted. The 'norm' that was being stressed was the exercise of sexual restraint until the independent economic means to support dependants was secured. This ignored that the traditional prenuptial and common-law marriages long practised in working-class communities represented acceptable sexual behaviour to the working classes; that it had its own morality. In the NPL reports and subsequent legislation working-class morality was reconstituted as immoral. Barbara Taylor (1983, p 196) shows this behaviour was "hardly the unregulated, unstructured 'promiscuity' which many middle class critics believed it to be, but a code whose norms were no less compelling for their lack of legal status". Social policy sought to override working-class rationalities and sexualities believing them to be debased by the material conditions of working-class existence. The new middle-class norm demanded that individuals/couples exercise sexual restraint, with sex and procreation taking place only within the confines of a legally sanctioned, economically viable and independent marriage. For women this meant celibacy until such a marriage could be secured.

Contemporary resonances?

One immediate reaction to reading the above interpretation of the 1834 NPL Reports is to notice how many of the discursive devices and ideas about unmarried mothers appear to have persisted throughout the 20th century and even into the 21st century. A word of caution, however. While comparisons can undoubtedly be made between the discourses invoked in the 19th century and contemporary discourses about lone mothers, it should not be assumed that the practices and discourses of the early 19th century can be straightforwardly and unproblematically applied to the 20th and 21st centuries. Nor can it be taken for granted that, when apparently similar discourses and practices are produced at different times, they can be assumed to have the same meanings and intents.

To begin with, the social, economic and political contexts informing the introduction of the 1834 NPL are significantly different from those of the 1980s or even those of the early 21st century. Any attempt to make comparisons between different periods needs therefore to take this into account. Similarly, the language used and meanings, values and understandings attached to actions, behaviours, practices and relationships in the early 19th century are also likely to vary considerably to those attached in the late 20th and 21st centuries. Contemporary ideas about morality, marriage, relationships, partnering and parenting, male and female sexuality, and acceptable sexualities differ from those of the 1830s. In recent decades, for example, there has been a considerable shift in the way people live as families and in what counts as a 'family' as well as in the meaning of 'family' to individuals. There is also a greater social acceptance in many areas of diverse family forms and intimate relationships – be they same sex, cohabiting, single parent and so on.

However, with this caveat in mind, it is interesting that despite unmarried motherhood being differently constructed at different periods (as a moral problem, as pathological, as mental deficiency, as a social problem) some discourses persist and are particularly potent – the idea, for example, of unmarried mothers deliberately getting pregnant to obtain welfare benefits – and we can find traces of 19th century discourses on marriage, family, unmarried motherhood and sexuality resonating in 20th and even 21st century debates on these topics. There is not the space here to undertake a detailed analysis of 20th century marriage, family and lone motherhood discourses so as to identify these traces. What follows therefore is a brief overview of those aspects of the discourse of bastardy which have persisted into the 20th century – specifically in the 1990s debates on lone motherhood.

In the 1990s lone mother discourse, unmarried mothers, lone mothers (through divorce, death or separation) and young single mothers tended to be grouped together and treated as homogeneous. A variety of discourses about family, marriage, morality, parenting, the underclass, dependency, and financial cost constituted lone mothers as a problem. A number of these echo themes evident in the NPL discourses on unmarried motherhood. Significant, was the reappearance, in the 1980s and early 1990s, of the moralising approach to unmarried and lone motherhood. Last evident in the 1950s and 1960s, the moralising discourse appears to be more forcibly asserted following periods when the stigmatisation of unmarried motherhood has declined (as in the early 1830s prior to the NPL, brief periods during the First and Second world wars, and the 1970s). That aspect of the early 1990s discourse, which was concerned with issues of morality, focused on the increasing numbers of women failing to marry who were having sex – and especially children – outside marriage. Many social commentators (see Dennis and Erdos, 1992; Morgan, 1995) and politicians found these shifts in family and marriage practice indicative of "a crisis in traditional authority relations and moral codes which [needed] to be addressed. From this standpoint lone mothers became both the cause and effect of this crisis in traditional morality and as a result were constructed as a social problem" (Lentell, 1999, pp 252-3).

As with 1834, the early 1990s discourse problematised unmarried motherhood by utilising ideas which linked unmarried motherhood with moral crisis, and stability of nation and family. Commentators spoke, for example, of the family as "the foundation stone of a free society ... today family life is breaking down ... growing illegitimacy and family breakdown, the reduction in the work ethic and rising crime are signs of a general malaise affecting British culture" (Green in Dennis and Erdos, 1992, p vii). Others spoke of the need "... to encourage proper family stability, because it is the bedrock of the nation ..." (Harry Greenway, *Hansard* (Commons) 6th series, vol 228, 22nd volume of session 1992-93, 5 July 1993, col 11).

Lone mothers, particularly never-married and teenage mothers, were seen as a threat to the traditional nuclear family and to the nation in part because of their increasing numbers and the signal that this was thought to convey about marriage and the traditional family. Through not marrying and by having children outside of marriage the increasing numbers of never-married mothers were presented as a threat to the stability of marriage and the traditional family both of which were seen, by the then Conservative government and others, as the cornerstone of the nation's morals. Teenage mothers were particularly threatening because, not only were they having sex outside marriage, and children which they could not support, they were, as far as many traditionalists were concerned, too young to be even having sex, let alone to be having babies. Teenage sexual activity was for many across the political spectrum a major threat to morality.

In a similar way to the 1830s, the debates of the early 1990s focused principally on unmarried mothers in receipt of benefits. These women were characterised as deliberately becoming pregnant, as sexually, socially, and financially irresponsible, as welfare dependent, and as a financial burden to the state and to taxpayers. A prevalent argument was that state benefits encouraged women to have children outside of marriage and produced fatherless families. In 1988 Thatcher, then prime minister, spoke of the problem of young single girls who were deliberately getting pregnant in order to obtain benefits and jump council housing queues (*The Guardian*, 23 November 1988). Again, in 1993 parliamentary debates resonated with the idea that "... the welfare system encourages young women to have babies out of wedlock so that they can qualify for council houses and benefits ..." (Mr Riddick, *Hansard* (Commons) 6th series, vol 228, 22nd volume of session 1992-93, 5 July 1993, col 11).

Through invoking a discourse of welfare dependency (a discourse that is still influential today) it was also possible to present lone mothers as irresponsible, and undeserving of welfare. After all, it was argued, they were irresponsibly having children without any adequate means of support (husband/marriage/work) and were a drain on the state's finances.

As with the 1830s, the early 1990s debate was also dominated by concerns about the cost of lone mothers to the state (Kiernan et al, 1998, p 1) and their role in producing an 'underclass' (see Roseneil and Mann, 1996). Single mothers were blamed for producing children who themselves were likely to be irresponsible and to become welfare dependent, an argument which, although not applied to unmarried mothers in 1834, was applied to poor families dependent on poor relief. In invoking the underclass discourse unmarried mothers were blamed for all sorts of ills – teenage motherhood, delinquent children, juvenile crime, a crisis in masculinity, and social and educational failure in fatherless boys (see, for example, Roseneil and Mann, 1996; Dennis and Erdos, 1992). These ideas were more forcibly endorsed in the run-up to the 1993 Conservative Party Conference making it clear that welfare services and benefits should be available only to respectable married mothers.

Although ideas about lone/unmarried mothers as welfare dependent, immoral, irresponsible and a financial burden and so on, may be less virulently and explicitly expressed in the late 1990s and early 21st century such ideas endure in, for example, the New Deal for lone mothers and policy proposals for teenage mothers. Marriage and work are now the preferred policy preferences of government for unmarried and single mothers.

This section has intentionally focused on those ideas about unmarried mothers which have persisted in one form or another through to the present day. More work, however, needs to be done to explain why ideas about, for example, women's sexuality, welfare dependency, and so on continue to be so potent. Finally, while it is interesting to focus on the continuities to be found in discourses of lone motherhood and the role played in those by sexuality discourses, we must be careful not to ignore the divergences in those discourses – the emphasis, for example, on the best interests of the child, women working, and the recent renewed interest in male responsibility.

Conclusion

At the start of this chapter I indicated that my aim was to look at social policy through the lens of sexuality. Analysing the influence of sexuality discourses in the 1834 NPL and related reports shows that, not only can poverty discourses be understood as a means of categorising the poor into deserving with rights (the elderly, widows) and the undeserving with duties and responsibilities, but that sexuality played a role in this. Second, it shows that the constitution of welfare subjects is the outcome of the interaction of multiple discourses. Further, the constitution of welfare subjects although clearly powerful and influential often bears little resemblance to individual experiences and 'realities'. Policy makers often dismiss, as this example shows, welfare subjects' economic, moral and sexual rationalities, believing them to be inferior, flawed, or as lacking moral integrity. Instead, they prefer to impose their own moral values and practices. Third, this analysis also illustrates that poverty discourses are concerned with much more than simply poverty. Not only are other dominant discourses 'played through' poverty discourses, but these discourses play a part in constituting those other dominant discourses. Thus, in this case, ideas and discourses about sexuality, morality, gender relations, the family and marriage are embedded in poverty discourses. Correspondingly, poverty discourses become a means by which appropriate sexuality, gender relations, morality, the family and marriage are spoken about. This process, albeit historically specific, is evident in contemporary analyses of social policy.

Notes

[1] The sources of data for this research are, primarily, the Reports of His Majesty's Commissioners on the Administration and Practical Operation of the Poor Laws with Appendices, Parts I, II, and III Reports from the Assistant Commissioners published by Irish University Press, Shannon: Ireland. Also used is the Pelican edition of *The Poor Law Report of 1834* edited by S. G. and E. O. A. Checkland (1973). Additional original sources used include, *Hansard* Parliamentary Debates, series 3, vols XXI–XXVI, London, *Hansard*; *Poor Law Commission Official Circulars of Public Documents and Information, 1840-1851*. vols VII–X, (Reprinted 1970), New York: Kelley; *Report of the Commissioners of Inquiry (South Wales) and Other Papers Relating to The Maintenance of Civil Order 1839-44*, vol 2, Shannon, Ireland: Irish University Press; *The Poor Man's Guardian 1831-1835,* H. Hetherington. London: The Merlin Press (1969 Reprint), vol 3.

[2] Both sexuality and heterosexuality are assumed to be socially and culturally constructed and historically specific.

[3] The abbreviation NPL will be used to refer to the 1834 New Poor Law Act and Commissioners Reports on the Operation and Administration of the Poor. The term commissioners used in this paper refers to all the contributors to the reports.

[4] For a detailed discussion of the discourse of bastardy and the ways the unmarried mothers were constructed within it see Carabine (2001) 'Unmarried motherhood 1830–1990: a discursive genealogical analysis', in M. Wetheral (ed) *Doing discourse analysis: A workbook*. London: Sage Publications.

[5] See Carabine (1996a) 'Heterosexuality and social policy' in D. Richardson (ed) *Theorising heterosexuality*, Milton Keynes: Open University Press for a discussion of this process within contemporary social policy.

[6] See Lord Althorp, the Lord Chancellor's comments (*Hansard*, 3rd series, vol XXV,1834, p 605).

[7] The commissioners indicate a desire to avoid "making her [unmarried mothers] an object of sympathy", Main Report, 1834, Remedial Measures, p 197).

[8] Under the old Poor Law system both men and women had been legally financially responsible for their illegitimate offspring.

[9] The influence of Malthusian ideas about population on the NPL are well documented (see for example, Huzel, 1986; Peterson, 1979).

References

Bland, L. (1983) 'Cleansing the portals of life': the venereal disease campaign in the early twentieth century', in M. Langan and B. Schwarz (eds) *Crisis in the British state, 1880-1930*, London: Hutchinson.

Carabine, J. (1996a) 'Heterosexuality and social policy', in D. Richardson (ed) *Theorising heterosexuality*, Buckingham: Open University Press.

Carabine, J. (1996b) 'A straight playing field or queering the pitch? Centring sexuality in social policy', *Feminist Review*, vol 54, pp 31-64.

Carabine, J. (2001) 'Unmarried motherhood 1830-1990: a discursive genealogical analysis', in M. Wetheral (ed) *Doing discourse analysis: A workbook*, London: Sage Publications.

Clarke, A. (1995) *The struggle for the breeches: Gender and the making of the British working class*, London: Rivers Oram.

Daly, M. (1994) 'A matter of dependency: gender in British income maintenance provision', *Sociology*, vol 28, no 3, pp 779-97.

Dean, M. (1991) *The constitution of poverty: Toward a genealogy of liberal governance*, London: Routledge.

Dennis, N. and Erdos G. (1992) *Families without fatherhood*, London: IEA Health and Welfare Unit.

Foucault, M. (1990) *The history of sexuality, Volume 1: An introduction* (trans Robert Hurley), New York, NY: Vintage Books.

Foucault, M. (1991) *Discipline and punish: The birth of the prison* (trans from the French by Alan Sheridan), London: Penguin.

Ginsburg, N. (1979) *Class, capital and social policy*, Basingstoke: Macmillan.

Hall, C. (1992) *White, male, and middle class: Explorations in feminism and history*, Cambridge: Polity Press.

Hansard Parliamentary Debates (1834) 3rd Series, vol XXI -VI *Hansard*: London.

Home Office (2001) *Supporting families* (www.homeoffice.gov.uk/cpd/fmpu/sfamr.pdf).

Huzel, J.-P. (1986) 'Malthus, the Poor Law, and population in early nineteenth century England', in J.-C. Wood (ed) *Thomas Robert Malthus: Critical assessments*, vol IV, London: Croom Helm.

Keirnan, K., Land, H. and Lewis, J. (1998) *Lone motherhood in twentieth century Britain*, Oxford: Clarendon Press.

Laslett, P. (1977) *Family life and illicit love in earlier generations: Essays in historical sociology*, Cambridge: Cambridge University Press.

Lentell, H. (1999) 'Families of meaning: contemporary discourses of the family', in G. Lewis, *Forming nation, framing welfare*, London: Routledge.

Morgan, P. (1995) *Farewell to the family: Public policy and family breakdown in Britain and the USA*, London: IEA Health and Welfare Unit.

Mort, F. (1987) *Dangerous sexualities: Medico-moral politics in England since 1830*, London: Routledge, Kegan and Paul.

O'Brien, M. and Penna, S. (1998) *Theorising welfare*, London: Sage Publications.

Perkins, J. (1989) *Women and marriage in nineteenth-century England*, London: Routledge.

Peterson, W. (1979) *Malthus*, London: Heineman.

Rendall, J. (1985) *The origins of modern feminism: Women in Britain, France and the United States, 1780-1860*, Basingstoke: Macmillan.

Reports of His Majesty's Commissioners on the Administration and Practical Operation of the Poor Laws with Appendices, Parts I, II, & III Reports from the Assistant Commissioners (1834), Shannon: Ireland Irish University Press.

Roseneil, S. and Mann, K. (1996) 'Unpalatable choices and inadequate families', in E. Silva, *Good enough mothering? Feminist perspectives on lone mothers*, London: Routledge.

Taylor, B. (1983) *Eve and the New Jerusalem: Socialism and feminism in the nineteenth century*, London: Virago.

Taylor-Gooby, P. (1994) 'Welfare futures', in R. Page and J. Ferris (eds) *Social policy in transition: Anglo-German perspectives in the new European community*, Aldershot: Avebury.

Thane, P. (1978) 'Women and the Poor Law in Victorian and Edwardian England', *History Workshop*, vol 6, pp 29-51.

Webb, S. and Webb, B. (1910) *English Poor Law policy*, London: Longmans, Green and Co.

Weeks, J. (1981) *Sex, politics and society: The regulation of sexuality since 1800*, London: Longman.

Index

NOTE: Page numbers followed by *n* indicate information is contained in a note on that page.

Russia 138, 139-40, 142, 143, 147,
150, 151, 152
see also Central and Eastern Europe

S

sadomasochism: consensual 16,
89-104
Sainsbury, D. 188
'Sarah's Law' 4
savings paradox 235-6
Scottish Nationalist Party 4
second-job holders 191
Seldon, A. 112
self-help
and active citizenship 209, 213, 221
in CEE countries 144
self-interest 64-5, 71
as human nature 247-8, 249-50,
257, 260
'self-service welfare' 212, 213
sexuality
consensual sadomasochism 16,
89-104
meanings of term 104*n*, 267
New Poor Law (1834) discourse on
205, 267, 270-88
'sexually transmitted debt' 31
Shelton, B.-A. 195, 196
Shildrick, M. 92, 96, 103-4
Shortell, S. 43
Siaroff, A. 198*n*
signs and signification 31-2, 33, 35
Silburn, R. 118
silo performance management 50,
51-2, 54
Simmel, G. 26
Singer, L. 103
Singh, S. 30-1
single currency debate 4
single mothers *see* lone mothers
Single Regeneration Budget (SRB)
51
skills for ICT access 218-20, 221,
222-3*n*
SMART targets 41
social capital in CEE countries 145
social contract 75-9

social control 71-5
social costs in CEE countries 134-5,
140, 148-9
social democracy and human nature
250, 251-5, 257
social democratic welfare model 187
social discount rate 235
social exclusion/inclusion
in CEE countries 143-6
communitarian approach 80, 81
and employment 139
financial exclusion 25, 34
and ICT access 211
Social Exclusion Unit 3
Policy Action Teams (PATs) 74,
217-18
social insurance *see* social security
provision
social justice 10, 113
and human nature 254-5
intergenerational justice 206,
227-43
social meanings of money 31-2
social model of disability 97
social movements 145-6, 159, 162
and active citizenship 209, 215, 221
social networks in CEE countries
144, 145
social organic model of human
nature 249, 250, 251, 255-6, 257,
260, 262
Social policy agenda (EU) 8-9
social psychology 26
social responsibility 75-9
social security provision
in China 170-1, 173
in Hong Kong 168, 169, 173
as intergenerational contract 227-43
marketisation of reform 107, 109-25
national insurance system 252-3,
258
for part-time workers 191-2
in Taiwan 165-6, 172
welfare to work schemes 69, 75, 78,
80, 257, 260-1, 262
see also welfare reform
social services: integration with
health services 42-3

THE NORTHERN COLLEGE
LIBRARY

10688   BARNSLEY